JESUIT HIGHER EDUCATION

Jesuit Higher Education

Essays on an American Tradition of Excellence

Edited by Rolando E. Bonachea

Duquesne University Press
Pittsburgh, Pennsylvania

Published by:
Duquesne University Press
600 Forbes Avenue
Pittsburgh, PA 15282

Library of Congress Cataloging-in-Publication Data

Jesuit higher education.

    Bibliography: p.
    Includes index.
    1. Jesuits—Education—United States.　2. Catholic
universities and colleges—United States.　I. Bonachea,
Rolando E.
LC493.J47　1989　　　　377.82'73　　　　88–33492
ISBN 0–8207–0208–0

Printed in the United States
of America

To my wife Nancy and daughter Anna Maria.

CONTENTS

Introduction

Rolando E. Bonachea

THIS collection of essays represents a revision of papers presented at the December 1984 St. Louis University conference
entitled *Jesuit Education: The Challenge of the 1980s and Beyond.* In
addition to the excellent forum the conference provided for reflection on recurrent themes facing Jesuit institutions of higher education, it is my hope that a critically reflective dialogue will ensue
among an even larger audience on the many topics included in this
volume. In doing so, we can prepare our institutions to meet future
needs and demands.

The inquiry into the Jesuit identity and mission has been an
ongoing process, as illustrated by the historical perspective in Father
McInnes's essay. In part, the distinctiveness of the Jesuit tradition
lies in the conviction that educating the total person entails a strong
liberal arts foundation, and a fundamental commitment to ethical,
religious and civic formation. As Father Biondi indicates, how to
promote and attain this development of the total person would
evoke many responses, but an important component must be found
in the philosophy underlying the core curriculum. A Jesuit education is not confined to ancient philosophy, literature or to history.
As Father Biondi points out in his insightful treatment of the liberal
arts curriculum, the core also encompasses the arts, theology, language; the natural, mathematic and social sciences as well as world
cultures.

Because a liberal education addresses questions of man's identity
and ultimate destiny, theology and philosophy must play a central
role in the curriculum. Both disciplines, Father Theodore Hesburgh
has argued, must not be included in the core as mere "window"

1

dressing.[1] Further, as Father Renard and Dr. O'Connell agree, theology must exist in "living dialogue with all the disciplines in the university."

In his creative essay, Father Renard observes that, through dialogue, such disciplines as art and theology "begin to discover that they have much in common, with respect to the values and attitudes they seek to foster in their students, and with respect to the various human operations required in their disciplines" (Renard, 55). Dr. O'Connell emphasizes the vital functions of religious and theological studies in the undergraduate humanities curriculum, and the role these studies play in the overall educational experience of students. He points out that our re-thinking of their role in the core leads to a reflection on our specific Jesuit identity.

In addition to the challenge of making theological and religious studies relevant to young adults and instilling a critical appreciation of the great religious traditions, we ask something more: that theology faculty enable students to think and act within a vision of life that includes religious values. A "critical," not "catechetical" approach, as Dr. O'Connell says, is crucial for the moral and spiritual development of our students.

Philosophy, like theology, plays a critical and unifying central role in liberal arts education. Its consideration of ultimate questions about God, the world and the human person, as well as its critical analysis of the presuppositions of other disciplines' methodologies, makes the study of philosophy central to the formation of disciplined and self-reflective thinkers. Father Tetlow discusses the role of philosophy in Jesuit higher education and traces its historical development in the core curriculum. Philosophy, he asserts, lies at the heart of the Jesuit liberal arts curriculum because it ". . . provokes the intellectual conversion of the conventional thinker to principled reflection" (Tetlow, 105).

One of the most important concerns of a Catholic liberal arts college is that of human values. This is an obligation which proves to be compatible with the advancement of human knowledge, the support of modern science and technology and other segments of higher learning. Both Father Brungs and Father Pollock remind us of the tremendous changes that technological and scientific advances have brought to our lives. We are all, each and every day, awakened to the moral implications following in the wake of the revolutionary changes in science and technology that have occurred during the course of this century.

Furthermore, we have an obligation to become conversant with the methodologies of the physical and natural sciences, the fledging social sciences, and other technical fields. In this manner, we can honestly prepare our students to live in a society where they possess an "adequate understanding of the scientific and technological basis of modern-day issues so that they can make intelligent decisions in their role as responsible citizens in their communities and nation" (Biondi, 96).

Likewise, we can hardly ignore, as Father Brungs poignantly says, the profound impact the ". . . spectrum of scientific and technological advances (the biological, chemical, physical, cybernetic, etc.)" wields on "personal dignity, personal freedom, and the integrity of the human body" (Brungs, 88).

Radical and far reaching advances have occurred in the fields of science and technology. Therefore, the acceleration of knowledge in these fields constantly reminds us of the need for Jesuit institutions to remain current. Father Brungs tells us that Jesuit education is "fatally weakened" without a serious commitment to and appreciation of the sciences: ". . . if we do not offer significant instructional opportunities . . . to our students, we are not preparing either a religious laity nor citizens competent to contribute to the cultural life of the Church and of the nation" (Brungs, 89).

In addition, our educational institutions have a responsibility to address moral questions that confront society as a result of these scientific and technological advances. We can only meet this responsibility in the same measure that we succeed in providing an ethical formation of our students. Father Pollock underscores the centrality of ethical formation and development of character, a message echoed by Frs. Biondi, Panuska and Brungs. Equipped with an ethical foundation, students will be better prepared to reaffirm essential values, for as Father Tetlow points out, "In our culture and time, collegians mature in a culture without coherent public discourse, in which values are incessantly trivialized, and in which pluralism of viewpoint is bewildering" (Tetlow, 116).

David Hassel, S.J., in his book *City of Wisdom: A Christian Vision of the University*, comments ". . . only such a community arising out of loyalty can appreciate traditional wisdom, develop it, and pass it on to others. For wisdom is more than techniques, more than specialized knowledge, more than routines; wisdom is interpersonal knowledge and deeply felt values."[2]

Another vital component of Jesuit higher education lies in the area of graduate students. As Father Panuska discusses, the long-lived contributions of Jesuit graduate and professional education have

4 INTRODUCTION

fostered an important tradition at our institutions. This tradition has been characterized by a commitment to advanced research and a distinguished record of public service. From the rosters of graduating alumni, many distinguished leaders have emerged and made their contributions to society. We must ensure that our graduate programs maintain a high-quality curriculum of study and that the degrees granted reflect a high caliber of scholarly accomplishments. This requires a committed graduate faculty who exemplify the dual qualities of productive scholarship and teaching excellence.

There are other issues germane to sustaining our reputation of excellence in graduate and professional programs. We must maintain our campus facilities, and make available student and academic support services. Furthermore, we must devote sufficient resources to provide extensive research opportunities, upgrade our library holdings and increase graduate stipends to an equitable level.

Undeniably, one of the greatest contributions that Jesuit education can make to men and women of this century — which is also integrally tied to our emphasis on values — is the type of education which offers society visionary leadership. As Father Biondi emphatically argues, our charge proves to be more than the intellectual, spiritual and moral education of our young adults. In addition to all these, "a remaining purpose of our educational enterprise is to help our students become *more effective leaders in our society*: to mold them to use their knowledge and expertise to serve and to lead others living and working in their communities" (Biondi, 99). Moral development is central to fostering good leadership potential. Father Biondi suggests that a leader is more able than others in identifying and solving problems. A leader has a clear-sighted and unobstructed vision of a goal, and conveys the "certainty of purpose to others" which leads to the realization of that goal (Biondi, 99).

How do we aid in the formation of capable and visionary leaders? We accomplish this through incorporating ethical and religious values into our curriculum and by being, as Newman suggests, "teachers and patterns of truth." "We need to foster leadership in our own standards by our own modeling of leadership and by acquainting our students with historical models of Christian courage and leadership" (Biondi, 99).

As Father O'Malley reminds us, the divergence of humanistic schools of education from scholasticism rests upon the conviction that education should effect a personal transformation of character and that, through education, an individual is led to productive service to God and the world (O'Malley, 15). Thus, our ultimate aim for educating is not merely theoretical. Instilling a deeply ingrained compassion for the plight of others is mirrored in the inner convictions of our forefathers who believed that the formation of character, which is education's domain, could bring about constructive reforms in society. This brings us to the issue of social responsiveness.

Jesuit education, as Father Kavanaugh indicates, must be translated into social reliance and action, a life-long commitment to peace, justice and human rights. "The great project of education which is that of human self-understanding in all its forms, is a project of human dignity. . . . Education's meaning and purpose is justice itself. Human dignity is its premise. Human freedom is its goal" (Kavanaugh, 173).

For what we are teaching, as Father Tetlow alludes to, is no doctrinal subject matter. We are after something much more profound — an intellectual conversion. This conversion instills a value-infused commitment to addressing social problems, issues of justice and injustice, world peace, nuclear war, and the increasing gap between the wealthy and impoverished nations of the world. Our responsiveness to society includes a striving for human equality, an eradication of abject poverty, hunger, disease and ignorance. In our outreach to society and our service to the community we, again, preserve our relevance — through action, not theory alone. As a reminder of our social responsibilities, the Bishop's pastoral letters have continuously called upon us to exercise moral courage on behalf of the oppressed. The Pastoral in 1980 on *Catholic Higher Education and the Pastoral Mission of the Church* places the challenge before us to be attentive to the educational needs of minorities and the disadvantaged.

In addition to a moral foundation, the formation of our students must also include an international experience or dimension. We live in an increasingly interdependent world, a world wherein ignorance of other cultures is inexcusable, especially in a university environment where the expressed task is to cultivate understanding and perpetuate knowledge. Father Sauvé challenges us "to recover our sense of an international system" so that we may promote greater international cooperation and understanding (Sauvé, 166).

As Father Pollock states in his treatment of "Ethics and the Challenges of Contemporary Society," modern means of transportation and communication make possible a closer union of the peoples of the world, diminishing the distance that separates us. The present climate of competition, hostility and violence must be replaced by a constructive sharing of the earth's goods in a peaceful environment. Developing this awareness is essential in the formation of our students.

In addition to the academic disciplines, non-academic support services such as Campus Ministry, the Office of Student Development, programs on Justice, retreats and other extra-curricular activities contribute to the formation of the total person. The presentations by Father Sutton and Dr. Schroeder emphasize the possibilities in these important areas.

As Dr. Schroeder tells us, a "rigid" environment thwarts growth. We must be cognizant of the fact that we are integrally linked to a social and physical environment in which our efforts at spiritual and intellectual formation occur. For example, many of our colleges and universities are set in an urban environment, an environment which — without attempts for beautification — can be harsh, to say the least. In order to foster the growth of individuals, we must promote a healthy and humane campus environment. This must be an environment that takes into account the "unique needs and preferences . . . exhibited by special student populations. . . ." Since the needs and characteristics of a student body are constantly changing, administrators and faculty must make frequent re-evaluations of the campus environment. they must make decisions to improve it, including: creating an atmosphere in resident halls conducive to study and productive social interaction, beautifying facilities that promote "physical" health (which is crucial for spiritual and mental growth), and devoting resources to strengthen student development programs (Schroeder, 144).

Dr. Schroeder also gives an informative and interesting discussion on significant variances in student learning habits. The more we know about the different behavioral patterns of our students' learning process, the better able we are to implement effective instructional methods in our classrooms.

The discourse on approaches for the development of the total person is inexhaustible. But the journey began at Manresa in 1548 when Ignatius of Loyola wrote the *Spiritual Exercises*. Ignatius represents the bond of all Jesuit colleges and universities, reminding us that the ultimate goal of our efforts in education lies in the service of God and the Church.

When Ignatius died in 1556, there were 35 Jesuit colleges in Europe. Today, there is a network of 90 colleges and universities, as well as 430 high schools in 55 countries. The importance here lies not in the number, but as a testament to the vitality of the religious humanistic vision that motivated Ignatius' conversion. As Father

O'Malley asserts, this Ignatian vision, 400 years old and evolving, remains vibrant and relevant today.

In this evolution lies its dynamism, for as Father McInnes says, there can never be a single, final and self-enclosed philosophy of Jesuit education. It is a dynamic vision that provides the permanence rooted in our own uniqueness as shared since Ignatius, and at the same time seeking action-oriented solutions to contemporary problems. Father John W. Donahue remarks that the unique combination of Ignatius spirituality and educational theory rests in Ignatius's "insistence on keeping simultaneously and steadily in sight the most exalted ends along with the most exact and concrete means of achieving them." Ignatius was committed to making ideas reality for all. "If to take means seriously is to be a modern man, Ignatius was preeminently modern."[3]

Reverend Ganss puts the issue aptly. The question, he says, is not the relevance, per se, of Ignatius's world vision for Jesuit higher education today, but to consider how to constructively and creatively achieve those objectives. How can we move closer to the Ignatian vision? There are of course different ways, but Father Ganss suggests that reflecting upon the documents left to us is a beginning. The *Spiritual Exercises* are an experience of God and contain many of the foundational principles of Jesuit educational philosophy.

I believe that Ignatius intended for education to be useful, adaptable, and humanistic, but also with a strong moral and religious orientation. The exchange of ideas between student and faculty in a constant dialogue about life and its many dimensions should be fostered. "At the heart of any Jesuit college or university are its students, staff, faculty and administrators and its Judeo-Christian principles, ethics, values and beliefs by which they choose to live their lives" (Biondi, 100).

Ultimately, we dedicate the vision to our students — not simply for education's sake — but for what may be achieved through that education, as Pope John Paul II so vibrantly summarized at an address at the Catholic University of America:

> To be what it ought to be, a Catholic College or University, must set-up among its students and faculty, a real community which bears witness to a living and operative Christianity, a community where sincere commitment to scientific research and study goes together with a deep commitment to authentic Christian living.[4]

As we prepare for the last decade of the twentieth century to unfold, the collective effort and reflection of these authors call for a rededication to several goals. First, we must devote ourselves to a liberal arts education that goes beyond secular humanism, uniquely infusing the traditional study of the liberal arts and sciences with faith to provide a sound guide to the moral dilemmas witnessed in society and technology. This goal is predicated on the inclusion of theological and religious studies in the core curriculum to enable students to think and act within a vision of life that includes religious values. We encourage our theology faculty to continue the reflection on this central role of theology in the core and to carry out their objectives with renewed enthusiasm. In addition, philosophical inquiry, with its questions about the world, humanity and God, also plays a critical role in the core curriculum.

Secondly, we reaffirm our belief that a creative student development office and an inspirational campus ministry are essential components in the formative process of our students. As Reverend Edmund Ryan remarks, "the level of esteem and the importance of student development of student affairs on each of our campuses can serve as an index to our dedication to the principles of total person development."[5] Likewise, Campus Ministry has the important responsibility of imbuing the campus with a practical religious dimension, exposing students to the Catholic tradition and to a sincere ecumenical spirit.

Thirdly, we assert the importance of strong emphasis on the mortal and ethical dimensions of each discipline and to fostering global awareness and acceptance of cultural diversity. In doing so, there is a commitment to society and the world and the belief that our students will be prepared "not simply to survive in that world, but to be an effective presence in it"[6] (Biondi, 99).

Finally, one additional challenge facing each of our institutions in the twenty-first century is to continue to strengthen Jesuit-lay collaboration in our common dedication to the Ignatian vision and to Jesuit education. Since the 1960s, the numbers of Jesuit faculty and administrators have continued to decrease. Reverend Edmund Ryan pointed out at the 1981 AJCU Conference held at Boston College that this fact could have profound consequences if the focus remains on numbers and called for renewing our spirit of Jesuit-Lay collaboration.[15] Three years earlier, in July 1978, Father Arrupe in his address "Jesuit-Lay Collaboration in Higher Education" at St. Joseph College said:

> In its early decades, St Joseph College helped immigrant Catholic youth find their place in an environment in which Catholic values

were always welcome. Now its task is to make the planet its concern in the sense that its campus, its buildings, and its entire education program provides the setting wherein teachers and students, men and women, Jesuit and Lay, can learn the attitudes, acquire the skills and win the knowledge that will enable them to engage responsibly in action promotive of faith and promotive of justice.[7]

Father Arrupe also called on us to direct our energies in the service of third parties and to do so on the basis of dialogue and trust. In this volume, the essays of Fathers Ganss and Sauvé reiterate this theme of Jesuit-lay collaboration. Father Sauvé calls for an international exchange of information, creating "an educational community in which Jesuits and lay persons can share a common sense of mission" (Suavé, 165).

This collection of essays represents one modest example of Jesuit-Lay collaboration that reaffirms our commitment to the Ignatian heritage.

1 / The Jesuit Educational Enterprise in Historical Perspective

John W. O'Malley, S.J.

EVEN the most innocent reader must realize that the vast subject indicated by my title requires considerable reduction if it is not to career completely out of control. What I propose to do, in fact, is to examine in some detail the origins of Jesuit education in the sixteenth century — the period of history I know best, and the one in which the Jesuit tradition was set for centuries to come. I shall attempt to set the Jesuit schools into the general context of the sixteenth century, as well as into an earlier context, and try to elicit some of the principles that animated them. In so doing, I shall be heavily dependent on the research of other scholars.[1] My purpose will be to show how the Jesuit schools were part of larger movements, yet somehow distinctive within them. Although some of the principles the schools operated on are well known, placing them in their historical contexts might cause us to view them in a slightly different perspective and thus help stimulate our thinking about directions in education today. I engage in the undertaking, hence, not under the illusion that the sixteenth century holds any pat answers for us, but out of the conviction that the study of the past helps locate us better in the present and thereby helps us plan more judiciously for the future; such study also enlivens our imagination by showing alternatives to "the way things are."

The history of education, like the history of any great and long-lasting institution, impresses us first of all with the tenacity of its traditions. From the fourth century before Christ until the beginning of the twelfth century A.D., for instance, education was dominated

10

by the learning of ancient Greece, soon joined by that of ancient Rome.[2] From the thirteenth century until the present, and presumably into the forseeable future, higher education has been dominated by an institution known as the university, where structures and goals have changed remarkably little since they were first devised around the year 1200.[3]

Nonetheless, within this long tradition there have been some turning points, some decisive moments, when notable shifts in outlook, purpose, curriculum, and even structures have occurred that have been determinative for centuries to come. Within a tradition that strikes us by its long continuities, there have been (I use the term made famous by Thomas Kuhn) some "paradigm shifts."[4] Old elements are newly configured, usually because of the influx of forces never before part of the mix and because of a new vision about how to "put it all together." These "shifts" and changes do not take place overnight. A long gestation period generally precedes them, and a long period of consolidation, of "mopping-up," and even of routinization, follows. The result of the "shift" or change, in any case, is something new, even if it takes place within a continuous tradition.

As I have already indicated, the thirteenth century was one of the great decisive moments, a judgment few would contest. What happened was not simply that the texts of ancient Greek philosophy, especially so-called natural philosophy or science, were recovered in the West and now confronted Christian revelation, but that out of this confrontation, and to a large extent as a result of it, a whole new style of learning was produced, along with an institution to advance it.[5] The style of learning was the "professional" style, and the institution was the university. No more apt title could have been devised for this style of learning than "scholastic," even though few persons today seem to realize how penetratingly accurate that description is. The same is true for the designation of the practitioners of this new learning as "schoolmen" — that is, persons whose adult training took place not in the privacy of their own studies, *scriptoria*, or salons at their own leisure and according to their own pace, but rather was conducted during a protracted period of time in a highly formalized institution, the *school* — that is, the university. The university was the first step in displacing the haphazard, varied, and informal learning situations that had long held sway. Aristotelian science was its centerpiece.

Antiquity had produced nothing that resembled the medieval — and, hence, the modern — university. The gentleman (or gentle-lady) scholar was replaced by the "professional." Although this change touched only an extremely small percentage of the population, its impact was immediate and its implications for the future enormous. The characteristics of this style of education are familiar to us, for they have endured in only slightly modified form to our own day: an ideal of "learning for its own sake" (pure research), a carefully delineated, graduated, and monitored program of instruction within an institution and leading to a degree, the marginalization of the self-taught or amateur scholar, the emergence of a publicly certified class of professional educators whose training had been effected in the schools, by the schools, and to some extent, even for the schools.

When Aquinas insisted in the first question of the *Summa Theologiae* that theology was first and foremost a "contemplative" discipline, and only secondarily practical, he touched the nerve center not only of scholastic theology but of the whole university system: academia is, according to that formula, academic.[6] One might further infer that it is, according to that definition, the preserve of the few, for most persons have neither the time, wealth, or inclination for a life of academic contemplation or for the many years of training it now required. They must be about the business of life.

The next great moment came in the sixteenth century. Aside from the religious controversies, nothing is perhaps more striking about that century, at least from the cultural point of view, than the great "war against ignorance" that it waged on so many fronts. That war was characteristic of both Protestantism and Catholicism, a fact that implies a common and deeper origin for the phenomenon, an origin not easily discerned or described.[7] By the middle of the sixteenth century, we must note, the church-related school, in the stricter sense of the term , had thus come into being. These schools were spread all over Europe, especially as secondary schools, and by 1581 the Jesuits alone operated 150. By 1599 they operated 245, and, by 1626 the number had risen to 441 schools. They had created a vast educational empire. This phenomenon marked a major shift in the way Christian ministry was perceived and practiced, even though it generally receives little notice in standard histories of Christian ministry.[8]

Two factors, surely, helped give birth to this mighty impulse. The first was the call for the reform of the church. This preoccupied western Europe at least from the time of the Council of Constance, 1414–1417, all the way through the sixteenth century. The complaints about an ignorant clergy and an even more ignorant laity were heard on all sides and from almost every quarter. Although only one factor in a much larger concern, it was an important one and seemed to be an evil whose remedy was possible even on the local level, here and now. Perhaps the best indication that education had in fact already improved by the late Middle Ages and that literacy was more widespread than before was this growing conviction that these were goods and that their absences were evils, deleterious to both church and society.

It is against this background, and against the catalyst of the Reformation, that in many parts of Europe catechetical instruction of children on a widespread and systematic basis emerged by the middle of the sixteenth century as a major cultural force, little studied though it has been until recently. We often associate this phenomenon, or at least the origins of it, with the Lutherans — and their initiatives should surely not be minimized — but it seems to have emerged almost simultaneously, and only in part as imitation and reaction, in areas of Catholic Europe. Professor Paul Grendler of the University of Toronto is now engaged in a comprehensive study of the phenomenon in Italy, and has already published some of the results of his research.[9] A man by the name of Castelino da Castello, for instance, founded his first School of Christian Doctrine in Milan in 1536. Note the early date. By 1564 Milan had about twenty-eight such schools, taught by about two hundred adults, mostly lay men and women. The idea and the model spread. By 1611, Rome had seventy-eight such schools with about ten thousand boys and girls from ages five or six to about fifteen. Similar figures could be adduced for other Italian cities.

Classes were held on Sundays and feast days; instruction was graduated and books were provided free of charge. The classes were intended principally for the lower classes of society, for those who did not have opportunity for regular schooling. Hence, the great cultural importance of these so-called schools; they taught not only catechism but, in order to do so effectively, also taught the children how to read and sometimes even how to write.

The Jesuits were from the beginning heavily involved in catechizing both in Europe and in their foreign missions. Teaching catechism was one of the "experiments" through which the novices of the Society had to pass, and the professed members of the order vowed "special care for the instruction of children." Catechetical instruction played a role in Jesuit schools through the centuries, and two of the most important catechisms of the Counter-Reformation were authored by Jesuits — Peter Canisius and Robert Bellarmine. I have neither the space nor the competence to develop this aspect of Jesuit education, but I make mention of it here simply to illustrate how widespread was the "war against ignorance," how it was related to the problem of church reform, and how it invented strategies for touching even the humbler levels of society.

The second factor that gave impulse to this new enthusiasm for education, and that at many levels interpenetrated the first, was the humanist movement that began with Petrarch in the middle of the fourteenth century and reached maturity by the beginning of the sixteenth. This was — let it be said at the outset — an elitist, not a popular, movement. Although susceptible of many interpretations, Renaissance humanism can perhaps most intelligibly be viewed as a movement calling for the reform of education.[10] To a large extent, especially in its foremost representatives like Petrarch, Lorenzo Valla, and Erasmus, it reacted against the style, aims, content, and product of the scholastic system of education. By the middle of the fifteenth century, it had through Pier Paolo Vergerio the Elder, Vittorino da Feltre, and others codified its own style, aims, and content, and in Italy had even incarnated these in a few new institutions, the humanist schools.[11] It was only in the sixteenth century, however, that this movement had a general and profound impact on all of Europe.

In what did this impact consist? In the first place, the humanists articulated almost for the first time the importance of education, and they explicitly related it to the formation of character, and, thus, to the reform of church and society. The scholastics never did this in any formal way, and indeed their presuppositions about the academic nature of learning would seemingly preclude at least part of it. Difficult though the assertion might be to prove in any satisfactory way, I propose that the most striking achievement of the humanist movement was its role in having its convictions about the importance and goals of education permeate the most influential levels of society by the time the Reformation broke out. These convictions were common to Protestants and Catholics alike. Just how successfully the humanists correlated their high goals with their classroom techniques is a further question into which I cannot enter at present; evidence suggests that, almost from the beginning, propaganda about the transforming effects of their style of education outran accomplishment.[12]

In the second place, the humanists formulated and promoted an ideal of education that was a live alternative to scholastic learning. Humanistic learning was known in many parts of Europe as the "new learning," but in fact the universities were what was really new. Humanism derived its content and aims from the educational system of antiquity that dominated the Hellenistic and Roman worlds and that endured (in radically transformed conditions) as the normative style down to the thirteenth century.[13] Humanism in the Renaissance was "new" only in the sense that it newly articulated its aims, in that it codified anew its curriculum and content, in that it now had a notably Christian ethos, in that it girded itself for battle against a newly invented adversary, the university — or at least against the schoolmen who embodied the education that the university provided.

I am without doubt overstating the opposition between the humanists and the scholastics, but I do so to make a point. I am very much aware that even before the sixteenth century there were many persons, including members of the mendicant orders, who had had a university education and who at the same time were deeply influenced by the humanist movement.[14] Moreover, by the early years of that century, even the University of Paris, that vanguard and mother of scholastic learning, was being influenced by humanism in some of its colleges.[15] Nonetheless, there were significant differences between these two systems, based on a different vision of education. But these differences were fully appreciated and articulated, it would seem, by only a few unusually perspicacious individuals.[16] Erasmus would be oustanding among them.

What was, in brief, the humanist ideal, and how did it differ from scholastic presuppositions? First of all, it was not academic or speculative education. That is to say, it retrieved the ancient ideal that education was to prepare the individual for the "active life" of service to the common good of society and, in a Christian context, of service to the church. It would terminate, therefore, when persons were still in their teens, and not require long years of adulthood in school; it at first, in fact, assumed that its students would not need or want to go to the university. It was, unlike scholastic education, open to both boys and girls. It was principally literary or rethorical, not scientific or speculative, and thus it could exclude a large component of the university curriculum and reshape the rest of it. As has been well said, the Renaissance began "when Petrarch besought his countrymen to close their Aristotle and open their Cicero".[17] "Good letters" became synonymous with good education.

Intimately related to its literary base was perhaps humanism's most telling challenge to scholasticism. The humanist movement subscribed to the proposition that truly good literature was didactic, and hence assumed an intrinsic connection between the study of good letters and the formation of character.[18] The very aim of humanistic education dramatically contrasts with that of the universities: not the pursuit of knowledge for its own sake, not academic "contemplation," but the formation of good taste and right values, and the cultivation of the ability to *act* effectively and responsibly in the public sector, especially through the ability to persuade.

Perhaps the deepest conviction of the humanists was that a reform of education was the primary instrument for the reform of society and church, for good education produces good persons. Good persons would engage in the active life of the polis — they would not withdraw to the cloisters of academe. By their learning and the example of their lives they would reform taste, and they would especially reform the morals of public life. Not a "reform of structures" (a quite modern idea), but a reform of persons was the goal at which humanist education aimed. The Spanish Jesuit, Juan Bonifacio, who published in 1576 probably the first educational treatise by a member of the Society of Jesus, fully appropriated this ideal when he said, *Puerilis institutio est renovatio mundi* ("The education of youth accomplishes the reform of society").[19]

This brings me, finally, to the Jesuits of the sixteenth century. When one reads their pertinent documents on education, especially the fourth part of the Jesuit Constitutions and then the *Ratio Studiorum* of 1599, the magna carta of the Jesuit tradition, what immediately strikes one from this perspective is the attempt to conjoin elements from both the scholastic and the humanistic tradition. The evolution of this endeavor is complicated to trace in the sources and need not concern us in its details at this time. Its seed was surely the experience of Saint Ignatius and his first companions at Paris, where the components were already in juxtaposition, if not in synthesis, when they studied there. The future stance of the order was already adumbrated by Ignatius in his famous "Rules for Thinking with the Church," where in number 11 we are enjoined to praise "the positive doctors" like Augustine and Jerome, whose object is to "rouse the affections so that we are moved to love and serve God our Lord in all things" — a goal consonant with the humanistic tradition and with the humanist's interest in the fathers of the church —and at the same time to praise "the scholastic doctors" who "define and state clearly" what is to be learned. As I said, I will not concentrate on the evolution of this conjunction of scholastic and humanistic elements, an enterprise in which Jerónimo Nadal played, as always in this early Jesuit history, such a pivotal role, but rather I will try to call attention to the reciprocal influences that manifest themselves especially from a study of the matured instrument codifying them, the *Ratio* of 1599.[20]

Before I undertake that task, however, I must take a look at the more general plan of education envisioned in the *Ratio*. After the careful and effective study by Gabriel Codina Mir, we are well informed about the model for the system, the so-called *modus parisiensis* that the first Jesuits experienced during their own studies at both Alcalá and Paris itself.[21] Unlike other systems, particularly the *modus italicus*, the Parisian system provided a determined progression in classes and subject matter. It was also based on the principle of self-exertion and practice on the part of the student — *usus, non praecepta* — and this would be true of the study of both letters and then later of the so-called arts and sciences (sometimes called "philosophy"), and finally of theology.

Particularly distinctive of the *modus parisiensis* by the time Ignatius and the others studied in Paris was, in fact, this threefold set of colleges. The most recently constituted of the three colleges was in fact the first the student entered, the college of humane letters, in which literary studies were pursued under the influence of humanistic methods. The Italian humanists of the fifteenth century had envisioned their program apart from the university and even as an alternative to it, but their very success in propagandizing that program resulted in its partial incorporation into the rival system. This was part and parcel of the Parisian system that the Jesuits adopted, and it was surely from Paris that they first imbibed the notion, put baldly and somewhat anachronistically in our terms, that humanism and scholasticism were compatible educational visions. Clearly incorporated into their system were the three faculties already operative at Paris: the college of humane letters (where grammar, rhetoric, poetry, and history were studied with somewhat humanistic methods); the college of arts and sciences (where metaphysics, psychology, mathematics, and especially the natural sciences were studied according to the scholastic method), and finally theology, also a scholastic discipline. The thesis can be advanced that by the time of the *Ratio*, 1599, the Jesuits in fact gave more attention to the study of the humanities than did Paris in their day,

that they pursued them with more enthusiasm and had appropriated more completely and authentically the humanistic vision of
their purpose and intrinsic value. Nonetheless, these studies were
incorporated into a larger system and to a considerable extent were
ordered toward the higher discipline par excellence, theology. That
ordering towards theology was at the heart, at least in theory, of the
modus parisiensis.

It is at this point that the central problem emerges. Did the Jesuits
simply lay two systems — two educational visions, really — side by
side, so that these systems and the values inherent in each of them
were not both affected in the process? I have already suggested that
they did not, and I would here like to detail some of the modifica-
tions that resulted.[22] I will concentrate on theology, for that is the
area with which I am most familiar and also in which the central
problem most clearly manifests itself.

Before I descend to details, however, I must state the reason why
the Jesuits even during the lifetime of Saint Ignatius thought it
necessary to provide special lectures and repetitions in theology for
younger members of the order who were following courses at a
university. As Miguel Batllori has shown, it was so that these young
Jesuits would receive a more practical and pastoral approach to
theology than the style of teaching and the content of the courses in
the universities provided.[23] This fact might shock some persons,
who even today see little difference between academic and minis-
terial theology. The first Jesuits surely wanted their younger breth-
ren to have an academically rigorous training, comparable to their
own in that regard, but they also wanted that training ordered to a
life of ministry. That early orientation of theology in the Society
frames the interpretation we must give to the *Ratio,* published half a
century later.

We might begin our examination of the *Ratio* by taking a look at
the critique the humanists mounted against scholastic theology,
especially in their most eloquent and widely read spokesman, Erasmus. Erasmus's plan for the reform of theology was based on the
conviction that the "modern theologians" — that is, the scholastics
— had abandoned the rhetorical and more authentic theology of the
fathers of the church and were in their enterprise almost a contradic-
tion in terms. As early as 1497 he scathed them in a letter to Thomas
Grey, which I cannot refrain from quoting. Erasmus says:

> There is nothing more rotten than their brains, nothing more barbaric
> than their tongues, nothing more stupid than their wit, nothing more

thorny than their teaching, nothing more crude than their conduct, nothing more counterfeit than their lives, nothing more virulent than their languages, nothing blacker than their hearts.[24]

In speaking of the scholastics, Erasmus was not always as intemperately vituperative, and over the course of the years he elaborated a reasonable critique of them that can be gleaned from his many writings. That critique can be summarized under four major headings. I should like to show how the *Ratio Studiorum* correlates with each of these criticisms. I am not of course postulating that the compilers of the *Ratio* had Erasmus, or any other humanistic critic, explicitly in mind when they composed their work, but I want to indicate how the study even of scholastic theology was modified in the *Ratio* in a way that, in fact, manifests in almost every instance sensitivity to the shortcomings of that theology as contemporaries, especially the humanists, perceived it.[25]

Erasmus's first criticism was that the scholastics did not know "the sources" of Christian theology. By this he meant that they did not study the texts of scripture and the fathers with the literary and historical methodology developed by the humanists, so that they lifted verses out of context as proof texts and thus distorted the meanings to serve their own dialectical purposes. Moreover, they did not know Hebrew and Greek, the languages in which the Bible was written. Their enterprise was thus vitiated at the outset, vitiated in its very methodology. Granted some exaggeration in Erasmus's critique, there is no doubt that in the sixteenth century many scholastic theologians resisted the new humanistic program for the study of sacred texts.

In the *Ratio*, on the other hand, the first subject treated in the whole document is scripture.[26] Scripture is thus given primacy of place over all other subjects in the curriculum, at least on this prescriptive level. Knowledge of Hebrew, Greek, Syriac, and other languages of the ancient Near East is insisted upon in the teacher, and the scholastic method of exegesis is explicitly rejected. Teachers of scripture are to render the sense of the text from its context and not approach it in search of proof texts. Study of the fathers in their integral works is also enjoined, and their explanations of the meaning of scripture is commended.[27] We perceive from the preliminary draft of the *Ratio*, 1586, that these are not casual or perfunctory injunctions, but were conclusions arrived at after long debate and a certain alarm that the humanistic methods were in fact not being as assiduously and consistently employed as was thought desirable.[28]

Erasmus also criticized the theology of the schoolmen for being detached from the realm of the affections. We might rephrase his criticism and say that the point he was making was that the scholastic method, with its pursuit of conclusions for their own sake, had detached theology from spirituality. The adjective that Erasmus most frequently employs in describing the result is "cold," "frigid." The scholastics did nothing to warm the affections and thus promote a life that was in accord with the scriptures. Thus the true purpose of theology — to promote "theological *life*" — had been lost.

Correlative to this was his criticism of the scholastics for their "immoral" lives. Taken baldly, this criticism is unfair and could just as well be turned on some of the humanists. But it has a logical connection with the previous criticism. The frigidity, even sterility, of their studies rendered the scholastics susceptible to seeking satisfaction by giving free play to their vanity, to their ambition, and to even worse vices. That is to say, in its method and content the scholastic enterprise was not humane, and, according to Erasmus, this defect was reflected in the lives of its practitioners.

The second level of this criticism was directed at the lack of concern in the scholastic system for virtue and the spiritual growth of students. The scholastics' "professionalism," their concern with abstract truths, and their ardor for the advancement of truth left no room for edification and for the personal relationship between teachers and students that was at the heart of good education.

The *Ratio* meets these points head-on. The remedy against the frigidity of theology is the one Erasmus himself would have adduced — the study of rhetoric, the discipline of persuasion, by which persons are moved to love what is good and despise what is evil. And there are the injunctions to professors of scholastic theology that they are to teach so as to strengthen the faith and nourish the devotion of their students.[29] It is perhaps considerations like these that induced Nadal to describe teaching in the schools as part of *ministerium verbi Dei*.[30]

Nothing, surely, is more central to the *Ratio* than the principle that all studies are meant to lead the student to virtue and probity of life. The idea recurs in a number of crucial passages in almost every major section of the document. The aim is to be accomplished by the manner in which subjects are taught and by the example of the teacher's own life.[31] One can assert, I believe, that the humanistic ideal that formation of character is the first goal of education thoroughly pervades the *Ratio* and to a large extent animates it, even in the sections dealing with scholastic philosophy and theology. Nadal stated the goal succinctly: *Ut in studiis primum locum pietas obtineat.*[32] A slightly tendentious translation points up the paradox: "So that in academic matters, religious formation hold the primacy." If Nadal's assumptions were scholastic, not humanistic, one would have expected him to insist that in academic matters the untrammeled *pursuit of truth* was what was at stake.

Erasmus's final criticism of scholastic theology was perhaps the most central in his attack, and it to some extent summarizes all the others. For Erasmus, scholastic theology was simply irrelevant. It was pursued by egghead professionals in a way that made it irrelevant to life, to the needs of society, to spirituality, and even to ministry. The scholastics were concerned with trivial, obscure, and purely academic questions, and these shortcomings became evident whenever they engaged in ministry, especially in preaching. Moreover, they in fact showed precious little concern for ministry, and engaged in it all too seldom, taken up as they were with their disputations and internecine debates.

As must be evident by now, the *Ratio* tries in a number of ways to obviate these problems, real or imagined. It explicitly warns against the teaching of trivial and obsolete issues.[33] It commends the study of Aquinas, the scholastic master perhaps least vulnerable to these criticisms.[34] The early Jesuits themselves criticized professors of theology at Paris who never left their classrooms and studies to minister to persons in need.[35] Most important of all, perhaps, is the first "rule" for the rector of the Jesuit school: the purpose of the schools of the Society is stated in terms of aiding one's neighbor.[36] Even the study of the sciences and of theology had a goal beyond speculation, a goal of service.

My purpose in presenting this counterpoint between Erasmus and the *Ratio*, sketchy though it is, has been to show how the Jesuits wanted to preserve the best of two great educational ideals even in their universities: the intellectual rigor of the scholastic system and the more personalist, societal, and even practical aims of the humanists. I am not trying to say that they were altogether successful in doing so. Does not any attempted synthesis of the two ineluctably run the danger of blunting the internal dynamics of both? Indeed, I wonder if a final resolution of such disparate goals is possible within any educational vision and, unless we clearly opt for one of the two alternatives, if we are not perpetually condemned to some compromise rather than synthesis.

I think I can illustrate this juxtaposition of goals in a concrete way.

Every American educator is familiar with the motto of Harvard University — *Veritas*. It would be difficult to express the aim and dynamism of the scholastic vision more succinctly and forcefully, and Harvard stands in the eyes of many as a symbol of that vision in its modern guise. Less well known is the fact that the original motto of that university, still visible on some of its older buildings and present even over the main entrance to Harvard's great Widener Library, was more complex and suggested the scholastic-humanistic duality about which I have been speaking. The original motto was *Veritas pro Christo et ecclesia*. The briefer version does not necessarily reflect only a process of secularization, but also an option for one horn of the perennial dilemma in education. I do not of course mean to imply by this illustration that Harvard is today unconcerned with the broader range of its students' needs. In fact, in recent years there has been considerable discussion at Harvard about the ethical and humane development of students, which again indicates that the problem will not go away. On the other hand, the motto of the university in its present form does indicate a clear priority.

It seems to me, in any case, that a certain ambivalence about the purpose of university education was introduced by the Jesuits and others in the sixteenth century and that that ambivalence persists even today. The terms in which it manifests itself are of course quite different. Perhaps one of the purposes my exposition has served is to illustrate how far removed we are today from the specific concerns over the compatibility of humanistic and scholastic education in the strict sense of those terms.

Through the past four hundred years, university education has undergone profound changes. Nowhere in the world today, for instance, is either Aristotle or his sometime rival, Cicero, the center of the curriculum. In fact, they are probably not studied at all. Moreover, just in the past fifty years the universities, instead of being the preserve of the leisured few, have become the goal of vast numbers of young persons, few of whom ambition either a life of cloistered research or a life of service to public causes. Today university education is generally conceived of, and even explicitly presents itself to the public as, a way to "get ahead" — socially and financially — whereas before the two world wars it was designed almost exclusively for those who already "*were* ahead." For those who "*were* ahead," it provided a sabbatical of contemplation, leisure, and cultural nourishment before they moved into their secure places in society — a far cry from the rat race of undergraduate and graduate competition in the "better" universities today. The convergence of these recent changes indicates, in my opinion, another real paradigm shift. We are again at a crossroads.

No doubt, in any case, our situation is quite different from that of the sixteenth century. Nonetheless, many of the problems we face and debate about have ancient roots, or at least ancient counterparts, though they now take different forms and are quite differently contextualized. One issue is fundamental: How do we reconcile with current practice our high rhetoric about education ideals — ideals that hark back to both the scholastic and humanistic traditions?

But more specific issues also reflect the older debates. I mean even questions about "life in the dormitories," the place and purpose of the theology department (especially in its undergraduate instruction), the role of campus ministry, the kind of faculty we seek and why, and, perhaps most tellingly, the formation of students "in the service of faith and for the promotion of justice," about which those in Jesuit schools have heard so much in recent years.[37] How can especially this formation in faith and justice avoid, on the one hand, the pitfall of crass indoctrination and, on the other, the pitfall of mindless do-goodism — neither of which is consonant with genuine education? Other contributions in this volume will deal explicitly with some of these issues.

The main point I have been trying to make is that the documents and institutions I have spoken about pose, in different terms and in a different context, the fundamental and perennial questions facing every educational enterprise: Why are we engaged in the task? What is education *for*? What is *this institution* for? Is there any way to join personalist aims with the untrammeled pursuit of knowledge and truth? Or must we rest content with the axiom "a school is a school is a school," aimed by its own intrinsic dynamism not at affective life or at public service, but at the pursuit of knowledge, either for its own sake, or for the sake of preparing persons to get a job that will enable them to make more money than their parents did. It is that last purpose that has obtruded itself into higher education in a massive and almost overpowering way only in relatively recent times. But it does seem to indicate were much of higher education, even in the oldest and most traditional institutions, has in fact been heading, as the panel convened by the National Endowment for the Humanities informed us in November 1984.[38] The panel did not consider it a good sign.

In any case, as I hope my exposition has at least suggested, the Jesuit tradition in education is complex and not without its ambivalences for us today. Whether or not the early Jesuits successfully resolved some of these ambivalences in their actual practice is a matter of historical interest that cannot detain us at the present, for no matter what the answer, we must work toward our own solutions in the situations that we currently face.[39]

Before concluding, however, I should like to point out one key area in which Jesuits did find, it seems to me, genuine agreement between scholasticism and humanism, to which they subscribed wholeheartedly. That area was a fundamental principle, or even religious worldview, that in different forms has been consistent in Jesuit education, at least in theory, from the origins of the Society down to the present. That principle is, put in its most traditional terms, that "reason and revelation" are ultimately reconcilable. This is what Jesuit universities seem to me to symbolize by the very fact of their existence, and that is one area in which scholasticism and humanism agreed.

Let me slightly rephrase the principle in words that I believe are historically more accurate and presently more helpful: culture and religion interpenetrate, and religion is impoverished and ultimately distorted when it runs from the challenges of the culture in which it lives, painful though it may sometimes be to face those challenges. More fundamentally, culture and religion are reconcilable, and the Jesuit order is committed to a theology — or a philosophy — of *reconciliation.* "Grace builds on nature" is a scholastic dictum, but it is perfectly consonant with the worldview of Renaissance humanists.[40]

When in the Constitutions Saint Ignatius made Thomas Aquinas the theological master for the order, he was reflecting his own experience of the study of theology at Paris and the favor Aquinas enjoyed in Rome.[41] But, in fact, of all the scholastic theologians Aquinas was the most committed to the reconcilability of reason and revelation, which for him meant the Bible and Aristotle. As the early Jesuits become ever more imbued with enthusiasm for the study of the literary and rhetorical texts of antiquity, they did not view those texts merely as models of eloquence but also as sources inspiring genuine growth in virtue and religion. The idea appears in the *Ratio* and in many of the other writings from the early period of the Society.[42] As far as I know, no Jesuit ever went so far as to repeat Erasmus's most famous line, "O Saint Socrates, pray for us."[43] But some of them came close. I recall for you only the words of the famous Jesuit exegete, Cornelius à Lapide, on reading a passage from the philosopher Epictetus: *O Stuporem! verba haec sonant Evangelium, non philosophiam moralem* ("O wonder, these words ring of the gospel, not just moral philosophy").[44]

I submit that, as we work toward solutions to the problems that face us, we must do so in the context of this principle to which, it seems to me, the Jesuit tradition in its deepest impulse obliges us. This principle implies, of course, a critical attitude toward general culture and a slowness to accept the latest idea as automatically the best. But it at the same time forbids any return to a narrow sectarianism, to a "sacristy Christianity," and, a fortiori, to Catholic varieties of fundamentalism, a danger not unknown at the present time.

2 / The Current State of the Jesuit Philosophy of Education

William C. McInnes, S.J.

JESUIT education is a living tradition. It is based on a specific heritage and it is being continually shaped by current decisions. Even to begin to understand the current state of the Jesuit philosophy of education in the United States — or to determine whether there is one — requires, therefore, a review of both writers and decision-makers. Inasmuch as no definitive philosophy of Jesuit education has ever been written and no ultimate decision as to its form has ever been made, all analyses must be tentative. The definitive work will probably be assigned to an archeologist rather than a philosopher.

The complex system of Jesuit higher education in the United States — with its twenty-eight institutions, two hundred thousand students (of all ages), one thousand Jesuits, twenty six thousand lay colleagues, and one million graduates — is unparalleled in any other part of the world.[1] The evolution of this enterprise with its foundations in a remote phrase, *Ad Maiorem Dei Gloriam*, and a continual reference to a work entitled the *Spiritual Exercises*, is unmatched in Jesuit history. Thus the American system of Jesuit higher education must be looked at in its own context and with some of its own norms.

In this paper I will first consider three stages of development in Jesuit education. Next I will review some of the authors — corporate and individual — who have analyzed the meaning of that development. I will then describe some of the major decisions that have shaped that system without systematic philosophical reflection.

Finally, I will offer some conclusions for both thinking and acting to meet "the challenges of the 1980s — and beyond." For the sake of brevity — and relevance — I will largely confine myself to the years following World War II. These years witnessed a remarkable development of Jesuit schools in terms of governance, academic standards, student enrollments, mass education, community relations, financial underpinnings, and public policy. They provide both a heritage and a laboratory for review.

THREE STAGES

Since World War II, Jesuit colleges and universities have traversed roughly three stages: (1) a search for academic respectability in the 1950s; (2) a search for a new citizenship role — social and legal — in the 1960s; (3) a search for identity — specifically religious — in the 1970s. Each of these stages was initiated from outside the university. But what is significant is not the source of the challenge but the quality of the response.

Academic Respectability

Reflection upon the academic excellence of Jesuit colleges and universities in this country began, not with an isolated scholar, but with a central committee.

In the early 1920s the Jesuits themselves began to have "serious doubts about the calibre of Jesuit education."[2] Their schools were not well received in the groves of American academe. They were threatened by new demands from accrediting associations — a unique American phenomenon. In 1921 the provincials, concerned about the lack of uniformity of the schools and the lack of acceptance by other educators, formed an interprovince committee on studies to promote a more coherent central direction to the higher education apostolate. Their concern was justified — but the direction of their thrust was finessed. Two decades of committees, commissions, and reports marked the struggle to raise standards and at the same time counter the strong individualism of independent-minded presidents and rectors.

The drama played out in the 1930s even had its own central character: a commissarius — Father Daniel O'Connell, S.J. He is evaluated by Fr. Paul Fitzgerald, S.J., as "the major architect of higher standards and professionalism" of Jesuit education.

Fr. O'Connell cut a wide swath through the plans of those centrifugally oriented presidents and rectors who were attempting to match aspirations with resources and to move with a rapidly changing world. O'Connell recommended that Boston College discontinue all its Ph.D. programs. He wanted Greek to be an elective at Holy Cross. Georgetown, he alleged, was competing with the Catholic University of America in graduate programs, and so should end them. St. Louis should be built up as the education center for the Midwest, he prescribed, noting gratuitously that the president was a "charming gentleman but no educator or executive."[3] Marquette should settle for a smaller regional role. Fordham, he proposed, had the best opportunity to become a national graduate center for Jesuit education. Thus spake O'Connell.

The end result: not a new idea, but a new organization — the Jesuit Education Association (JEA). It was formed in 1934.

That association became the major spokesman for Jesuit higher education, especially in the postwar period. That was a time in which the vast influx of postwar students inserted a new style of mass education into the Jesuit system. Enrollments quadrupled in fifteen years. A new partnership of government and the academic community evolved in those years, not so much as a master plan but as a series of pragmatic political and academic choices. In 1982 Jesuit schools received $94 million in benefits from the federal government; they collected $139 million from private sources.[4] A new closeness to the surrounding community as well as to the government had developed. Professional schools expanded greatly, diverting — if not draining — the financial and human resources of the system and threatening the very soul of Jesuit education. Some allege it killed it, though they can find no corpus delecti or produce any autopsy report.

Rapid expansion threatened quality, and fostered a philosophical dialectic. A countervoice demanding a higher quality of intellectual leadership in the Catholic school system emerged — most visibly in the widely distributed article of Msgr. John Tracy Ellis of Catholic University in 1955.[5] An attempt was made the following year by Dean Arthur North of the Fordham graduate school to put a bright face on a sad situation. He responded to Msgr. Ellis in an article in the National Catholic Education Bulletin.[6] The content of the response mattered less than the enlivening of the dialogue. The public began to take academics more seriously.

It was action, however, more than reflection, that was closing the gap between intellectual aspirations and accomplishment in the

Jesuit system. The JEA had already formed a commission in 1948 to improve the quality of Jesuit education, especially in the graduate schools.[7] As a result, provincials had committed themselves to improve the graduate programs in the universities and to assign young Jesuits to doctoral studies. Those important decisions were reshaping the system even before the question was raised philosophically by critics. The commitment to doctoral studies is operative today — a tribute to the succession of provincials who have supported it.[8]

The 1950s were, in fact, a decade of navigators rather than of philosophers. The system was being determined by a series of pragmatic actions rather than by a centralized reflective philosophy. Jesuit education moved into the mainstream of American higher education in the 1950s primarily because of the concerted efforts of many Jesuit leader-activists and decision-makers.

Civic Responsibility

Academic respectability took a back seat to civic involvement in the 1960s. In that decade the citizenship function of the college and university in the world was thrust peremptorily by external events to center stage. Once again, the initiating force came from outside: the desire to tap more government funds for burgeoning student enrollments, the new scientific competition with the Soviet Union, unresolved church/state issues, and — increasingly — the rising clamor of students challenging the prerogatives of the lords of the ivory towers.

Colleges were being asked to justify themselves not as educators but as citizens. The demand brought forth a whole new set of questions, not easy to resolve, and a whole new body of decisions, not always quietly made.

In the 1960s the Jesuit schools evolved as civic institutions: legally and socially. The twenty-eight Jesuit colleges and universities fought for their social identity both in the courts and in the streets. There was much more doing than reflecting.

The *Tilton* and *Roemer* church-state litigation took the schools into court.[9] The *McGrath* and *Cessna* theses took them into the arena of public debate.[10] In both areas Jesuit schools struggled to proclaim a new rationale for their citizenship responsibilities. It was not easy, nor was it readily accepted. Through complicated and expensive legal cases, religiously affiliated colleges and universities won the right to be treated as first-class citizens. Through messy legal and psychological rearrangements of their structures and operations, they realigned themselves somewhere along the new spectrum of church-state relationships in a pluralistic society.

One consequence of the embroilment in legal and social activities was the growing recognition of public policy as a worthy apostolic ministry for Jesuits. Jesuits realized that if the air was going to be made clean, they would have to help clean it. Since 1970 Jesuit schools have been actively involved in the apostolate of educational public policy — a field never envisioned when the JEA was established. Jesuits have accepted the premise that one of the most significant areas for leadership is the influencing of public policy. It has become a primary foundation in the search for justice.[11]

Jesuits in the 1960s sought not only legal but also social acceptance for their schools. The challenge — again — had come from outside. Restless and anxious students were challenging — sometimes violently — the perceived stand-off positions of their alma maters. In their intense view the schools were confronting the horror of racism and war with the bland response of discussion. That was not enough — either for students or for many Jesuits.

A major attitudinal change within Jesuit ranks occurred in the late 1960s. Fewer younger Jesuits felt attracted to the education apostolate. A wave of anti-institutionalism rolled across the Society of Jesus, rocking it from top to bottom.[12] The tremors carried many from the campus into the streets and on to the barricades. The new thrust was even baptized (but not canonized) by a decree of the 32nd General Congregation calling on all Jesuits to promote faith and justice, suggesting to many that new approaches and commitments were required for a new age. It was hard in those years for the schools to ponder reflectively their role as citizens. Many decisions were made under pressure, often without sufficient reflection or context. Events more than philosophies were remolding the academy in that era of upheaval.

For some, the late 1960s and early 1970s was the moment of Camelot. For others it was a radical interruption of the serious work of the university, which they could never excuse, let alone forgive. For still others, it was an inchoate realization of idealistic service, clinging to the heart of Jesuit education. For all it ended after a short, vigorous adolescence — following a brief, exciting whirl. Jesuit schools were never at the center of the storm. But none was untouched by the impact of the social and legal phenomena of the 1960s. All were changed to some degree.

As with all waves, the wave of social action eventually subsided.

The schools survived — even grew. The work of education continued. A new world of opportunity in high technology, a new
fascination with self-improvement and individual careers shifted the
thrust of the challenge to Jesuit education, even as it cooled the
ardor both for political action and social crusades. Even litigious
matters became less-than-earthshaking preoccupations.

No major historical or philosophical study has yet been written
about this amazing decade of transformation in Jesuit higher education. Its meaning still lies hidden in some as yet unwritten work.[13]
Its consequences, however, are evident on the twenty-eight campuses — in new sensitivity to surrounding constituencies, new
campus community action groups and organizations, such as the
Jesuit Volunteer Corps, a new legal sophistication, and even a new
rhetoric in the school catalogues. No Jesuit school tries to define
itself today without taking into account its social dimension and the
legal implications of its statements. That was the heritage of the
experience of the 1960s.

Search for Identity

The search for academic responsibility and social responsibility
yielded (inevitably?) to a third quest — for identity. The big question
in the 1970s was no longer "what should we do?" but rather "who
are we?" — the most agonizing of the searches for self-realization.
Not accidentally, this search on the Jesuit campus became specific as
a search for religious identity — "who are we as a Jesuit college or
university?" The search for the identity of the college or university
as such was left to others.

The search for identity washed up against the campus walls from
the outside. It was not born in the university. A new personalism
had swept the country. The successes of developmental psychology
were being widely publicized and seemed to offer novel insights
into the nature of change in the intellectual and cultural worlds.
Narcissism became legitimate as a style of living and philosophy of
life. Vatican II, with its emphasis on change and growth, provided
new sanctions for experimentation.

Jesuit vocations declined precipitously after 1964. Even though
the schools continued to increase their enrollments, their anxieties
were increased. Questioners wanted to know whether all this activity and effort in education was really worthwhile — especially for
them!

A worldwide sociological survey of Jesuits in 1969 had noted:

. . . it used to be sufficient to answer the question *who we are* in terms of *what we did*. If you asked a person, even as late as a decade ago or in those benighted years of the 1950s, it was often sufficient to respond that the Jesuits taught schools, ran parishes, gave retreats. But this response will not answer the question being asked in the Society today. The question today is: "What really is a Jesuit like?" Or again, "What is the intrinsic worth and benefit of this lifestyle to which you are asking me to commit my life?"[14]

The authors catalogued the malaise of Jesuits around the world. They identified, as one of the nine major obstacles to any change necessary, an "identity crisis, affecting priests and religious in numerous countries."[15] They tried to calm some anxieties by claiming that the Society of Jesus had not really shifted in its fundamental spirituality, but only in its orientation — from a traditionalism and classicism to an experimentalism and historicism. But they had to concede that at the heart of the malaise was a fundamental disagreement:

> Almost all of the basic problems which the Society of Jesus in the United States is currently experiencing stem from a lack of agreement regarding fundamental beliefs and rationales underlying the assumptions, values, and practices relating to religious life, the role of the Church in the modern world, and a choice and role of Jesuit ministries.[16]

In brief, there was a substantial identity crisis in the Jesuit Order. Jesuit colleges and universities could hardly escape the fall-out.

The clamor to know *who we are* became acute as the decade wore on. In 1974 the ten American provincials began to probe the future through a process of centralized planning — Project One. It was an exercise not so much of philosophical insight, as a practical method for determining priorities and the choice of ministries.[17] The conclusions of Project One focused on context and direction, not on identity. A series of practical suggestions for ministry, it committed the Society of Jesus in America to a national corporate apostolate in higher education.[18] A final document wrapping up Project One — *The Mission of Jesuit Higher Education* — appeared in 1978. It was the result of a joint effort of provincials, rectors, and presidents. Eight concrete actions for the "national corporate apostolate" were stated. But implementation was left to local communities and institutions. The results of that implementation have never been evaluated systematically.

A follow-up to Project One, attempting to specify the context of our ministries, began in 1980. A set of papers appeared. But the project ran aground on the rocks of weariness with grand statements and distraction.[19]

CORPORATE REFLECTIONS

The efforts to situate Jesuit identity stayed alive through the 1970s. Both corporate and individual reflections — as well as many different decisions and events — were writing the narrative of Jesuit education and revealing its spirit — though many could not give it a precise name.

Outside leaders came to Jesuit assistance.

A major effort at self-definition by a hundred Catholic college presidents (including some Jesuits) opened a new horizon for thinking about Jesuit education. *The Catholic University in the Modern World* was a philosophical/theological insight into the distinctive nature of the Catholic university.[20] The 9–page document suggested that a Catholic college was distinctive because it has a corporate Christian inspiration, engages in a continuing reflection on human knowledge in the light of faith, prizes fidelity to the Christian message, and has an institutional commitment to the service of all humankind.[21] The statement was produced in 1969 after wide discussion; it was again revised, and finally acknowledged — though not officially approved — by Rome in 1972.

It is a serious statement, the most comprehensive ever to be produced. It has a special foundational significance for Jesuit education, which is certainly one species of Catholic education. For those who believe that "Jesuit indicates a special style or mode of carrying on this Catholic education," it should have a particular meaning. There are many who feel the real identity of Jesuit education in the Catholic tradition is found exclusively in its style and not in any substantial distinctiveness. Others disagree. The issue has never been definitely resolved, but it has been the subject of discussion, which has helped to illuminate it.[22]

Denver Workshop

Eighty-nine Jesuits gathered in Denver in 1969 to reflect corporately on the nature of the Jesuit university and college and its commitment to a world of change.[23] The workshop was designed to be more than an academic exercise. Confusion and uncertainty about the future of Jesuit education demanded clarification. Originators of the workshop recognized the need to set new directions. There were sessions on philosophy and theology, the role of lay persons, and the role of chaplains and campus ministry. Each presentation raised practical questions of policy as well as of theory. More importantly, the workshop probed the issue of the uniqueness of Jesuit education. The principal paper on that subject was prepared by Fr. William Richardson, S.J., a philosophy professor at Fordham. He argued that Jesuit education is not unique, but it is distinctive. He wrote:

> Jesuit education means a style of maintaining colleges and universities that is grounded in a certain mode of religious experience — that of Ignatius — and is reinforced by a certain historical, or historically contingent, vision.[24]

This is one of the first reflections to emphasize a specific religious experience (the *Spiritual Exercises*) over a pragmatic set of rules (the *Ratio Studiorum*) as the real foundation of Jesuit education. The debate continues even to today.

At the conclusion of the workshop the participants agreed on a statement about the distinctive characteristics of Jesuit education. The official report of the meeting noted:

> The word "Jesuit" indicates a special style or mode of carrying on this Catholic education [outlined in the Land O' Lakes Statement]. Its characteristics include: an apostolic intent, a lived witness, a pragmatic strategy of education, an emphasis on intellectual development, and a world-affirming spirituality (or secular mysticism). Tracing its origins to the *Spiritual Exercises* and the Jesuit Constitutions, the delegates declared it leads to a "mysticism of service" to both God and man.
>
> Catholic educational institutions, therefore, differ from other such institutions because their perspective is enlarged by the understanding that everything human is also divine and that commitment to man is radically a commitment to the fullness of man, who is Christ.
>
> "The special mark of Jesuit education," they wrote, "is this absolutely critical position of secular mysticism, an action-oriented Christian humanism."[25]

The language was lofty and esoteric. But the implication is clear: a system based on a religious experience manifested through a pragmatic strategy makes impossible a single philosophy of education. Any specific philosophy, therefore, would have to be subordinate to a theological foundation and be subject to change in practice. That is an important insight in the evolving discussion of the specific nature of Jesuit education. There is no one philosophy of Jesuit education, or any particular form.

The participants acknowledged this when, looking to adaptations needed in the future, they concluded:

> No particular juridical structure, no formal control on the part of Jesuits or Board of Trustees, Administration or Faculty, or by any specific curriculum, as such, specifies the Jesuit system. It is distinguished by a way a significant number of men — Jesuit and lay — express that secular mysticism in their professional and personal lives, win a consensus and design an effective educational enterprise aimed at developing all of the dimensions of the human person.[26]

They looked ahead to experimentation, commitment, acceptance of provisional answers, a creative humanity, a genuine ecumenism, an openness to mystery, a true community, and a prophetic witness. They had touched all the bases! The statement was more revolutionary than perhaps many realized at that time, or realize today.

The future, noted the delegates, depends not on a central philosophy, but on each school "critically reading the signs of our times and flexibly adapting to meet them successfully through an experimental orientation, a consensus on commitment to human values (including the freedom of the student), an acceptance of provisional answers, and open dialogue, a creative humanity, genuine ecumenism, openness to mystery, a true community of Jesuits and laypersons, a prophetic testimony on pressing human and social problems."[27]

That workshop was the last national corporate effort to try to elaborate a general philosophy (theology) of Jesuit higher education. It is an intellectual landmark — defining the heritage while opening the system to living change. Presumably its conclusions filtered down into the thoughts and decisions of many who heard about it. But we are not sure. No one has ever checked.

At least it touched the minds of certain Jesuit leaders.

Association of Jesuit Colleges and Universities (AJCU)

One year after the Denver workshop the centrifugal force of the system spun off a new national organization from the JEA: the Association of Jesuit Colleges and Universities (AJCU). The new directors of AJCU — now presidents instead of provincials — took over. The office moved from New York to Washington. It began a new life under a new president.

The directors of its board were the twenty-eight Jesuit presidents. They resolutely tried — in the face of much other pressing business — to keep alive conceptually the issue of the distinctive nature of Jesuit education. It disintegrated, however, in the pluralism of opinion and action.[28]

The directors took up the subject of Jesuit distinctiveness at their October 8, 1971, meeting. The reason was pragmatic rather than philosophical. The directors had gained autonomy of direction from the provincials. They now needed to reestablish some kind of link with the directions of the Society of Jesus. That bridge came in the form of a provincial request to spell out for them the criteria for "Jesuitness" of a college or a university. Though distracted by the battles over separate incorporation, the onslaught of campus demonstrations, the rising concern with federal relations, mounting litigation and chronic financial squeezes, the presidents tried sincerely to respond to this request. The request became more emphatic when the presidents learned that the provincials had copyrighted the word "Jesuit" and therefore, could control its application.

Father Michael Walsh, S.J., president of Boston College, was chosen by the directors to prepare a statement. He elected to move off a philosophical (or theological) base to a functional, operative one. Looking back to the Denver workshop, he outlined some "characteristics" that made a Jesuit college or university distinctive: individual Jesuit presence, witness, and influence; a strong campus ministry; good departments of theology and religious studies; placement of Jesuits in key and critical positions. These, he claimed, were the criteria of the "Jesuitness" of a college.[29]

The presidents received the report and mulled over it. The following year the directors returned to the list, adding to it "a concern for the social apostolate." Father Robert Henle, S.J., president of Georgetown and chairman, led a wide-ranging discussion of the criteria. But the session ended with only a general understanding that the presidents truly desired a "functional statement" on criteria and could produce one by the spring of 1972. No neat list of characteristics was accepted by all!

An ad hoc committee (Frs. Henle, Baumhart, Hanley, and Fitterer) worked on. The presidents met with the provincials again in April. Result: the provincials repeated their request for a "functional criteria for Jesuitness."[30]

"We need to do this . . . by the fall," agreed the chairman, stressing the obvious and hoping to raise flagging interest in what some now viewed as sterile discussion.

That fall Fr. John Fitterer, S.J., AJCU president, presented the committee's revised findings to the board. The findings came in the form of a position paper with nine criteria for *membership in AJCU* (note the shift in the *status quaestionis*). The criteria: official commitment to be a Jesuit college or university, a corporate commitment by a visible group of Jesuits, an institutional arrangement to perpetuate the Jesuit character of the institution (e.g., through the trustees), a Jesuit president (in good standing), Jesuits in key spots and one in every major department, the acceptance of the educational ideals and the spirit of the Society of Jesus, with a strong campus ministry and department of theology, discussion of the philosophical questions in the curriculum, and a genuine effort by Jesuits to share their Ignatian vision.

Secular mysticism had become engulfed by membership criteria. And another difficulty had surfaced: specificity had been gained at the cost of increasing disagreement.

Discussion at the meeting proved inconclusive. Fordham's representative found legal difficulties with the paper. Marquette's preferred *regional* statements between provincials and the school. One president denied the possibility of describing any commitment in univocal language. Fr. Walsh wanted something more general. Another president favored more individual essays and studies as a better solution to the problem. Still another questioned the very possibility of ever coming up with anything. With resignation, the chairman asked the members to write in any comments they might have to Fr. Fitterer before the next meeting in January.[31]

In January 1973, the directors returned to the question for one last go-around.[32] The results were again inconclusive. Fr. Toland, president of St. Joseph's, submitted a lengthy summary of the discussions to date. He prodded the members to decision with the threatening analogy of the preamble that the high schools had so successfully submitted to the provincials. There was a marathon discussion. The minutes record the final moments:[33]

> Fr. Tipton: "We seem to be passing the problem back to the provincials and the Jesuit communities."
>
> Fr. Mitchell, provincial: "The provincials are not questioning AJCU membership, but rather asking what AJCU institutions are all about."
>
> Fr. Reinert: "Perhaps we should have a standing committee or commission, continually dealing with this problem."
>
> Fr. Henle, chairman: "In summary we are saying that a checklist is not the answer. Do we want Frs. Fitterer and Mitchell to work out a membership committee?"

The motion was formally made. It was rejected. The question never reappeared on the agenda of the AJCU.

Ironically, down the street another document had been introduced at a parallel meeting of the academic vice-presidents. It had to do with something called "the principle of attraction," an operational guideline for personnel assignments, which was to shape the system more than any statement of criteria. The provincials were no longer waiting for further presidential reflection. Project One was now underway.

In summary, the 1970s were not noted for conclusive philosophical reflections on Jesuit identity. But the decade was marked by a strong growth — qualitative, as well as quantitative — of the Jesuit educational system. The search for identity remains unresolved today — even as the mission continues and the system grows.

INDIVIDUAL REFLECTIONS

Corporate statements, commissions, workshops, and directors' reflections have faded away. But individuals are still intrigued by the subject of Jesuit identity. Philosophers and theologians — and the professor in the classroom — are still asking: Who are we? Unknown to many Jesuits, there is in fact a substantial amount of literature on this topic. But it is scattered, fragmentary, and infrequently referred to by others.

In the past three years new individual reflections on Jesuit identity have surfaced.

At the AJCU meeting of the academic vice-presidents at Santa Clara in 1981, Fr. Michael Buckley, S.J., theology professor at Berkeley, presented to a group of pragmatically pressed AVPs an answer to their question of Jesuit identity to try to help them understand the strange animal that they were administering.[34]

He did so enthusiastically. To the door of their concerns, he nailed twenty-one theses based on the fourth part of the Constitutions of the Society of Jesus.

Why did he do this?

> I do so because I suspect that a central problem for many administrators of such institutions lies with the vagueness or even chaotic understanding of this governing issue: what is it that they are administering? What do you mean by a "Jesuit" university? . . . especially in a university there is a unique value in knowing what you are doing.[35]

Comfortably at home in an arena of protesting dialogue and not inexperienced in the game of debate, Fr. Buckley first of all rejected other earlier descriptions of the meaning of the Jesuit university: Fr. Tim Healy's institutional description of the relationship of the church and the university as two distinct, though interconnected, institutions, was inadequate.[36] "It does not do justice either to the historical nature of a Catholic university, nor to a Catholic university's extrinsic uniqueness."

Next on his list of "adversaries" came Fr. Ladislaus Orsy, S.J. Orsy had suggested that "to have a Catholic university means to have a Catholic presence at the university."[37] Buckley dismissed the approach out of hand: "This is actually a description of a secular university with an active and influential Newman club."

Out, too, went the organizational model and the polished language of the Santa Clara handbook. That publication described the university in terms of the activity of campus ministry, involvement of Jesuits and campus lay persons in all areas of life, presence of spiritual counselors in the dorms, exposure of undergraduates to courses in religious studies, and the role of the mission church. "All of these," claimed the handbook, "assure that Santa Clara remains a Catholic and Jesuit university in more than name only."

"Not true," retorted Buckley. "Most of the presence of the church is assigned to the campus ministry and segregated from the more general intellectual life of the university."

His own response ultimately identified the university as a whole presence of the church, one form of the church, one of its integral communities striving to relate all human cultures to the gospel of salvation.

"Hence the Catholic university as a unique Catholic community . . . is essentially sacramental. . . . It makes present for all human beings now the reality of Christ drawing all human culture to himself."[38]

Applying the fourth part of the Jesuit Constitutions to the Jesuit college, he wrote:

> The entire college/university is a Christian religious community oriented and ordering both schools of humane letters and of natural science to their integration with theology, insisting upon the Christian service for which these studies are undertaken. It follows that academic administration is essentially a religious ministry, its leaders committed to learning and the Christian life as a single finality.[39]

As a corollary he noted that "a Jesuit school does not depend upon the presence or absence of any particular discipline (including theology), but by the order of the questions which are entertained and by the kind of knowledge which is considered most worth having, the quality and influence of theology as the principal and governing discipline, and an environment of general Catholic culture."

The group had time — and breath — for only the first six theses. There was no follow-up.[40] A bright and provocative theological presentation from a serious thinker; perhaps too abstract for deskbound administrators, yet worthy of further consideration.

But with no forum for continued dialogue, the topic has rested there ever since.

A philosophical approach to the issue of identity is outlined by David Hassell, S.J., in his book, *City of Wisdom*.[41] The book does not identify the specific nature of a *Jesuit* university, but it does offer "one vision of the ideal Christian university." The author notes that the university is essentially a wisdom community; a Christian university is a university informed by Christian wisdom. The source of that Christian wisdom is the religious founding group and the constituencies of the university. Its authority comes from the knowledge and the discussions and decisions of the faculty. Its unity is rooted in the unity of Christian philosophy. The role of the religious founding group is to integrate Christian wisdom with university knowledge.

There are no names or places in this book. It is, rather, a framework for abstract philosophical thinking. It offers a penetrating insight into the Christian university, but yields few suggestions — or directions — for resolving practical problems. Perhaps that is why it did not become the subject of much campus dialogue. After a few reviews it went on to the back shelf.

Not all reflection has been deductive. There has also been an inductive approach to the analysis of the identity of the Catholic (and implicitly, Jesuit) university.

A remark of Pope John Paul II when he visited the United States in 1979 occasioned an empirical attempt to describe a Catholic university.[42] In his talk at Catholic University the pope had referred to the Catholic university as "a community of faith" — a very broad and inclusive term. A follow-up task force of the Association of Catholic Colleges and Universities (ACCU), intrigued with that insight, conducted a conference the next year on the relationship of the campus ministry to the community of faith. The thought deepened with exposure. A preliminary survey of thirty schools had shown strong interest in discussing the problem further. The survey had also suggested that most respondents recognized the community of faith primarily in terms of programs of the campus ministry. The task force sought to broaden the concept — and its application — for its own conference. So it drew up at a brainstorming session a list of thirty-four characteristics, which might be included as signs of a community of faith, many of them not involving campus ministry at all.[43]

At the conference the concept of the community of faith was discussed — and even separated from campus ministries. Six workshops followed at Barry, Mt. St. Mary's, Seattle, Riviere, St. Edward's, and Xavier (Chicago). They were held to flesh out the original "characteristics" of a community of faith. Input from faculty, administrators, and students, lay and religious, campus ministers and placement officers, broadened the concept considerably. Interestingly, the final list converged on three broad aspects of the school: mission, faculty, and social justice. The resulting checklist — suitable for institutional self-study — eventually included fifty-three specific items under five categories — religious, academic, extracurricular, administrative, and organizational (social and political) — to describe an academic community of faith.

It was a promising beginning. But after the conferences, interest waned. The effort has since stalled.

Fr. Joseph Tetlow, S.J., has attempted to describe panoramically *The Jesuit's Mission in Higher Education.*[44] His study, published in 1983, is a historical, philosophical/theological treatise. He locates the Jesuit college in the environment of the American higher education scene and within the philosophical framework developed by Merrimon Cunningham of "embodying," "proclaiming," and "consonant" colleges.[45]

He evaluates the Jesuit schools in terms of their "common mission," a phrase that is largely unspecified.[46] Today, he concludes, the Jesuits and the AJCU are seeking to reestablish their "common mission," clarifying the apostolic purposes of the community and the academic purposes of the institution.

His historico-impressionistic narrative notes that Project One, the provincials' attempt at national planning, was flawed, not because of the concept, but because it detached institutions from the process. He agrees, with Bangert, that the Jesuit colleges and universities are the uniquely American contribution to the history of Jesuit education. But he never settles what their identity — or even mission — really is.

42   JESUIT HIGHER EDUCATION

FRAGMENTED REFLECTIONS

Corporate and individual reflections on the identity of Jesuit education do not exhaust the possibilities for imaging concepts.

Top-down investigations and systematic philosophizing may have languished, but individual fragmented insights are circulating in a kind of underground movement and nonpublic dialogue. Fr. Sullivan, president of Seattle, speaks about the meaning of Jesuit education at a Fairfield convocation.[47] Fr. Padberg opens a workshop at Loyola (New Orleans) with a paper on the history of Jesuit education.[48] Frs. Loughran and O'Hare, new presidents in 1984, touch on the topic in their opening speeches.[49] Fr. Monan and Fr. John Langdon present the case to fund-raisers.[50] Fr. Rewak talks to the faculty on Jesuit distinctiveness.[51] Fr. Raynor summarizes his insights in his annual report.[52] Provincials in the past three years have begun to appear at trustee meetings to make presentations. Jesuit community meetings open up the question to a wider audience of Jesuits and to lay faculty. Fr. McBrien writes of the Boston College Community rationale in *Commonweal*.[53] Prof. David O'Brien of Holy Cross discusses lay-religious collaboration in a pamphlet of *Jesuit Studies*.[54] Dr. Jeanne Neff, academic president of Wheeling College, meditates quietly on the vision of Jesuit education.[55] Quentin Quade, executive vice-president of Marquette, trumpets unabashedly about *Jesus Christ and the Complex Institution*.[56]

Not surprisingly, Fr. Barry McGannon, S.J., of St. Louis University, was able to fill two loose-leaf volumes with these scattered presentations on the meaning and identity of Jesuit education.[57] In the AJCU offices today are the rationales of twenty-eight Jesuit schools, along with the rationales of several Jesuit communities about who they are and what they are doing.[58] It is not the library that is lacking; it is a general and sustained interest in the topic.

There is a new interest in this issue of identity in the AJCU conferences.[59] Very often the question is articulated in terms of mission rather than of identity, which should not be too surprising given the Jesuit orientation of the conferences.[60] But the probing is reaching out to new insights into what it means to be a Jesuit school. The Conference of Business Deans, reflecting on the distinctive characteristics of service, curriculum, stewardship, moral values, and leadership, has produced a document for the use of its members.[61] The Conference of Teacher Education has developed a mission statement to explain how its operations — relatively new — fit into a Jesuit philosophy of education. The Conference of Nurses is trying to produce a statement that locates them in the mainstream of the Jesuit system.[62] All of which is evidence that sober inquiry at the grassroots level — sometimes from surprising quarters — is still being made.

These efforts result only in fragments. The pieces have not yet been integrated into a whole. Perhaps they cannot be. But they do illuminate a continuing interest in the question. That may be the healthiest sign of all.

CONCEPTS VS. ACTION

One conclusion seems evident: to articulate the distinctiveness of any Jesuit philosophy of education — through theological insight, philosophical reflection, or empirical investigation — is only half the story.

The other half is narrated by the actions of decision-makers in the system. Jesuit education is being moved not just by what is said or written, but by what is being done. Decentralized decision-making in the system has sometimes brought more significant changes than centralized reflections. Action has brought the tradition to life.

The impact of external events on the Jesuit system of higher education has been great. Some of the most notable of these include: (1) a shift to a mass education system following World War II when federal funds became available and the clamor for new services was urgent; (2) a period of "radical restructuring"[63] of academic governance patterns — for example, lay trustees, separate incorporation, charter revisions — to adapt to modern times;[64] (3) the burgeoning of professional schools, especially in law, business, medicine, nursing and social work;[65] (4) a growing shortage of Jesuit personnel after 1964, depleting the visibility of a Jesuit presence on the campus and forcing Jesuits to explore — and embrace — unprecedented forms of lay-religious collaboration; (5) adherence to a core curriculum in spite of all of the temptations to abandon one, especially in the 1970s; (6) the rapid influx of women on Jesuit campuses — with both deliberate and indeliberate adjusting — and little conceptual reflection, even as their numbers reach a majority in over 50 percent of the Jesuit schools; (7) the increasing presence of minorities on our campuses, now over twenty-six thousand Blacks, Hispanics, and Asians, many of whom are almost completely ignorant about the fundamental nature of Jesuit education — an ignorance reciprocated by many Jesuits and their colleagues; (8) the opening of our doors to international students — now over seven thousand — with widely varying cultural backgrounds and social experiences;[66] (9) the rapid influx of adult learners with nontraditional needs and outlooks.

Like water dripping on granite, these and other factors are altering the rock of the Jesuit system. They are forcing decision-makers to reflect on Jesuit traditions, even as they struggle to adapt programs. Changes are coming not so much from a central philosophy as from decentralized decisions adapting to new circumstances and environments. Some changes have never been centrally approved by anyone — in fact, some were opposed. But changes came as a response to a practical need and to a local initiative. They could not be predicted from the *Ratio Studiorum*; they might be firmly educed from the activism of the *Principle and Foundation*.

Today the Jesuit system of higher education is a sprawling, vital enterprise with an undigested and eclectic philosophy. It is not built on any a priori forms or structure, but on a deep spiritual conviction that colors all that Jesuits do and yet solves none of the problems they confront.

Jesuit education not only reflects a Catholic philosophy of education. It is a creator of one of its own — a manifestation of a vision, more than an implementation of a blueprint. It is an unfinished *Spiritual Exercise*, not a *Ratio Studiorum*.

Some conclusions that might be pondered, for present and future thought and action:

1. *There is not — nor can there be — one canonized philosophy of Jesuit education.*

We must look beyond philosophy for the meaning and foundation of the system: to a religious experience and commitment. Jesuit educators may define many things and they may experiment with many different structures and still be true to their Jesuit heritage — as long as they do not violate the basic religious conviction that gave rise to the system. On the other hand they can betray their tradition by refusing to adapt to the "signs of the times."

2. *The philosophy of Jesuit education is formed not only by what philosophers think, but by what decision-makers do.*

Decisions, as well as thoughts, determine the historical manifestations of the underlying philosophy/theology of the system. Activities and experiments, therefore, should be communicated and shared, not privatized. Centralized communications provide a valuable service for a decentralized system, but centralized decisions would be clumsy, and probably fatal.

3. *The philosophy of Jesuit education is evolving.*

Today Jesuit education has reached only one of its possible mutations. Further changes are inevitable — and desirable. Serious reflection on the source of our heritage and courageous experimentation to adapt to shifting needs are both needed in order to keep abreast of the reality of the system and to ensure that the vision of the past will be ready to serve the needs of tomorrow.

Perhaps it is once again opportune to bring the dialogue on Jesuit education out of the closet and into the national forum. Should we think of another national workshop on the meaning and directions of Jesuit education? Since 1969 there has been no major national workshop devoted to the discussion of Jesuit mission and identity. The system seems to have grown more rapidly from an organizational and political perspective than from an intellectual and dialogic one. We have more good persons than good thoughts in our midst. We need to encourage more reflection and serious dialogue on the subject.

A condition for a renewed public dialogue is the recognition that the enterprise itself is a public one and not a private affair. Ignatius's vision was elaborated to be personalized — but not privatized. It was intended to flow from a private, personal experience to a public, global mission — not to be hoarded. National dialogue, therefore, presupposes a renewed sense of academic and spiritual citizenship, a new respect for a public vocabulary, rules of evidence, and pluralistic public forms that can stimulate ideas and encourage experiments.

The standard rhetoric of every Jesuit college and university today proclaims that the institution serves a public purpose. The facts need to catch up with the rhetoric. The case for the public nature of the Jesuit college or university must be proven not only to the judge and the surrounding community — and not only expressed in the public *worship* of the campus. It must be demonstrated to all those who by their thoughts and actions are participating in the living tradition that is Jesuit education.[67]

3 / The Role of Theology in the Liberal Arts Curriculum

Laurence J. O'Connell

IN 1980 the dean of the College of Arts and Sciences at St. Louis University initiated a revision of the core requirements of the college. During the revision process it became increasingly difficult for those of us in the department of theological studies to clearly articulate and defend a rationale for the proportionately large role that we had traditionally played in the core curriculum. As a consequence the Executive Council of the College voted overwhelmingly to reduce the required hours in theology.

Although this outcome might have been attributed to the malicious mischief of self-interested colleagues or incompetence on our part, I suspected — and indeed I preferred to think — that the underlying cause of our predicament was situated elsewhere. Upon reflection I concluded that the nature and function of religious or theological studies in the undergraduate curriculum had been changing — or better, developing — in recent years. It was time to come to terms with these developments and translate them into cogent and respectable curricular offerings that would be unmistakably recognized as contributing to a well-rounded liberal arts program.

Consequently, I submitted a proposal to the Frank J. Lewis Foundation, which agreed to fund a study directed toward clarifying the nature and function of religious/theological studies in the humanities curricula of church-related colleges and universities. As the study began to take shape in early 1982, five areas of concern began to emerge as the principal vectors of inquiry:

1. The relationship between, on the one hand, religious studies and, on the other hand, theology in colleges and universities with a strong orientation and devotion to classic Christian traditions.
2. The function of religious/theological studies in the educational experience of students in a church-related institution.
3. The function of religious/theological studies in the undergraduate humanities curriculum.
4. The function of religious/theological studies in relation to the specific identity of the educational institution.
5. The need to develop teaching methods and a curricular model(s) that would be consistent with the findings of the foregoing inquiries.

Although all five areas were considered, the first (the relationship between theology and religious studies), the third (the undergraduate humanities curriculum), and the fifth (curriculum design) demanded and ultimately received greater attention.

I had based my proposal to the Lewis Foundation on the premise that the role of religion in the curricula of many church-related schools had changed. Over the years, due to several cultural and religious shifts, there had been a gradual movement away from the notion that the inclusion of the study of religion stems primarily from the religious character of the institution. The view has emerged that the study of religion, especially on the undergraduate level, finds its validation and role, not primarily in reference to the religious identity of the institution, but in connection with its own identity as a legitimate humanities discipline. Thus, the study of religion in many church-related colleges and universities has transcended the reductionist view that its sphere of activity is circumscribed by the sponsoring church's religious doctrine. The study of religion takes its place among the humanities without, on the one hand, making apologies or, on the other hand, claiming a privileged position. It is now accepted in most circles that, within the context of the humanities curriculum, the study of religion should be critical rather than catechetical. In short, the study of religion, whether it be in a church-related college or a state-supported university, should draw its identity from the humanities.[1]

This view of the study of religion is reflected in the considerable structural changes that have occurred in the humanities curriculum of many church-related colleges and universities. In the 1960s what had been a religion department became a theology department and in many places evolved into a religious studies department or, in the 1970s, into a hybrid of theology *and* religious studies. Parenthetically, it might be noted that many of the same forces that fostered a broadened understanding of the function of the study of religion in church-related schools opened the way for the wide emergence of religious studies departments in state universities. Once the study of religion had been emancipated from the strictures of denominational identity, it was free to assume its rightful place within the general humanities curriculum.

Yet, problems remained. On the one hand, how were church-related schools to incorporate the scientific study of religion — that is, religious studies — into a curriculum that had been heavily informed by a specifically theological agenda? And on the other hand, could religious studies in fact be taught in state-supported universities without some direct reference to the theological sensibilities of both students and professors? Is it possible to teach *about* religion without venturing into the lived experience of religion?

Many church-related colleges and universities handled the problem by devising a double set of courses, thereby giving rise to the forementioned departments of theology *and* religious studies. However, little or no explicit attempt was made to critically interrelate the two fields of study. Oftentimes, the end result was a hybrid department in which the constituent parts were not well defined or integrated. In state universities the situation was different. The so-called objective, nonnormative nature of religious studies was championed against the supposed subjective, ecclesiastically controlled character of theology. Suspicion reigned supreme. In some church-related colleges religious studies were caricatured as a vehicle of creeping secularism that, if given too prominent a place in the curriculum, might tend to undermine the personal appropriation of religious values. Likewise, theology was ruled out of state-supported schools on the grounds that its inclusion in any fashion would be tantamount to the unconstitutional establishment of religion.

This insistence on the almost absolute distinction between theology and religious studies within the context of university education in the United States has been increasingly criticized. In his rigorously argued and brilliantly written book, *Mended Speech: The Crisis of Religious Studies and Theology*, P. Joseph Cahill provides a heuristic structure that supports the contention that, although differences exist between theology and religious studies when they stand in isolation, they can be powerful allies when they meet as mutually supportive dimensions in the general humanities curriculum.

As part of the study funded by the Lewis Foundation and with additional support from the National Endowment for the Humani-

THE ROLE OF THEOLOGY

ties, St. Louis University sponsored a conference aimed at exploring the relationships between theological studies and religious studies in a manner that might enable the two fields to establish a close working partnership within a coherent undergraduate liberal arts curriculum.

Along with several members of our own department of theological studies, the conferees included Dr. Bernard Cooke, president of the Catholic Theological Society of America; William F. May, of Georgetown's Kennedy Institute of Ethics; Dr. Vera Chester, former president of the College Theology Society; Dr. Jacob Neusner, Ungerleider Distinguished Scholar of Judaic Studies at Brown University; and Prof. Walter J. Ong, S.J., university professor of humanities at St. Louis University.

Also taking part were Harvard's Dr. Wilfred Cantwell Smith, an authority on the scientific study of religion; Dr. P. Joseph Cahill, founder-chairperson of the religious studies department, University of Alberta; Dr. Jill Raitt, chairperson of the University of Missouri's new department of religious studies; and two consultants to the general research project: Dr. Walter Capps, president of the Council on the Study of Religion, and Dr. John Orr, dean of the School of Education, University of Southern California.

Although the St. Louis conference did not resolve many of the thorny theoretical issues surrounding the problematical relationship between theology and religious studies, it did have the practical consequence of creating a climate in which the department of theological studies could rethink its understanding of how both theology and religious studies relate to the undergraduate core curriculum. In short, the department realized that both religious studies and theology had a role to play in the core curriculum. Religious studies — that is, the investigation of humankind's religious experience in the most general sense — provides a humanistic framework within which to interpret other academic pursuits, while providing a foundation and point of reference for the more focused study of specific religious traditions in theological studies.

Consequently, the department of theological studies decided to develop a single, first-level course that would draw its predominant identity from religious studies, while working out a set of complementary second-level course that would be more frankly theological. The first-level course has been taught during the last two semesters and we expect to phase in the second-level theology courses in the near future. Although we have had little in the way of in-depth evaluation, our initial experience seems to vindicate the belief that both theology and religious studies belong in the core humanities curriculum at a Catholic, Jesuit university. In excluding religious studies, on the one hand, we would run the risk of teaching our theological tradition in isolation, severing it from the broader religious concerns and convictions of humanity at large. In neglecting theology, on the other hand, we would risk losing sight of the tradition that is our raison d'être.

The role of theology becomes more specific beyond the confines of the undergraduate core curriculum at a Jesuit university. Although I have argued that both religious studies and theology should be part of the undergraduate requirements, I would not argue that religious studies in the strict sense must be incorporated beyond that level. Theology, however, can and should be present on the senior under-graduate and graduate levels of a Catholic, Jesuit university whenever possible.

A Catholic, Jesuit university has a responsibility to provide academic opportunities for students to critically appropriate their religious faith. Building upon the foundation laid down in the core curriculum, a student should have access to a theology major or some similar set of organized courses in theological reflection. On the senior undergraduate level, the faculty should strive to provide a set of clearly articulated, well-integrated courses in the Catholic theological tradition.

On the graduate level, theology lives an amphibian existence. The graduate theology department has a responsibility to both the university and the church. In reference to the university, the theology department is responsible for fashioning an academically respect-able and practically feasible program of graduate studies in theol-ogy. In reference to the church, the theological enterprise at a Catholic, Jesuit university has special responsibilities. Theologians must serve the church as well as the university. While strictly adhering to the principles of academic freedom, our theology facul-ties have the right and responsibility to take an active role in developing the Catholic theological tradition. The theology faculty at a Catholic, Jesuit university should be recognized for its ability and willingness to involve itself in public dialogue of critical issues affecting Catholicism today.

Theology, then, plays a variety of roles in a Catholic, Jesuit university. In the core undergraduate curriculum, theology teams up with religious studies in an effort to provide a comprehensive, humanistic framework, thereby, on the one hand, preparing the way for a more specific consideration of theological traditions and, on the other hand, encouraging an openness to cross-disciplinary approaches by highlighting the congeniality between religion and the other humanities. Beyond the core curriculum, theology provides for the critical appropriation of one's faith tradition in an academic rather than a catechetical setting. And, finally, on the graduate level, theology serves the university and the church by providing for the preservation and advance of our theological tradition.

In conclusion, then, I should like to suggest that the task of theology and of the theology faculty at a Catholic, Jesuit university is pluriform. The discipline and the faculty function differently on different levels and within variable contexts. In short, theology is, as Bernard Lonergan and David Tracy have demonstrated, characterized by functional specialization. To the degree that we recognize and build upon this functional specialization, we shall, in my opinion, be better able to carry out the comprehensive task of theology in a Jesuit, Catholic university.

4 / Lonergan in Flatland: Reflections on the Role of Theology in the Liberal Arts Curriculum

G. John Renard, S.J.

W AS it not Shakespeare who said, "Curriculum doth make cowards of us all" — or words to that effect? Had he been involved in formal educational endeavors, the thought would surely have crossed his mind. Had he lived to see this age of growing interest in things cross-cultural, interdisciplinary, and the like, he might well have said instead, "Curriculum must make missionaries of us all." Allow me to elaborate, borrowing from the droll and charming *Flatland: A Romance of Many Dimensions*, written by a nineteenth-century British mathematician named Edwin A. Abbott.

Flatland is the memoir of an inhabitant of a region of only two dimensions: length and depth, but no height; no up or down, only north, south, east, and west. It is a land without sun or other heavenly luminaries, and so without a sense of directionality of light source; light is always and everywhere more or less equal. Flatlanders have no inkling of interiority as distinct from exteriority. All citizens are distinguished purely by the number of their angles, but because they appear only as moving lines, as "sides" without elevation, the number of their sides must be inferred. A dense fog pervades all the land, and although it sounds terribly gloomy, the fog serves a critical function: it allows Flatlanders to infer the number of sides of their compatriots by discerning their relative "brightness." The sharper the angle of an approaching figure, the more rapidly will its sides diminish in brightness from the viewer's perspective. The more dramatic the decrease in brightness, the

smaller the number of sides, and the lower the social rank of the
oncoming Flatlander. From the nearly perfect circles of the priestly
class to the humble isosceles triangles of the peasantry runs the
social scale.

So much for the author's description of "This World," in Part I.
How the Flatlander who wrote the memoirs came to experience
"Other Worlds" is the crucial part of the story.

Imagine that it is the second last day of the year 1999. While
asleep this night, the Flatlander has a dream of a land of but one
dimension, where only a point-horizon can be seen. One *sees* only
points, but can infer length and distance, even though distance
never actually changes. Hearing is critical, and is the only way to
determine size: every male inhabitant has two mouths, one bass and
one tenor, and size is determined by calculating the time-lapse
between the arrival of the sound of the first voice and that of the
second. Here in Lineland, inhabitants move only alone a line, and
there is no "place" or position except on that line.

Our Flatlander dreams that he encounters the Monarch of Line,
and tries at length but in vain to explain to his punctilious Majesty
the existence of a world of more than one dimension. The king
cannot imagine a world in which seeing is so important and where
even touch is deemed essential to survival; where right and left
mean something more than merely northward or southward; and
where one can see, not only infer, straight lines, and can even infer
triangles, squares, polygons, and so on. The breakfast bell rouses
the dreamer to face the last day of the old millennium.

That very night, however, after his four pentagonal sons and two
hexagonal grandsons (each generation has one side more than the
preceding one — evolution in Flatland) had been put to bed, the
Flatlander and his wife sat up to usher in the new millennium. As
the hour approached, the Flantlander sensed an alien presence in
the room. The visitor appeared at first to be a circle, for though it
was actually a sphere, the Flatlander could make it out only as a
circle whose diameter varied as the sphere ascended and descended
through the plane of Flatland.

After gaining the Flatlander's confidence, but also becoming convinced that mere words would not persuade him of the existence of
a three-dimensional realm, the Sphere led the Flatlander Beatricelike
to Spaceland. There the traveler experienced firsthand the wonders
of height, of solids, of interiority and exteriority, of the fifth and
sixth dimensions (up and down). Needless to say, the Flatlander did
not go gentle into that good night. Of the fearful wrenching from

the security of his comfortable plane he wrote in his memoirs:

> An unspeakable horror seized me. There was a darkness; then a
> dizzy, sickening sensation of sight that was not like seeing; I saw a
> Line that was no Line; Space that was not Space; I was myself, and
> not myself. When I could find voice, I shrieked aloud in agony,
> "Either this is madness or it is Hell." "It is neither," calmly replied the
> voice of the Sphere, "it is Knowledge; it is Three Dimensions: open
> your eye once again and try to look steadily." I looked, and, behold, a
> new world![1]

From his new vantage point, the Flatlander was granted a view of
his own world as though from above. He marveled to see even the
insides of things — of buildings, for example, as if in plan; he saw
light and shade and perspective. There, too, the Flatlander began to
imagine the still more outrageous possibility of rising to yet another
level, into the land of Four Dimensions from which one could look
down on that of Three, and so forth. He reasoned with himself,
"Was I not taught below that when I saw a Line and inferred a
Plane, I in reality saw a Third unrecognized Dimension, not the
same as brightness, called 'height'? And does it not follow that, in
this region, when I see a Plane and infer a Solid, I really see a Fourth
unrecognized Dimension, not the same as colour, but existent,
though infinitesimal and incapable of measurement?"[2] He there-
upon proceeded to convince the Sphere of the existence of other
worlds using the same notion of analogy by which the Sphere had
persuaded him there could indeed be three dimensions.

Time came for the Flatlander to return to that "dull level wilder-
ness" on his mission as "Apostle of the Gospel of Three Dimensions." He knew he would suffer much, but, now experienced in
the delights of moving into other worlds, he was resolved to spread
the message whatever the cost. Then, as if to encourage the apostle
by proving to him how much worse matters could be, the Sphere
conducted him in a dream to that underworld whither all epic
heroes must venture, to the "lowest depth of existence, even to the
realm of Pointland, the Abyss of No Dimensions."[3] There the
monarch of Pointland reigned: a totally self-satisfied, windowless
monad, who could hear nothing but his own voice, in a world
without horizons. At least, thought the Flatlander, my own people
will *hear* me. Later, however, he would write in some discouragement, but not utterly without hope:

> Hence I am absolutely destitute of converts, and, for aught that I can
> see, the millennial Revelation has been made to me for nothing.

Prometheus up in Spaceland was bound for bringing down fire for mortals, but I — poor Flatland Prometheus — lie here in prison for bringing down nothing to my countrymen. Yet I exist in the hope that these memoirs, in some manner, I know not how, may find their way to the minds of humanity in Some Dimension, and may stir up a race of rebels who shall refuse to be confined to limited Dimensionality.[4]

Now imagine a conference attended by all shapes and sizes of persons interested in curriculum — a potential "race of rebels" that would no doubt lift the spirits of the Flatlandian Jeremiah. At the conference, individuals from many dimensions (read disciplines) meet. Our attention is drawn to two in particular, from the dimensions of theology and the arts. Which is the Flatlander and which the Sphere, the reader may decide. It must be recalled that the Flatlander himself first experienced an authentic Sphere in only two dimensions, and that visitor and visited both regarded the other as somehow deficient, lacking in perceptive abilities, and, most of all, as operating out of a truncated worldview.

The conversation proceeds somewhat as follows. The theology person asks what language arts persons speak among themselves. He/She is shocked to find that although words are important, color, texture, shape, mass, volume, pitch, movement, gesture are equal if not greater importance. The arts person is likewise amazed to hear that theology persons manage to communicate almost exclusively through words and concepts. The theology person thinks, but does not say, "What kind of mundane discipline is this? No sense of transcendence!" The arts person muses, "These theology types are so otherworldly and abstract. No sense of immanence!" After a good deal of listening, however, both parties begin to discover that they have much in common, with respect to the values and attitudes they seek to foster in their students, and with respect to the various human operations required in their disciplines.

An earlier speaker at the conference happens to have handed out a pretentious but not unhelpful chart, claiming to summarize in one page Bernard Lonergan's *Method in Theology* by lining up the two "phases" in Lonergan's eight "Functional Specializations" with his four levels of "Conscious and Intentional Operations" (refer to Appendix). The two conference participants naturally fall to discussing the chart. They agree, first of all, that in both disciplines one can speak in terms of levels of conscious and intentional operations as a way of discovering mutual concerns about attitudes they would like to help their students develop. They agree that experience, understanding, judgment, and decision linked together in the postures of inquiry, reflection, and deliberation, are crucial needs in the study of all the liberal arts. More specifically, they agree that certain key themes can be said to characterize the approaches of both disciplines.

First, inquiry presupposes a kind of contemplative frame of mind, without which there can be no genuine creativity. The arts person recalls a chapter in Rudolph Arnheim's book *Toward a Psychology of Art*, entitled "Contemplation and Creativity." Arnheim suggests that, in spite of widespread "spectator" and "consumer" mentalities, contemplation is essentially active. It is a questioning approach to the world as it "invites the mind by its mysterious complexity." Contemplation is in no way a spectator activity. It demands questions that arise from the need to "give account of what it is like to be a human being in this world." On the other hand, Arnheim writes, "contemplation differs from a willful quest in that it is not an interview but an audience granted by the object which directs the conversation. Only by surrendering to the object will one obtain the answers to the questions that make the object speak."[5]

Secondly, according to Arnheim, widespread "naive realism" in our culture suggests that confronting the world is a matter of recording and manipulating objective data. One result is, for example, that a work of art is regarded as nothing more than a "faithful copy" of reality, or that a one-to-one relationship must be evident between every theological statement and the dominant mood of a culture or society. Contemplation, however, is more authentically experimental, and at the same time more respectful of the integrity of both subject and object.

Thirdly, our culture so often seems to equate success with competition, and hence regards contemplation as a way of latching onto aberrant ideas of the sort for which "creative" (read "different," "odd") persons are famous. But whereas contemplation may indeed lead the creative person toward views that are not widely held, its ultimate result is to enable the creative person to "analyze the potentialities of the object" for the kind of truth that fits "both object and subject." In other words, one is not forced to impose on an object the commonly accepted view merely because it is commonly accepted.[6]

Arnheim's reflections bring to the theology person's mind an article by Monika Hellwig, "Theology as a Fine Art," in which the author sees the fine art of theology as a "simultaneous cultivation of contemplation, empathy, and reason" (presupposing, of course, a broad acquaintance with a "tradition"). Mastery of argument must be secondary to vulnerability to experience and willingness to be taken by surprise. Both theology and the arts call for "allowing persons, things, and events to be, to happen, allowing them their full resonance in one's own experience, looking at them without blinking, touching them and allowing them to touch us without flinching."[7]

Inquiry, then, means an informed amazement, neither naive nor jaded and cynical. It means fostering an awareness of the spaces we inhabit and the ways we parcel out our time — a total environmental sensitivity. Inquiry involves an appreciation of the interdependence of change and continuity: just as there is stability in the changing experiencing self, so there is a core of revolution and renewal even in the most outwardly immutable of traditions and communities, both cultural and religious. Finally, all genuine inquiry needs to include a profound respect for the "preconceptual" dimension of experience.

Secondly, there is reflection. In both the arts and theology, reflection requires that one learn to think not only discursively/linearly or intuitively/circularly, but rather in a kind of spiral fashion. One needs to be able to think not only vertically or horizontally, but from a variety of angles and directions all at once. It requires a combination of acceptance of cultural and religious diversity with an unterrified realization of cultural relativity; a deepening knowledge of one's own religious and cultural traditions along with a growing awareness of those of other persons.

Thirdly, deliberation means a conviction that fostering an atmosphere of tolerance and acceptance is not the same as settling for a totally value-free response to one's world. Both theology and the arts call for social and individual commitment, a willingness to evaluate, to offer judgment and preference. Even as one becomes more aware of the world of experience as a horizon of mystery, one cannot lose sight of the need to address and solve problems. There is no escapism in authentic self-transcendence. Hellwig's description of "empathy" is helpful in this context: it is a link between "the reality revealed in contemporary experience both of suffering and of hope, both of conflict and of peace, on the one hand, and the gospel of salvation with its doctrinal elaborations through history on the other."[8]

As they begin to talk about Lonergan's "Functional Specializations," the two conference participants discover more common ground in the areas of method than they had previously suspected. Both theology and the arts have traditionally thought of themselves as rather naturally divided into both "fields" and "subjects," the former divided largely according to types of *data* and the latter categorized according to types of *results*. So in theology there are the *fields* of scripture, patristics, medieval and Reformation studies; and in the arts, such fields as history of theater, art, music, criticism; and numerous subdivisions such as early Christian, Byzantine, and so forth. In theology there are the *subjects* of fundamental, systematic, moral/pastoral; and in the arts, such subjects as music theory and composition, theater production and direction, sculpture, painting, and the varieties of work in other media and techniques.

Just as in theology one can speak of encountering theology that has already been elaborated (Phase I: Theology as Indirect Discourse), so too in the arts. Here, in general, is the province of the "field" specializations. There are, to be sure, significant differences in the methodological needs of theology and the arts, and it is not profitable to minimize them. But there are some important analogies by which the theology person and the arts person can begin to discern some measure of affinity, if not consanguinity. In both areas, students need to learn how to go about *experiencing* the "raw materials," whether in the form of texts, scores, artifacts, sherds, or architectural complexes. This is Lonergan's "research" specialization. In both areas of study, *understanding* relies on more or less established principles and methods of "interpretation," ranging from scriptural exegesis, to iconology, to the study of commentaries on Shakespeare, and far beyond. "History," with its evaluation of materials, exposes students to the classic *judgments* that have been passed on the classic works. Finally, the need for informed *decision* is highlighted by the function of arts criticism, or what Lonergan calls "dialectic."

It is at this point that activity in the arts and in theology may pass over from reflecting on and appreciating the artistic and theological works of others in the past, to actually doing art or theology. But what Lonergan calls Phase II: Theology as Direct Discourse, and what might be called firsthand artistic activity, both depend on an intangible element. I hesitate to draw too close an analogy between what Lonergan calls intellectual, moral, religious (and, later on, also affective) *conversion*, and that most rare and indefinable gift called *inspiration*; but I do not hesitate to suggest that there is some correspondence between them, if only to the extent that some change in direction and approach to life that is more than merely technical must occur if the would-be theologian is not simply to parrot the greats of yesteryear as though in possession of a magical formula, and if the aspiring artist is to produce art rather than craft. Assuming that such a point or stage of transition is experienced and negotiated successfully (though it is always in progress and never completed), one can move toward doing art or theology.

In Phase I Lonergan sees a movement from multiplicity of data toward a dialectical unity out of which choice and conversion emerge. Phase II then proceeds back through the four levels of conscious and intentional operations in reverse order, moving from a unified horizon of meaning toward the production of a multiplicity of new data arising from a variety of interests, cultures, tastes, and so on.

It is possible to understand the specialization of "foundations" as in some ways analogous to a new way of viewing one's place as an individual and social being in the human situation. For Lonergan, foundations is "concerned with the origins, genesis, present state, possible developments and adaptations of the categories in which Christians understand themselves, communicate with each other, and preach the gospel to all nations."[9] Foundations requires a conversion from the inauthentic and arbitrary, to a deliberate "surrender to the demands of the human spirit: be attentive, be intelligent, be reasonable, be responsible, be in love."[10] I imagine artistic inspiration involves something like that: a perhaps dramatic revolution in one's horizon, outlook, worldview. However else one might describe conversion and inspiration, they must be seen as providing the contexts within which all subsequent theological or artistic expressions have meaning. Because both experiences have their social as well as intensely personal dimensions, both must in time effect new social groupings, new ways of belonging, as well as changes in the individual's horizons. In sum, foundations "determines which views (artistic works) are the positions (creations) that proceed from . . . conversion (inspiration), and which are the counter-positions (results of craft) that reveal its absence."[11]

Just as theology has its "doctrines," selected from a broad spectrum of possible modes of expression and interpretations of human experience — possibilities juxtaposed and sorted out by "dialectic" and given sharper focus in the context provided by "foundations" — so do the arts. There one finds the more or less conventionally accepted limits of certain media, favored techniques and their experimentally discovered strengths and weaknesses, iconographic repertoires, decorative and formal vocabularies, canons of composition and perspective, and so on.

Theology's doctrines are in turn shaped into what Lonergan calls the specialization of "systematics," whose task it is to develop "appropriate systems of conceptualization, to remove apparent inconsistencies, to promote understanding of realities affirmed by doctrines, to show how it could be possible that the facts are what they are,"[12] to make the facts into an assimilable whole. Clearly, the arts do not systematize quite the way theology does (although art history and criticism surely classify into "schools" and trends); nor do the arts speculate as theology can (although some might argue that the subject of esthetics belongs as much to the arts as it does to philosophy). Nevertheless, there is in the arts that which provides internal consistency, without which their products would be as incomprehensible as a jumble of disconnected theological pronouncements. It is style. How can one establish with confidence the ways that styles develop in the arts? I believe there has to be an integral relationship with cultural trends. One can identify, for example, "impressionistic" elements in music, painting, poetry. Though I am not prepared to venture a lengthy analysis of this question, I have found in Lonergan's *Method* a remark about "systematics" that is quite tantalizing in this context:

> Because a theology is the product not simply of a religion, but of a religion within a given cultural context, theological revisions may have their origin, not primarily in theological, but rather in cultural developments. So at the present time theological development is fundamentally a long delayed response to the development of modern science, modern scholarship, modern philosophy.[13]

"Interesting suggestion," replies the arts person; "and I recall reading an article some years ago called 'Emerging Images in Teaching Religion and the Arts,' that made some complementary observations." The article, s/he recalled with a nearly photographic memory, had remarked that the comprehensiveness and coherence that are so central to the specialization of "systematics" are actually as much esthetic as they are rational. Coherence, the authors went on, "gains much of its force from metaphors or models of part-whole relationships." They give several cogent reasons for believing that theological discourse is shaped by esthetic consciousness relating to the esthetic criterion of "fitness." In other words, though theology is often mistakenly identified with "hard-core propositions," definitions, and abstract argumentation, it is in reality as much a matter of style as it is of content. As in the arts, so in theology, "style always determines content . . . in the sense that ways of seeing and speaking give rise to ways of believing and thinking which are noticeably different and elicit different kinds of response." One might regard style in both areas as a "web of presuppositions taken for granted in an epoch" — a kind of idiomatic usage, whether visual or audial or tactile or. . . .[14]

Lonergan's final specialization is that of "Communications." Both in theology and in the arts, the ultimate goal is to communicate the result of reflection and action. For theology, communication necessarily involves three levels of what Lonergan calls "external relations." First, theology must be able to move into other disciplines, such as art, language, literature, the history of other traditions. Secondly, theology must develop genuine intercultural sensitivity while retaining its own identity. Thirdly, it must acquire the technical skills needed to use various communications media. Communications requires that theology persons enlarge their horizons so that a religious tradition can pass along its essential message, rather than merely some trappings of a particular culture. This specialization therefore demands an appreciation of human communities of all kinds and of cultural pluralism.

In a similar way, the arts are oriented toward communications in various media. Technical skills are only the beginning. Also presupposed are financial support or patronage, and a reasonable market. Given those necessities, the arts gear up for exhibits, plays, concerts, readings, which in turn furnish fresh experiences, data, research, and so forth.

As the signal was being passed around that all participants were returning to the auditorium for the next session, the theology person and the arts person found themselves agreeing that both are engaged in what must be both a reflection on "givens" from the past and a creation of new "givens." If either theology or the arts is relegated to a defense or idolatry of inherited, fossilized structures, death is at the door: art becomes craft, theology the trusty sidekick of magic. On the other hand, if either loses its moorings in the past, equally sure disaster awaits: the arts become a matter of sheer whim and inarticulate chaos, and theology degenerates into the mouthpiece of a religion that is subjectivist and elitist. Both areas of activity are focused on the need to maintain a harmony between a fascination with limits, measure, and order, on the one hand, and the terror and adventure of confronting possibilities for growth, on the other. One is well advised to be wary of theology and arts persons who are utterly in control of what they do and coolly assured of their results. Equally a waste of time, however, are the works of those who are not convinced with every fiber of their being that what they do is of great importance.[15]

At the last session of the conference, participants voted almost unanimously that a time-honored Curricular Creed (now popularly known as the Flatland Quadrilateral) was no longer adequate. They discussed its four points and resolution, rejecting each in turn. The old document read:

1. Each individual field can legitimately be regarded as "queen of the sciences." None of what any given field/subject tries to accomplish can be effected by any other discipline.

2. Each field/subject is by definition exclusively monocultural and monocreedal, with its primary task to defend its own pronouncements.

3. The effectiveness of any liberal arts curriculum will be in direct proportion to the easily countable hours on a student's transcript.

4. The more uncontaminated a field/subject can be kept, the clearer will be our idea of how to define the field/subject still further, and the greater the chance that the field/subject will be duly credited with producing a recognizable and measurable body of knowledge.

Resolution: Any person who fails to agree with the above is to be considered a running-dog interdisciplinary rebel.

A committee was appointed to draft a new creed. After the conference they assembled and worked out the following, dubbing it the Multidimensional Manifesto:

1. Any discipline, understood not as field or subject, but in terms of functional specializations, times any other discipline equals both disciplines squared.

2. Any two disciplines squared and then raised to a "global" power (i.e., taken beyond one societal framework, religious or cultural tradition, etc.) equals both disciplines cubed.[16]

3. The effectiveness of any liberal arts curriculum will be in inverse proportion to the methodological isolation and content-purity of the fields and subjects that make it up.

4. The more areas of interest are interrelated, the less will anyone be tempted to waste time defining them, the less likely will anyone be to worry whether the area is getting its due credit, and the more time will be devoted to exploring possibilities.

Resolution: Any person who fails to agree with the above is to be considered an unregenerate angle-jerk isosceles who needs a swift kick in the hypotenuse. (Because the first draft was thought to be perhaps too strident and intolerant, it was amended: ". . . to be considered a reactionary field/subject specialist.") The Manifesto has yet to be voted on.

As one contemplates the task that faces liberal arts educators at the turn of the curricular millennium, it may be helpful to remember the words of the Flatlander concerning his noble missionary calling to preach the Gospel of Three Dimensions:

> My volition shrinks from the painful task of recalling my humiliation; yet, like a second Prometheus, I will endure this and worse, if by any means I may arouse in the interiors of Plane and Solid Humanity a spirit of rebellion against the Conceit which would limit our Dimensions to two or three or any number short of infinity.[17]

Only in that spirit can theology fulfill its role in concert with the other liberal arts. For when all its functional specializations are integrated, theology's ultimate function is twofold: to lead toward the comprehension of the "length, and breadth, and height, and depth" and the knowledge of that love that surpasses all knowledge (Ephesians 3:18–19), and to heighten awareness of the Mystery that "no eye has seen, nor ear heard, nor any human mind conceived" (1 Corinthians 2:9).

JESUIT HIGHER EDUCATION

APPENDIX

BERNARD LONERGAN'S "FUNCTIONAL SPECIALIZATIONS"

Four levels of
conscious and   Phase I
intentional   Theology as Indirect Discourse
operations   Mediating theology: encounters the
(cumulative but   past. Reflects on a religion's documents,
open process)   Joined by   beliefs, ideals, performance

(right margin, vertical: Movement →)

1) Experience ⎫   1) Research: gathers data, whether
              ⎬ Inquiry   human, religious, Christian,
2) Understanding ⎭   Roman Catholic

              ⎫   2) Interpretation: meanings uncovered
              ⎬ Reflection   via principles (hermeneutics) and
              ⎭   application (exegesis), re: object
                                   of text, words, author, self;
                                   criteria for accuracy: exposition
                                   of text's meaning.

3) Judgment ⎫   3) History: narrative of themes of
            ⎬ Deliberation   "fact and value" — people, places,
4) Decision ⎭   events, results; cultural,
                                   institutional, doctrinal movements.

                               4) Dialectic: Sorts out conflicts re:
                                   fact/value, meanings, experiences;
                                   challenges one to choose (religious
                                   but not yet "theological" event) —
                                   hence, change (conversion) needed.
                                   Renders' interpretation
                                   appreciation, and history evaluative
                                   (good/evil). No longer merely
                                   approaching past — now genuine
                                   encounter: meeting persons,
                                   appreciating values, criticizing
                                   defects, facing personal challenge.
                                   (Apologetics)*

(right margin, vertical: Multiplicity of data ————→ Dialectical unity)

Rel. of Func. Spec. to other   "Field Specialization" subdivides materials
"Models": Func. Spec. sees *stages*   on which these operate: division of *data*
in process from data to results.   (i.e., material objects)

Movement →

Phase II
Theology as Direct Discourse
Mediated theology: confronts the future. Reflects on conversion as horizon of religious meaning; decides truth issues; how to reconcile with science, philosophy, history; and how communicate to peoples, cultures

Multiplicity of interests, cultures, tastes, societies

8) Communications: Interdisciplinary, intercultural, multimedia production of data (pastoral/execution — feedback to judge policies and planning)*

7) Systematics: Establish core of message to be communicated; internal conceptual consistency (Speculative planning for optimum use of existing resources)*

6) Doctrines: selects from among alternatives presented by dialectic, using foundations' horizon of meaning as guide (Dogmatic policy-making re: attitudes and goals)*

5) Foundations: objectifies horizon of meaning effected by intellectual, religious, moral conversion; thus provides context within which doctrines are meaningful — transition from saying "So and So said . . ." to "This or that is so. . . ." (Fundamental)*

Unified horizon of Meaning

[*indicates, first, traditional labels of theological "disciplines," and then Lonergan's suggestions for "Integrating theology with scholarly and scientific human studies . . . to generate well-informed and continuously revised and plans."]

"Subject specialization" classifies results obtained by these (i.e., formal objects)

5 / Ethics and the Challenges of Contemporary Society

James R. Pollock, S.J.

I N a world in which our assumptions are regularly, if not methodi-
cally, challenged, one assumption should remain safe and un-
questioned — that is, that ethical discourse take place in an atmosphere of honesty, even of humility. So let me begin by saying that I
am certain that I am not even aware of all the challenges of
contemporary society and equally certain that I do not have answers
to all the ethical problems and dilemmas they pose. Similarly, I
speak as a Christian ethician or moral theologian, and therefore my
remarks will call upon the data of revelation and the experience of
faith that are also presupposed as a framework for discussing Jesuit
education. This is not, by any means, to downgrade or exclude
insights of non-Christian moral thinking, of Christian moral philosophy, or, most fundamentally, of the experience of ordinary Christians and non-Christians alike. It is simply to state at the outset that
my remarks are consciously, if not surprisingly, those of a Jesuit
priest who is a moral theologian. Although I do not wish to differen-
tiate myself excessively from other moralists or ethicians, and most
emphatically do not wish to deny my common humanity, the
distinction is important because I want to sketch briefly some salient
aspects of contemporary society and I shall begin with the ambivalence of modern humanity in the face of differentiation. I say
ambivalence because, at the same time we speak of a global village,
of ecumenism, of instantaneous and mass communication, of human rights for all guaranteed by all, we live the tensions and
realities of parochialism and nationalism, of a preoccupation with

discovering our roots, even when these roots join us to different groups, different lands, and even different values; we live the tensions and realities of a need for privacy and individuality — we experience the fact that the more fundamentally we acknowledge the ties that bind us all together, the more we yearn for more freedom to be ourselves, often in contradistinction to one another and at the expense of one another's freedom and its concomitant rights. As Catholic moralists, by way of example, we want to speak of a morality that is essentially and truly human, lest we run the risk of leaving anyone out, and *as* we run the risk of neglecting the faith experience and commitment, the faith life, that animates, motivates, and gives ultimate meaning to our ordinary, everyday human choices and lives.[1]

The world of today calls us to be universal and international at the same time that our own society demands that we prize our individuality, our uniqueness, our privacy, and, especially, if we are educated and affluent enough, our own innermost feelings. In an educational and even a Jesuit setting, our solidarity with one another, our obligation to the less fortunate, our contemporary global, international, and universal outlook are all taught and preached and exhorted in a university setting whose departments and schools often continue to vie with one another even as they reinforce the competitive and individualistic spirit that can run counter to the values being proclaimed.

Surely another characteristic of contemporary society is its overwhelming definition by technology and its products. Our lives are enhanced and determined and in some ways threatened by the dizzying speed with which the new replaces the old and out-of-date. We are in unending danger of identifying the new with the better (not just the good) even when this reflects itself in an option for the young and the beautiful as opposed to the older and the more seasoned or mature, not to speak at all of the oppressed or disadvantaged. We have not lost our sense of discrimination when it comes to recognizing the better quality of the old days when we had home-cooked meals, instead of frozen delights. We are beginning to appreciate the quality and character of older ways of building homes or cities, though there is still a lag in appreciating or really reverencing older models of the human person. To an extent this story is as old as the human race itself, but the rapidity of change in our society, the universal demand for immediate satisfaction of our whims and desires, the addiction that we flirt with succumbing to that demands the new and the now and the fast for its own sake —

these characteristics are particular to our own age in a way no previous age could have experienced them. Clearly it is not change or even rapidity of change that is the problem — we Jesuits have even been encouraged to be agents of change in our lives.[2] The problem is one that touches on values and even priorities, which centers our discussion squarely in the realm of ethics and morality.

A beneficial aspect of the rapidity of technological change in our society relates precisely to the moral area of our lives. In all fields today, technology has advanced and is advancing so rapidly that, before the ethical questions relating to a particular issue are formulated and articulated, they are often outdated. Normative statements are difficult to come by, as the American bishops admitted in 1983, when one is discussing weapons systems that no one seems to understand completely and that will soon enough be outdated anyway.[3] The maze of ethical and moral issues that are beginning to surface in the fields of health care and bioethics present similar difficulties. Heart transplants, for example, were already problematic enough in terms of a host of concerns, not the least of which is their enormous cost, when Baby Fae arrived on the scene and moralists had to shift their attention overnight to the ethical implications of transplants across species. *Time* magazine had a cover story entitled "Making Babies: The New Science of Conception."[4] Two elements about its coverage were immediately noticeable — the careful job it did to survey the variety of technological aids available today (even the first test tube baby, born in 1978, is considered by some to be the "product" of already obsolete techniques)[5] and the almost entire absence of any discussion of the human, let alone Christian, values involved. Ethical problems that relate to such issues as the astonishing panoply of drugs now being prescribed, and the new kinds of experimentation on human embryos and other human subjects that are being suggested, cannot be "solved" quickly enough to satisfy the demands of medical professionals, technicians, and researchers. Members of the medical profession itself are increasingly called upon to act more like technicians than doctors in the more classic mode, dealing more often than not with the figures that represent bodily functions in computer print-outs, rather than with the actual persons whose lives and health are in question.

Business ethics, a field that until recently was practically unheard of, has assumed an important position in ethical discussion and is a profession where today demand far outstrips supply. Naturally, the pastoral letter being prepared by the American bishops will call even greater attention to this area. Additionally, a wide variety of new questions is emerging with regard to such issues as computer piracy and even the more prosaic areas that computers have served. One thing is clear from this very brief sampling of examples — the traditional practitioners of moral theology and ethics know less about these highly specialized, emergent subjects of ethical discussion — and conversely, the dominant technologists of our society tend to be relatively unfamiliar with the ways of moral and ethical discourse. This suggests a point to which I will return — namely, the responsibility of academicians to collaborate across disciplinary lines in the kind of university setting where this particular kind of interdisciplinary work can take place — that is, the Catholic and, in our case, the Jesuit university.

I mentioned that I consider the rapidity of technological change in our society beneficial from the point of view of morality. This statement requires some explanation. The very fact that moralists and ethicians cannot phrase many of the questions facing us rapidly enough to attempt to solve them before they have been replaced by other, more burning and confusing questions, should prompt us to arrive at a fundamental methodological conclusion regarding the role of ethics in Jesuit institutions of higher learning. We will not serve our students well, nor will we serve ourselves well, nor, in fact, will we serve the church well, if we focus our energies around trying to provide solutions to the moral problems that our students face and will continue to face, along with ourselves, once they finish school. Trying to accomplish this would make us uncomfortably similar to the casuists of the seventeenth and eighteenth centuries who tried to solve every doubt that the Christian conscience could face — the books kept getting bigger and bigger, filled with more and more detailed "cases of conscience" that were, unfortunately, reflected on less and less in the context of the real life of Christian persons. I am not suggesting that we have no obligation to respond to the most up-to-date problems that arise in the field of morality. What I am suggesting is that our response needs to be characterized by something other than devising answers to questions, answers that we can then pass on to our students who will have a ready-made blueprint for moral action. What I think our efforts should center around is an attempt to provide our students (and, of course, ourselves) with a methodology for dealing with and confronting moral issues that will arise in their lives, a methodology that will enable them to recognize the human and Christian values that are important and that surface in varying constellations around various problems and life choices.

Allow me to appear to digress briefly. In a more traditional setting, it was possibly sufficient to expect that a moralist — or any Catholic teacher, for that matter — could and would provide students with the church's normative responses to life's fundamental moral questions. The norms condensed and distilled the church's wisdom and the wisdom of the race; and in a generally more obedient and docile Catholic population, the norms were to be respected and followed. The difficulty today, apart from the fact that our world is increasingly pluralistic and secularized (in both the good and bad senses of that word),[6] is that norms, particularly as they are more specific and concrete, really are the conclusions to rather lengthy processes of reasoning — and the processes are either largely unknown or have been at least in part rejected or modified in the face of additional and often scientific claims. Norms, in short, enshrine and promote values; often they also hierarchize them. But it is precisely the values that are no longer clear in many areas of contemporary life. What the values are and how they relate to one another, especially in conflictual situations, are not immediately evident. To attempt to formulate new norms, though a necessary and important contribution to our students and to humanity in general, is to miss the point. New norms, and indeed many of the old ones, for that matter, will be formulated and reformulated in the course of a process that highlights the discovery and hierarchization of values. It is *this* process, however, that is both proper to an educational setting and likely to prepare students for the new and hitherto unanticipated specific issues that they will continue to face throughout their lives.

I have deliberately avoided making values appear to be the exclusive domain of moralists, because they obviously are not. It is true that in exercising moral responsibility, persons need to choose the values that they feel obliged to realize in a particular situation. But the values themselves are the proper domain of any academic discipline or part of life. In terms of some of the problematical areas I alluded to earlier regarding medical ethics, values exist on a number of different levels — there are the values of the owner of a pharmaceutical company, for example, the values of reduced pain versus reduced consciousness, the values of a doctor confronting a particular patient, the values of patients and their families — and this is just to scratch the surface of the host of values involved. Naturally, specifically moral analysis of values is central from my point of view, and this analysis must be rooted in a clear understanding of who the human person is, how human community relates to that person, and indeed how the person relates to other persons — in short, what are the human goods involved in human living. My point here, however, is that never before have moralists and ethicians been more dependent on co-professionals in the university to discover precisely which values attach to the biological, linguistic, social, political, and other phenomena that they study. Values are, in the last analysis, matters of importance to human persons and thus are intimately linked up with basic and not so basic human needs, with human rights and obligations. It goes without saying, then, that if our goal must be to provide our students with a methodology for uncovering, discovering, and hierarchizing values, then each of us must make the effort to demand of ourselves a keen awareness and ongoing evaluation of precisely the valuational elements of our disciplines. Similarly and correlatively, we need to speak out our values to one another in a collaborative effort to share them and to assist one another in prioritizing them.

Providing our students with a methodology for discovering and ranking values in their lives is only another way of saying that we have an obligation to assist our students and ourselves in the ongoing process of character formation. Our goal, stated simply, is to facilitate growth in the life of virtue. Unless we view moral choice and decision-making as an atomistic or fragmented part of our lives, a view that is consonant in some respects with an abstract focus on acts as opposed to persons, we surely recognize that choice, even in a severely conflictual situation, is the property of persons. The rather exclusive focus on norms alluded to earlier has as another of its liabilities the fact that it tends to assume a static and fragmented person who "remembers" the "right answer" to this particular "question." It is clearer to us today, however, that for a normative response to fit a particular situation, it must be that the person in question has interiorized the values involved in the norm. Even more, to avoid moral paralysis in the face of conflict, it is desirable that a person have the ability to set aside certain values when they must, in fact, cede to others, or better, to be able to realize as many of the values as possible in a given situation. Because this paper is only a sketch, after all, I will not here enter into the complex question of what is actually happening in a conflict of values situation, how precedence is decided, and which "normative" statements transparently state values that must be realized, whatever the cost.[7]

Growth in the life of virtue, then, places ethical or moral decisions and choices in the context in which they belong — that is, in the ongoing life of the person. What we must communicate to our students, then, is that the answers to questions will not suffice, nor will isolating moral choices from the rest of a life suffice, any more than relegating religious worship to Sunday morning or Saturday evening serves to illustrate the integrating force in a life that religious commitment entails and provides. Although the college or university setting provides the ideal setting for rediscovering the age-old fallacy that knowledge is virtue, this is a temptation that must be strongly resisted. It may be correct to say that knowledge is its own end, properly understood, just as it is correct to say that academic disciplines and research flourish in an environment of freedom and can never be allowed, or rather forced, to be the slaves of a moralizing penchant that masquerades as orthodoxy.

It is abundantly clear, however, that knowing the right answer never guarantees that it will be chosen or followed unless, under ordinary circumstances, the values that it incarnates are values that the chooser has gradually and consciously interiorized and assimilated so that they act, in fact, as quasi determinants in practice. This is a painstaking process that flourishes best in a communal setting where values are continually brought to light, shared, weighed, and gradually owned. Academic freedom, though certainly no more an absolute right than human life itself, rightly has a significant place in such a communal setting and process.

The very rapidity of change, and especially of technological change, that is so characteristic of our society and even of our world, lends a special urgency of its own to this task of promoting a life of virtue. Perhaps an example will clarify this aspect of the problematic. Consider the means of communication themselves, those means that have so enriched human life in our century. The instantaneity with which they transmit more than events, even values themselves, from one end of the globe to another, is a dazzling tribute to human creativity. That humanity could watch, together, the landing on the moon, the contests of athletes from many parts of the world celebrating the triumph of freedom and the human spirit, the simultaneously emaciated and distended bodies of fellow human beings suffering the rages of famine and war, and even the funeral of a pope, the election and coronation of another, and still more both the attempted assassination and the pleas for the disadvantaged throughout the world of the present pontiff — these are value-laden experiences that have the capacity to touch the human heart and set its spirit free. And yet, though they are also capable of being replayed, their very instantaneity and fragmentary nature, as well as the purportedly value-free (curiously identified as "objective") nature of the commentaries that accompany them, reveal some of the complexities and limitations of this particular means of communication.

Turning to the ordinary fare of television reveals more, which strikes at the core of our comments on the life of virtue. Putting the matter simply, the nature of television, with its images and its rapid story-telling in constrained amounts of time and its assumptions (apparently well founded) about the attention span and interests of its viewers, lends itself much better to the portrayal of vice or at least human weakness than it does to the portrayal of virtue. Vice and weakness themselves are distractions of the human spirit, among other things; they are a kind of preoccupation with immediacy that distract from long-range, valuable goals. How much easier it is to depict a breach of marital fidelity in a brief period of time than it is to unfold the nobility of a fidelity wrought painstakingly over a long period of time. Good or virtuous characters, who are exceedingly complex at the same time that they are simply integrated, are most often portrayed as persons without passion or interest or concrete motivation or depth. My purpose here is not to fault television or the purveyors of mass communication in general. My purpose is to point out that, negatively, the nature of the technical art itself poses serious problems to the faithful depiction of virtue.

More globally, however, my purpose is to suggest that we cannot stand idly by, but must give testimony to the reality that virtue is passionate, fundamentally human, intensely satisfying and integrating, and, perhaps most important for our society today, simply that virtue is possible. It is vice and the glorification of human weakness as determining our choices and our lives, rather than as reflecting and feeding into the nobility of which we are capable, that serves to disintegrate our personal and communal enterprises. Holding out the possibility of a patiently woven life of virtue, carefully constructed with the threads of fidelity, honesty, chastity, wisdom, self-control, and the like, is an arduous task, and a task proper to education, certainly in a Jesuit setting, and one whose tempo or timetable of accomplishment can often appear to be at odds with the fast pace of television and of contemporary life in general.

Statistics, surveys, and opinion polls are other products of contemporary society that exercise powerful influence over any consensus of values that we might share, any virtuous life that we might try to pursue. As with other elements of the mass media, claims for objectivity and facts in contradistinction to values, are hard to resist in evaluating these fashionable tools of the modern scene. Statistics, surveys, and opinion polls can of course assume a prophetic quality for all of us when they support our own positions and hopes — even the church often appeals to the common sentiment of humanity in support of certain positions, although wisely stating that "statistics do not make objective morality" when the figures in question lend credence to attitudes and practices that the church condemns.[8] Again my point of view is not to undermine these tools, or to suggest that they cannot perform a worthwhile service for us. Let me cite just two commonly asserted statistics to illustrate what my point is. We hear frequently that almost half of the marriages in the United States end in divorce, and we hear that most males either have practiced or will practice masturbation at one point in their lives. I do not particularly doubt the truth of these statistics, but I would submit that this truth is very partial and not at all characteristic of the process that our lives really are. These "facts" themselves are frozen, atomistic distortions of human life in community. How many divorced persons felt certain that most of the blame rested with their partners five years ago and are as certain of that today? What does the phrase "irreconcilable differences" really mean? How many would rather not have divorced or see their divorce as a failure on their part? Did sin enter into the failure of their marriage — whose, and was forgiveness extended or withheld? It can also be claimed that many marriages endure because of a failure of nerve or interest or preoccupation for children or unwillingness to incur the financial disadvantages that child support and alimony entail. Again, let me stress that my interest is not in judging the parties of failed marriages (or of today's no-fault divorces); my interest lies rather in the direction of questioning what values are involved in this enormously complex phenomenon and what values are truly represented by the statistics. It is a question of assumptions not being stated, of options not being provided, of values not being clarified, and of the virtuous life being sold short. It is an unworthy pastoral practice in the church to point to these numbers in a way that says that sin and selfishness are alive in the world. Only a fool would think that they are not, and it is more dangerous than indulging in folly to presume to be able to judge one's brothers and sisters. These contemporary facts are deficient, however, precisely as facts — they do not tell us enough of the reality that lies behind the statistics, the real human suffering and joy, dashed hopes, painful awakenings, and so many other value-laden factors. When young persons suggest rewriting their marriage vows to promise themselves to each other as long as their love lasts, it is time to call for a deeper appreciation of the relationship between values and facts that this rate reflects. We have the capacity in our institutions of higher learning to help our students realize that, if facts do not lie, neither do they tell the truth, nor do they faithfully reflect on their own the values they often reveal and those they often hide. We like our "statistics" to be tidy and easily memorized and recounted. But this is not the way of values in our lives, nor is it the way that the virtuous life is discovered, admired, treasured, and loved. There is no need to comment in detail on the statistics I mentioned concerning masturbation — acts that are isolated from their context and meaning in the lives of human persons over a long period of time shed relatively little light on the depths of the values embedded in human sexuality. A culture that is as orgasm-conscious as our own may have good reasons to be so, but without a better sense of the human and Christian values that are involved in human sexuality and how these can be patiently and progressively lived out over a lifetime, we run the risk of guessing at an interpretation that may do nothing more than continue to isolate a part of our lives and let it dominate us, as it diminishes our hopes and expectations.

In a Jesuit school one legitimately expects to encounter an emphasis on specifically Christian values, and it may be thought that this emphasis, while further defining and refining a Jesuit education, at the same time removes us, so to speak, from the mainstream of values in our society, arguable as it is exactly what that mainstream might be, and granting that it exists. This latter is an important qualification, for much of our society deliberately attempts to present itself as value-free, and those values that are most often articulated tend to cluster around the pursuit of an individual and autonomous life as undisturbed as possible by outside interference. Nonetheless, it is true that to speak of Christian values (implied all along in our discussion of the virtuous life) is to introduce another factor into the equation that must be discussed. After all, Pope Paul VI stated, in his exhortation on evangelization:

> For the church it is a question not only of preaching the gospel in ever wider geographic areas or to ever greater numbers of people, but also of affecting and as it were upsetting, through the power of the gospel, mankind's criteria of judgment, determining values, points of interest, lines of thought, sources of inspiration and models of life, which are in contrast with the Word of God and the plan of salvation.[9]

Stated perhaps more positively and linked up more clearly with the notion of the virtuous life is his comment that:

> Above all, the gospel must be proclaimed by witness. Take a Christian or a handful of Christians who, in the midst of their own community, show their capacity for understanding and acceptance, their sharing of life and destiny with other people, their solidarity with the efforts of all for whatever is noble and good. Let us suppose that, in addition, they radiate in an altogether simple and unaffected way their faith in values that go beyond current values, and their hope in something that is not seen and that one would not dare to imagine.[10]

The fact that these comments come from a statement on evangelization does not render them foreign to a discussion on ethical concerns in Jesuit schools today — rather, it serves to reinforce the fact that Jesuit education, when all is said and done, is itself a form of evangelization. This can appear to be a very threatening statement if it is not properly understood and explained.

Before attempting, however, to elucidate this statement, let me add a few comments of the American Jesuit provincials, comments found in a letter they addressed in 1978 to all the Jesuits in the United States who serve in Jesuit institutions of higher education. They describe higher education as "an enormously valuable apostolate in which the time, energies, and love of our men should be expended — to the service of our neighbor and the greater glory of God."[11] They add that "our Jesuit purpose in professional education is to train men and women of both competence and conscience."[12] Further,

> All Jesuit undergraduate colleges and schools are committed to a liberal arts curriculum, or a core program of humanistic studies, especially congenial to the fundamental human values we cherish. In face of the strong inclination of many students toward career specialization and narrow professionalism, Jesuits have the opportunity to offer them a curriculum that frees them to act thoughtfully rather than to be mastered by circumstances or unexamined convention.
>
> We endorse the high priority being given to carefully designed programs of liberal studies that integrate human and ethical values, because we all share the conviction that through them students gain freedom from undue preoccupation with security, from insensitivity to the plight of the morally deprived and the socially oppressed, and from paralysis before seemingly unchangeable political, economic, and social mores.[13]

Perhaps the simplest way to address some of the issues these various statements raise is to ask a series of questions. Is Jesuit education, after all, beneath a veneer that gleams with worldly wisdom and tolerance for great diversity, really in the business of keeping Catholics in the fold and of luring others into it? Is there a fundamental dichotomy between the values of this world, espoused by so many of our colleagues, and Christian values, which serve to illuminate the hollowness and emptiness of this world's values? Was all our earlier discussion of the arduous task of uncovering, revealing, and hierarchizing values from a multidisciplinary point of view only empty verbiage, because the values and priorities are already clear and subtly programing the mechanisms of our schools? There is neither time nor space to substantiate the resounding no's I want to answer to these and similar questions.

In effect the Christian vision of values and the hierarchizing of them that must animate Christian life and choice flow from an experience of faith that can be shared but never forced. The depth of that faith vision, grounded in the saving action of God in human lives and our world, serves simultaneously to ground all that is truly human and noble and good. That some of our colleagues and many, perhaps, of our students do not share that vision serves ultimately to testify to the mystery of God's ways and the fact that God is to be discovered in a variety of ways and experiences that are greater and more profound than any one of us. Just as many manifestations of God's love are obscured in practice by those of us who believe, so other manifestations are clarified by the testimony of many lives lived outside the formal parameters of the church. One thing is certain, however: there are no truly human values, no moral values, no virtues, that are alien to the Christian vision.

The fundamental point I am trying to make here is simply this: faith and the Christian vision of values and their prioritization in the living out of the virtuous Christian life can only illuminate values and convictions about the nature of the virtuous life that come from any other source. They add depth to our vision and clarity to the formulation and articulation of our values, needs, rights, and du-ties. From a Christian point of view, dialogue with other systems of value is itself valuable not only because of the illumination that Christianity can shed on other systems but because of the reciprocal illumination that it can and must receive. We live in a world where the light of faith itself can be dimmed by the limitations and even the evil of those who believe and can be brightened by the values lived out in an integrated and committed way by nonbelievers.

To put some flesh on the skeletal ideas I have been outlining, I should like, by way of conclusion, to suggest a theme that seems to me to be well suited to a discussion of education, ethics, and morality, and of the potential that Christian insight has for illuminating the virtuous life that we are attempting to facilitate for our students. This theme further seems particularly appropriate to me for our discussion today, for it serves as a symbol of the challenges of contemporary society. The theme I have chosen is that of communication. I will briefly attempt to describe its nature, and some of the insights that Christian belief and values can contribute to an understanding of it. Throughout this brief section, I will suggest how it can serve as one model of both the virtuous life and the moving force of education.

I have already discussed at some length several aspects of communication. In fact, in addition to my remarks about the effects of mass media and means of communication in our lives, the entire discussion of values and the virtuous life is an effort on my part to communicate to you what I think we should be trying to communicate to one another and to our students. If education is anything, it is certainly a lengthy process of communication! We all probably have departments of communication in our schools — we even have one that specializes in communication disorders — and our country reelected a man the media have named "the great communicator." And yet, what exactly is communication? Standard dictionary entries here, as in many other cases, are not very helpful. Let me share with you, instead, some thoughts on communication derived from its root words, and aided and abetted by some theological and moral reflection. I will certainly not attempt to exhaust this issue, nor do I feel I can. But I can suggest some possibilities for a reappraisal of communication and a recognition of it as one of the central moral issues of our time.

Communication is a process, the process of establishing union with the self, others, God, and the world. It is thus, first of all, a process, an ongoing event in our lives, that includes words, gestures, looks, self-images, attitudes, affects, and worldviews. On a radical level, when we communicate, in fact the object of our communication is our self. If morality can be described as a quest for integrity, for coherence and integration between the levels of our being and doing (or saying, and so forth) or between who we are and what we do, we can see immediately that communication is certainly not value-free. If, for example, what I say to you is not coherent with who I am and what I believe, if it does not flow in some continuity from the more transcendental levels of my being, then you may rightly conclude that I am either confused (perhaps tired) or a liar. The truth of what I say or of the way that I act has meaning beyond the moment because it is grounded in the truth of who I am, and this simple fact of experience both illuminates and is illuminated by Christ's statement that "I am the way, the truth, and the life."[14]

Let us proceed further. Communication is certainly a radically human type of activity; but more than that, it is a radically human way of being. Reflect that, in the Christian tradition, creation is an act of communication on God's part — it is God's Word that is creative, that brings order out of chaos, that brings our world and ourselves into being and continues to sustain us because the Word continues to communicate and reveal God's self to us and, greater still, because the Word made Flesh has dwelt with us and sent his Spirit to dwell within us, continuing to share God's own life, a life of love, with us. God's Word, in creation, is powerful, is dynamic, and it transforms nothingness into our world — and it continues to transform us into creatures who have the capacity to be more and more like God.

When God created humanity, which still happens today, God made us in the divine image — that is to say, we are created to be like God, to be powerful and dynamically creative and transformational through the process of our own communication. Adam's naming of the animals in paradise is a testimony to our partial dominion in the world, just as surely as the names we give to one another reflect everything from our claim to membership in a family, to the life-giving warmth of endearment and the icy death of disdain and contempt. Precisely this process, however, reflects the intimate relationship between who we view ourselves to be and who we consider others to be.

If we continue, in another simple example of communication, to repeat, out of our cultural heritage, that God is only masculine, surely we continue to reinforce the limited boundaries of ourselves and our creativity. We create God according to distorted images of ourselves. And we fail to penetrate the mysteries of what it means to be men and women. In the very act of speaking about God we expose the radical shortcomings of our view of ourselves, of one another, and of God. Because, in effect, we each expect less of ourselves than we have both a right and an obligation to do, we expect and hope for less from one another, and we confine the mystery of God to the relative impotence of our description of God, an impotence that limits us more than any physical impotence could, because it strikes at the very heart of our humanity.

For, returning to God's mystery, we are confronted with the reality of perfect unity and individuality within the very paradigm of community, the Trinity. The inadequacies of our frequent vacillation between dependence and independence, between submission and domination, may be relieved by a model of fundamental interdependence. If, very simply stated, God's self-understanding, self-acceptance, and self-expression *are* the very Word of God, the Son, it is clear that such perfect self-knowledge is incapable of addressing itself beyond itself except in the moving force of community, of love — that is, the same Spirit who labors mightily in us and in our world.

It is obvious, then, that entering into the process of establishing union with the self, others, God, and the world — which is what communication is — is to engage in a lifelong task, a process of growth that is not compartmentalized but that is, in reality, one process. Becoming godlike is to recognize our individual and common dignity, grounded in God's own image and likeness, and to affirm our destiny, the gradual growth in love that characterizes virtuous persons, that renders them a dynamic, passionate sign of God's presence and a bond of unity within our world. To love the Lord, our God, and our neighbor as ourselves is not, then, a task riddled with contradictions and dichotomies. It is to recognize, simply, who we are and who we are called to be.

One of the moral excesses of our own day is the privatization of conscience. My choice, my good, my evil, for that matter, my life and my virtue — these words and phrases that belie the very meaning of communication are commonplaces today, and surely not without reason. True communication, however, is impossible and meaningless except in the context of an interdependent and radically relational model acknowledging that our needs, our desires, our hopes, our rights and obligations, for that matter, are just that — ours. The quest for personal identity, so seductive in our age and so normal for students in any age, must be seen to be a quest whose accomplishment lies in the recognition of our radical need for one another and for our world, a need that focuses our attention on the God who is both the ultimate cause of our restlessness and our only and common hope for reaching a passionate rest.

Communication, the process of establishing union, is not value-free, as I mentioned. And a host of specifically ethical questions is raised by this simple fact. For communication can be seen, by its very nature, to offer us the possibility of creating our community, our world, even of creating ourselves as we interact with one another and with the mystery of our own lives. Just as easily, however, we have the awesome power to destroy, to create limits where there need be none, to tear down the often fragile peace that houses our hearts and spirits in a consensus of values that reflect the grandeur and the agony of our calling to be who we are meant to be.

Perhaps, most of all, we will need discerning eyes to recognize the stages of achieving union, which represent the real hope that we have of achieving one of our day's great goals, the goal of progress and growth. For the Christian vision that inspires us to trust and to love our world, to believe that revelation is truly and constantly ongoing in our lives, is a vision that calls us to new life and thus to growth through the reenactment of the suffering, death, and resurrection of our Lord. If we will be faithful to ourselves and to our students, we must help one another to see that the easy answers and the painless solutions, the immediate satisfactions and gratifications, are not in themselves the road to truly human and Christian growth. The ongoing process of communication that describes our lives must endure disunity and suffering even as it realizes its possibility of achieving transcendence and new life.

This is a lifelong task and process for us all, rich in the very need it uncovers to discover values, to estimate them, and to allow ourselves to be possessed by those of them that point us along the path of a life of virtue, lived in common, in the shadow and the luminescence of our God and the world that speaks God's mysteries to us.

I freely admit that I have offered here only the barest sketch of the possibilities and demands that contemporary society presents us with — the slow and common effort to discern what we care for, and to what extent — the ever-present need to state and articulate, to communicate this to one another as we foster in each other a sense of the attractiveness and radically human possibility of the virtuous life — the wealth of meaning, of responsibility, and conjoined pain and exultation that Christian faith suggests as the underlying driving force of our lives. Ironically, I may myself have communicated well or badly as I have tried to describe a task that the ethical concerns of our age offer to us all. It seems clear, however, that this is a task presented to educators and students alike, that nowhere, from my point of view, should there be greater hope of achieving this than in a Jesuit educational setting, and that the challenge itself offers us all hope for lasting satisfaction as we cooperate in our common enterprise, an enterprise that truly has light to shed on a troubled world never richer in possibility.

6 / Science and Technology in Jesuit Education

Robert A. Brungs, S.J.

THERE are almost as many aspects of Jesuit education as there are persons and institutions involved in it. If we are to talk reasonably about the place of science and technology in Jesuit education, we should offer a rationale for its being there at all. It is possible that there may be some repetition between my approach and what has already been presented earlier in this collection. I would be truly consoled if there were some repetitions, for that would indicate that I am not alone in all my idiosyncratic glory!

I wish to confine myself more or less to Catholic aspects of Jesuit education — its church relationships — though, of course, not denying in any way its civil obligations and its strictly intellectual (and, therefore, human) obligations. This is done for purposes of simplification and personal preference, not for purposes of ideology.

THE NEED

Christianity is a faith that is necessarily and solidly based on the belief that the Son of God became human in the womb of the Virgin Mary. He became, as St. Paul tells us, one like us in all things except sin. He became so much a part of the nature and the history of the world that St. Luke can date the beginning of his ministry among us with a listing of those in power in Palestine at the time: "In the fifteenth year of Tiberius Caesar's reign, when Pontius Pilate was governor of Judea. . . ." More, we firmly believe that after his death and resurrection he ascended bodily into heaven, retaining his full humanity in glory. Thereby, he instituted a new state of bodily life, one to which we are called and destined.

As Catholics we live in a world we believe to be sacramental, a world in which "material" things are seen to be of "spiritual" value, to have an everlasting destiny in God. We live in a world where, we believe, bread and wine become the body and blood of Christ, where water is a substance that washes us clean of the sin into which we are born and is the material agent (indispensably material) of our introduction into the life and love of the Blessed Trinity. In short, God in Christ has so deeply and permanently penetrated the created world in his body that part of the universe has become a part of him. Thus in him and in us, through him and through us, the physical world itself is somehow redeemed. We are all familiar with St. Paul's triumphant cry of joy: "creation still retains the hope of being freed, like us, from its slavery to decadence, to enjoy the same freedom and glory as the children of God."

This statement of St. Paul is echoed in the Vatican II statement in *Gaudium et Spes*, no. 34:

> Throughout the course of the centuries, people have labored to better the circumstances of their lives through a monumental amount of individual and collective effort. To believers this point is settled: considered in itself, such human activity accords with God's will. For mankind, created to God's image, received a mandate to subject to itself the earth and all that it contains, and to govern the world with justice and holiness, a mandate to relate itself and the totality of things to Him who was to be acknowledged as the Lord and Creator of all. Thus, by the subjection of all things to human beings, the name of God would be wonderful in all the earth. . . .
>
> Thus, far from thinking that works produced by human talent and energy are in opposition to God's power, and that the rational creature exists as a kind of rival to the Creator, Christians are convinced that the triumphs of the human race are a sign of God's greatness and the flowering of His own mysterious design. For the greater human power becomes, the farther our individual and community responsibility extends. Hence it is clear that human beings are not deterred by the Christian message from building up the world, or impelled to neglect the welfare of their fellows. They are, rather, more stringently bound to do these very things.

So the world, this beautiful blue and white planet, in what still appears to us to be an otherwise sterile universe, is the arena for our service and our worship. The council, in that passage, tells us many things about the place of science and technology in Catholic consciousness. Therefore, it should say something about their place in Jesuit education. Science (as a method of intellectual search whose conclusions are mathematically consistent, measurable, and verifiable through experiment) is a still increasingly effective way of human laboring to better the circumstances of our lives. Science and technology have become twins in our effort at understanding the structures of creation and at turning our planetary environment into a world apt for human betterment.

The council tells us that science and technology (among other things) are a sign of God's greatness and a sign of the flowering of God's own mysterious design. As such they should be seen as a part of the human worship of the Creator, especially so for us Christians, rooted as we are in the world by the body and blood of the Lord. If the pursuit of knowledge of the world and the attempts to alter it to make it a place more apt to human living are parts of our Christian worship, then they must be part of our intellectual and spiritual patrimony. What better place and what better mode is there for this understanding and changing than Christian institutions of higher learning, including Jesuit institutions. As Christians, we must live in the world penetrated and transformed by the life and death of Christ. We must love that world for its own sake as well as because of God's further will for it. The understanding of it as well as love for it must be a conscious part of Christian education.

Since the beginning of Jesuit education to the present, we have gone:

1.) from the telescopic discovery of the moons of Jupiter to close-up (relatively speaking) photographs of those same moons;

2.) from the beginnings of understanding of the vascular system to bypass surgery, arterial replacement, and heart transplants;

3.) from gunpowder to thermonuclear bombs;

4.) from the abacus to computers;

5.) from primitive understanding of the reproductive system, through the discovery of the ovum, to in vitro fertilization;

6.) from zero to recombinant DNA;

7.) from alchemy to the multitudinous products of chemistry without which our society would no longer function;

8.) etc., etc., etc.

There is really no way to compare the times when Jesuit education began with the present times. Much of that difference is directly the result of science and the technology that has grown from it. This is true of the products in our everyday lives (cars, refrigerators, televisions, etc.) as well as the more exotic products like space probes, bacteria-producing human insulin, "test tube babies," and so forth. Educated persons ought to be aware of how such things have come about and how they are to be put together. This is certainly a part of all education, Jesuit higher education included.

Also, in a society where science and technology are so central, persons must be educated to quantitative appreciation, to a sense of scale. I should like to quote from a friend of mine at Penn State — Rustum Roy. He was commenting on the failure even of educated persons to develop a sense of quantity:

I was involved with Three Mile Island. And the rubbish you had to put up with was so extreme. Take my students . . . thirty seniors at Penn State. I got back to Penn State from Harrisburg. They said:

"We're afraid."

"What are you afraid of?"

"We're afraid we'll die of radiation."

"How much radiation are you going to die of? How much radiation was there at Harrisburg?"

"We don't know, but it sounds pretty big."

"How's it going to get up here?" They weren't sure. I asked how radiation travels. Nobody had the foggiest idea. Little creepy-crawlies? They had no idea. How much radiation? Someone recalled reading a big number — 1120. I asked what the unit was. It was 1120 picocuries. Sure sounds like a big number! So, I said to them: We were talking about a nuclear war the other day. We were talking about megacuries. Which is bigger, megacuries or picocuries?"

Remember these are seniors at Penn State. We had a vote on this, since that's the way to get the truth in our democracy. Some of them allowed as how megacuries were smaller than picocuries. Twenty three of the thirty students didn't understand 18 orders of magnitude. . . . How many of you know what 18 orders of magnitude is? Well, I could compare the diameter of a human hair to the distance to the sun. Then you get a little feel of how bad a mistake we can make. People simply have no feel, no scale, no sense of quantification.

In a society where quantification means so much, it is discouraging to hear that a sense of scale is that badly lacking. How would such a question be answered in any Jesuit college or university? Would our students do any better? Yet, many of the issues facing society and church — issues like nuclear power, nuclear war, acid rain, etc., etc. — depend on a sense of scale. Statistics — as the recent election campaign showed — are now the grist for public discourse. How many of our students (or ourselves) have an adequate feel for statistics?

Yet, as fantastic as the products of science and technology have become, as powerful as the techniques of science are, as great is the need for a quantitative sense — these are not primary reasons why the study of science and technology should be central to Jesuit higher education. As greatly as science and technology have altered the landscape of our lives, so greatly has it raised new questions or changed the status of all the old questions raised over the centuries. Unless philosophy and theology come to cope with these new questions and with the revised questions of the past, they will become simply vacuous.

Perhaps the perennially central religious quest is the search for unity. It assumes several different forms: the unity within God, God's unity with the creation, the unities that occur within the creation. These form the basis of many of the great philosophical and theological questions of the ages. Science of itself cannot help us much with the search for an understanding of the unity within God. Only indirectly can it help us understand God's unity with creation. But it is of major importance in our recognition of unities among creatures. Where has the knowledge about such unities come from over the last several centuries? We have learned an enormous amount about the unities within creation *from the sciences.*

In 1687 Isaac Newton published the *Principia*, in which he showed that the motion of celestial *and* terrestrial bodies was describable by the same equations. This was the final demise of Aristotelian spheres. Perhaps from our superior perch on the tree of knowledge we may yawn a bit when we hear it. But in its own day it represented a profoundly deeper understanding of a basic unity in the cosmos.

Approximately one hundred twenty-five years ago, Darwin, in his *Origin of Species*, maintained the unity of living systems at the level of the species, an idea overshadowed by the creation-evolution debate. Now, since 1975, scientists have discovered a much more profound unity in creation. Writing in *Science* in 1980 ("Recombinant

DNA Revisited,"vol. 209, no. 4463, Sept. 19, 1980, p. 1317) Maxine Singer stated:

> We have learned that genes are fungible; animal genes function perfectly well within bacteria and bacterial genes within animal cells, confirming the unity of nature.

Thus, in our own day, in the aftermath of Watson and Crick's identification of the double helix, and as a result of the extraordinarily rapid and significant development in recombinant DNA research, we are becoming aware of the *unity of all living systems* at the level of the nucleic acids. This development represents one of the greatest possible advances in the understanding of the unities with which God has constituted the universe. I personally find it difficult even to imagine a deeper physical unity. The discoveries of such unities within creation can be the springboard for a much more mature theology, a more profound philosophy, a more appropriate legal system, and the like, if only we would seriously reflect on what science has *already* taught us.

Father Walter Ong has stated that the central intellectual and emotional problem in the church's realization of its mission in the world today (and Jesuit education as a part of that mission) is that we have no cosmology. In a private letter to me he wrote, "We have had none [a cosmology] since the Aristotelian spheres and all that went with them were shown not to be there. The lack of a cosmology affects christology, ecclesiology, and just about everything else in evangelization, including especially any real planning for the real future. For metaphysics, you obviously need a physics." The same is true of an anthropology; we cannot have an authentic anthropology without a biology. Science has been a tremendously successful development; we can learn many things from it that are invaluable for progress in theology, philosophy, law, and so on. These are among things that Jesuit institutions of higher education are in existence to promote. If there is to be anything like a research and development operation in the church, it must come from Catholic (including Jesuit) universities and colleges. It is something that must motivate our efforts.

Biological science is now the center of interest in science, in development, in heavy funding — both governmental and industrial. I shall go further and say that it is at the forefront of human intellectual progress. It may well eventuate that the greatest intellectual watershed of the twentieth century was the identification of the structure of deoxyribonucleic acid, DNA. This crucial scientific, technological, and industrial revolution is seen in such things as "testtube" babies, recombinant DNA, neuroscientific advances, as well as other biological developments that have already had a significant impact on society and the church. The spectrum of scientific and technological advance (the biological, chemical, physical, cybernetic, etc.) will have an even greater effect, especially in the areas of personal dignity, personal freedom and the "integrity" of the human body. Twice before in human history our scientific and technological genius has so radically redirected the course of human life as to merit from historians of culture the title of revolution — namely, the Agricultural and Industrial Revolutions. A third scientific-technological revolution is already well begun. Its capacity to redirect the histories of peoples is *vastly* greater than that of either its predecessors. Biological industrialization has begun — on a very significant scale.

We have a great need for a much more positive approach to and appreciation of scientific advance. We in the university community need to be aware of where we are and of what is happening. In about thirty years the life sciences, under a very significant impulse from physics, have moved from an observational posture, through an intense and extraordinarily rapid analytic phase, to a synthetic capability. The life sciences have now become experimental sciences linked to technological and industrial capability. The late Charles Frankel has summed up the power and revolutionary character of these new techniques:

> Biomedicine has eliminated the insouciance with which most people have embraced technological progress. It forces consideration not simply of techniques and instrumentalities but of ends and purposes.

This should in its own right be a mandate for the place of science and technology in Jesuit higher education. Science and technology — especially now bioscience and biotechnology — are significant (perhaps the most significant) engines for changing the course of human history. To be weak in science is, these days, simply to be divorced from the real world. There may have been a time when this was not true, but that time passed fifty years ago. Without a deep commitment to scientific understanding and appreciation, Jesuit higher education is fatally weakened. Without it that education is of significantly degraded value to society and to the church in the realm of what we can loosely call "research and development."

More, if we do not offer significant instructional opportunities (the-transmission-of-knowledge part of education) to our students, we are not preparing either a religious laity or citizens competent to contribute to the cultural life of the church and of the nation.

Still more, unless we dare be prophetic in our approach to education, we fail to fulfill our mandate as Catholics. Transmission of knowledge is necessary to Jesuit education but it is not sufficient to it. Dare we be prophetic? If not, we should quit. If we do, we should be realistically aware of the quality of a prophet's life. Do we have the courage?

THE HISTORY

Does the historical place of science in Jesuit education inspire confidence? I think the place of science and technology in Jesuit education, if visually depicted, would resemble nothing so much as a painter's drop cloth. There is a significant amount of paint on the cloth, but it does not present an easily identifiable pattern. Because I have not been able to discover any real order in our approach to science, I plan to treat that history anecdotally.

In researching this subject, I looked up several Jesuit scientists of my generation and the generation immediately ahead of me. I figured that their experience would be a mirror on the place of science and technology in Jesuit higher education. That was and is my modest assumption here. I wanted, then, to check their reactions on the assumption that those reactions would be a significant commentary on the place of science in Jesuit education, say, for the last half century in the United States.

When I began my graduate studies in physics here at Saint Louis University thirty years ago, the older Jesuits, especially those in the sciences, used to speak of a priest who clearly belonged in anyone's pantheon of legendary eccentrics. The lore was that this man (a physicist) had written either a paper or a series of papers (that point was never very clear) on physics. The paper was never permitted to be published because it was considered to be irreconcilable with the then "official" philosophical doctrines. Theories proposed in that paper, the story continued, won a Nobel Prize for someone else years later. I cannot say for sure whether or not this story was true. If all the stories we heard in those days about our athletic ability had been true, then almost all of us had been all-Americans. Nonetheless, what is important to this discussion is that no one felt that this sort of thing could not happen. It would have been no cause for surprise.

Another interesting chapter in the lore concerned Father Teodore Wulf. In 1936 the Nobel Prize went to a student of Father Wulf, Victor Hess, for work on cosmic rays. Father Wulf was a pioneer in such work; he invented the early cosmic ray detectors. But after World War I he was sent to teach the philosophers at Valkenberg, and relinquished the cosmic ray work. To be scrupulously fair I do not know that there were not other factors at work in the decision to send him to Valkenberg. Father Wulf had been a divisional chaplain in the German army during World War I. He *may* have been, as we say now, "burnt out."

Anyway, beginning after World War II, times and personalities conspired to make something new under the sun. A number of Jesuit superiors sent increasingly larger numbers of Jesuits into graduate studies in science. For a while it looked as if the parousia had arrived. There was major commitment of Jesuit manpower to science. But many of those trained at the time have a suspicion that, in terms of Jesuit education, they were never any more than a highly trained labor pool, obviating the necessity of paying high salaries to non-Jesuit professors. Others felt that it was in response to the availability of federal money in science. Still, let us take the high road and assume that it was done out of the highest educational motives. Even in that case, the love of science for its own sake never really permeated the spirit of Jesuit education. Science, it is my opinion, never really occupied a central place in Jesuit education.

I have given these anecdotes not to suggest that we ought to send large numbers of Jesuits into science again, nor to say that all of the blame for the demise of science and technology in our universities and colleges is to be laid at the feet of university administrators. Cultural factors were at work as well. The decline in the granting of graduate degrees in physics matches very closely the decline in religious vocation — a very curious correlation. Financial factors were clearly involved. Finally, many of us who were brought along in the halcyon days have not stayed in the science in which we were trained. I myself am a perfect example of the syndrome that "old physicists never die, they simply become philosophers (or theologians)."

Yet, seen subjectively, many of the persons with whom I talked, were aware of an intellectual priority in Jesuit higher education: theology or philosophy was first, depending on whether you were talking to a theologian or philosopher. Then there were the classics, followed by English, maybe next by history, and then finally by the trade school courses like science, engineering, and law. The sciences seem to have been an aside to the essence of Jesuit education. Ours were liberal arts colleges and universities; seemingly there was little place for science and technology.

Over the years, several Jesuit schools had very highly regarded programs in astronomy and in seismology. Various reasons were given for this: some felt that astronomy was popular when Jesuits started their educational apostolate; some thought that we were not able to reestablish our efforts in physics and chemistry when the society was restored after its suppression; several pointed out that biology was eschewed because of a deep-seated malaise over questions of human origins. So, too, anthropology was basically ignored as dangerous.

Then, too, the *Ratio Studiorum*, at least as it was interpreted to us, was certainly orientated to the "liberal arts," which were so defined as to exclude science from an integral role. I am of the opinion, the validity of which I shall leave to you to decide, that in Jesuit education the theoretical was to be preferred to the practical, to the technological. The impression was given that Greek was better than Latin, pure mathematics better than applied mathematics, ontology more dignified than ethics, and so on. There seemed to be a set of preferences, if not formal priorities, that promoted the more theoretical over the more experimental. This also had the advantage of avoiding the raising of disturbing questions that called for a revision of thought or behavior.

My intention is certainly not to denigrate either the persons involved or the system itself. If my informal survey is accurate, then Jesuit education put rather little stress on *modern* science or technology. These were never a *central* concern in U.S. Jesuit education. We must steal a slogan from elsewhere: we were the "ones last hired and first fired." So it has seemed to eventuate. The Golden Years (roughly 1945–1970) seem to have been an anomaly.

SUMMARY

There can be no doubt that the fruits of modern science are not really a part of the church's patrimony. At best the church's conceptual life is finally Darwinian. It cannot be said to be Einsteinian, Heisenbergian, or Watson-Crick. The church's failure here is mainly the failure of Catholic colleges and universities, and, reductively, Jesuit institutions.

Theology is by nature involved with vast quantities of knowledge, all of which is radically beyond its control. It is not a research discipline, as that terminology is generally understood. It does not generate its own data, as many other disciplines do. It derives its basic information from sources other than itself. Science and technology are absolutely basic to this process. But what is true of individuals is most likely true of institutions as well. The individual who learns a discipline as a tool for another discipline rarely learns it as well as one who approaches it in its own right, for its own sake — things like talent being roughly equal. So, too, I think, our institutions must promote science and technology in its own right, because it is an acceptable, appropriate, necessary, intellectual enterprise.

If we are to be a serious intellectual force in our communities, in the nation, in the church, we will need excellent science programs, rather than continuing the retrenchment that has been occurring. Not all science (even research science) is necessarily expensive beyond our reach. We could pick and choose; we do not need bevatrons.

Let me conclude by urging a growth in our commitment to both research and teaching in science and technology. Until we do, how can we call ourselves universities? Until science and technology are a significant component of the intellectual air we breathe on our campuses, the church will not be able to have an intellectual presence in the contemporary world. Moreover the stakes presented by that contemporary world are probably the highest with which the church has been presented.

I believe that an objective appraisal of the issues facing our society and the church will reveal the need for Catholic institutions of higher education to be deeply involved in scientific and technological advance as well as in critical evaluation of the meaning of this advance. If the church as a whole is going to begin to think in categories appropriate to the issues raised by contemporary science and technology, it will have to begin on our campuses. If theology is to come alive again, it will have to learn to handle the vast, revolutionary, new concepts that have arisen in the last half-century. If philosophy (at least in its cosmological aspects) is to speak to the contemporary world, it cannot ignore the advances in physics. If law is going to be appropriate, it must be able to handle technologies like in vitro fertilization with its attendant issues like surrogate mothers, frozen embryos, and the like.

Our institutional currency depends on our ability to incorporate science and technology into our curricular imagination. If we do not, our educational approach will be simply quaint. Yet we can always look to the imagination of our educational leaders to spur their schools to leadership in at least the less expensive aspects of science and technology.

The society we live in needs it. The church needs it. If we are true to, the spirit of Jesuit educational life, we shall provide it — because that is our vocation.

7 / Educational Aims of the Liberal Arts Curriculum: Contextual Education

Lawrence Biondi, S.J.

IN varying degrees we educators wrestle with the complex concepts and perceptions, questions and issues, that touch something we all cherish so preciously and esteem so highly: Jesuit higher education. I am quite certain that despite all the differences in our backgrounds, all of us share at least one deep belief — a belief in the enduring importance of a liberal Jesuit education. Because there is no point in preaching to the converted, I will not belabor the point. Instead, I should like to consider the constituent parts of our common passion. Given the *contextual situation* of the diversity among our undergraduate students in terms of their age, sex, socioeconomic, religious, cultural, and political backgrounds, what disciplines and skills must our undergraduate students master in order to be truly educated not only today in the 1980s but tomorrow in the 1990s and, for that matter, in the next millennium? What, in other words, makes up a good undergraduate education?

GOOD EDUCATION: DIFFERENT PERSPECTIVES

Every epoch has had its own answer to the question: What constitutes a *good* education? In ancient Greece, the answer included politics and physical fitness; in the Middle Ages, the *trivium* — grammar, logic, and rhetoric — and the *quadrivium* — arithmetic, astronomy, geometry, and music; during the Renaissance, Greek and Latin language and literature.

Of course, your answer to what constitutes a good education depends largely on what you believe the *purpose* of an education ought to be. Plato thought it should produce good persons who acted nobly. St. Thomas Aquinas believed its goal was the love of God. St. Ignatius Loyola thought the purpose of education was to know and love God, to save one's soul, and to ameliorate society, all for the greater glory of God. And Rousseau thought it should help students realize their unique potential as human beings.

With the rise of science, particularly after Darwin, came the *great debate*. Should the curriculum for a good education be grounded in traditional humanistic studies such as philosophy, history, language, literature, and the fine arts? Or in light of the recent scientific developments, should students be trained in such disciplines as biology, chemistry, physics, and paleontology?

The issue was debated in nineteenth-century England by two great educators, Matthew Arnold and Thomas Huxley. Arnold maintained that being truly educated meant "to know the best which has been thought and said in the world." And Arnold firmly believed that this could be learned only through the study of the humanities, especially literature. Huxley disagreed, arguing that above all truly educated persons ought to understand themselves and the world in which they lived. And the only reasonable way to acquire such understanding was through mastery of the natural sciences.

In some academic circles, the debate goes on to this very day. Which shall it be: the humanities or the sciences? I said earlier that one's definition of a good education depends on what one believes is the purpose of an education. I have some ideas of my own on the subject, and I wish to share them with you.

Unlike Arnold and Huxley, I do not believe that a good undergraduate education is a matter of *either-or*; rather, it is a case of *both-and*. A good undergraduate education requires a sound grounding in the best that has been thought and expressed in both the spoken and written word — in scientific formulas; in clay, metal, marble or on canvas; in numerous forms of electronic media — all expressions that reflect the human race's collective wisdom.

The humanities comprise the body of knowledge that deals with what it has meant and continues to mean to be truly human, to make value-judgments, to choose the wiser course of action. This is achieved primarily through the examination of human experience and its implications for the present and the future. Inasmuch as the human race's experience has been preserved principally through books, art works, and other cultural objects, the humanities are often defined in terms of specific academic disciplines. However, the concerns of the humanities extend beyond the classroom, library, and museum to encompass a variety of social, ethical, and cultural questions that all persons confront periodically throughout the course of their lives. The humanities should, therefore, be regarded as the intellectual activities that help undergraduates deal with these questions and will continue to help them define their relationships to themselves and to their society.

Jesuit Education

Although the purpose of a Jesuit liberal education has always been to bring to contemporary issues, problems, and questions the collective wisdom of the ages, this can no longer be done so easily without a deep understanding and appreciation of the significance of the scientific and technological developments of our modern age. Our students need to have an adequate understanding of the scientific and technological basis of modern-day issues so that they can make intelligent decisions in their role as responsible citizens in their communities and nation. Drawing on a language and a perspective that is pervasive throughout our institutional literature, I submit that an excellent liberal, Jesuit education must be based on an integrated, coherent, and well-structured curriculum of humanities, social sciences, and natural sciences, because each of these three disciplines in its own way provides undergraduates with a body of knowledge and a methodology to develop their skills to analyze and synthesize for clear judgments and for application of academic learning to real-life situations.

The curriculum of a liberal education, grounded in the humanities, social sciences, and natural sciences, is the heart of any Jesuit college or university. It is in the arts and sciences that the central Judeo-Christian tradition affirms the dignity of the human person and embodies God. It is in this milieu that our students develop their intellectual discipline and their awareness of past and present dimensions of human culture, confirm their dedication and commitment to help and serve others, and strengthen their courage to build a solid future for and in solidarity with the human family. Theology and philosophy, history and communication, English and foreign languages and literature, fine arts and a variety of social and natural sciences all have their distinct, yet cooperative and integrative roles in developing our undergraduates to fuller womanhood and manhood. Such a curriculum provides our students with knowledge, expertise, and skills to find solutions to complex problems.

These are the *goals* that I consider to be the hallmarks of an excellent Jesuit liberal education. The courses that constitute its curriculum should be planned as an integrative and unified educational experience. Courses should introduce our students to the main questions asked by each discipline. The curriculum should emphasize the most important ways in which each discipline addresses these questions and thereby fathoms the chief categories by which each discipline interprets reality and human experience, and discovers the relationships between disciplines. This kind of education will not tell our students how to solve all the puzzles of humankind and the universe. However, it will make them wiser about the mysteries of humankind and the universe. It will not guarantee wisdom, but it will increase their opportunities to acquire wisdom. And wisdom does increase a person's ability to lead and to serve. In simplest terms, the curriculum attempts to state what we stand for in our Jesuit institutions of higher learning, what we believe to be our creed and our character. It is a basic, but indispensable, step in helping our students achieve a true Jesuit undergraduate education.

CORE CURRICULUM

The spirit of such an undergraduate curriculum is made incarnate through its core curriculum, which is an expression of the classic understanding of the human person as developed in the Judeo-Christian tradition. Jesuit education is one embodiment of that tradition. The core curriculum, which is fairly uniform in many Jesuit colleges and universities in the United States, endeavors to educate our undergraduates according to a set of goals: (1) that our students will become responsible members in American society; (2) that as individuals endowed with inquiring minds, they will seek their origins as cultured persons in order to discover their destinies; (3) that as persons with sensitive feelings and creative imaginations, they will be excellent users of words and of languages; (4) that as thinkers they will find their proper vocations in the world; and finally (5) that as believers in God they will come to understand God's intervention into history.

The purpose of the core curriculum, then, is to further the education this view of the human person implies and to foster the growth of each student in the Jesuit spirit in twentieth-century America. This means that our prime educational objectives are to form persons of reflective and critical judgment; persons broadened by literature and trained for expression and communication, comfortable in the contemporary world of science and technology; persons aware of history, cognizant of the present situation of human society, and actively concerned for the future of the human race; persons formed in love with a passion for social justice and capable of enjoying life in its highest forms; and, finally, persons for others — to become servant-leaders in their community.

When you strip away all the details and get down to essentials, the purpose of an excellent contemporary liberal Jesuit education is to help our students acquire the knowledge and expertise, the values and vision, to do three things: (1) to understand the world and how they are to live in it; (2) to enjoy the world; and (3) to contribute to the world.

To Lead and To Serve

Beginning with part 4 of the *Constitutions of the Society of Jesus*,[1] there are common threads concerning educational goals that run throughout the Society of Jesus' 444-year history. To summarize them in capsule form: the aim of our Jesuit enterprise is to help our students know and love God, and to save their souls; to help our students master and excel in many fields of knowledge; to integrate that body of knowledge with moral and spiritual values so that they can become effective leaders in society and, as leaven, help others reach the same goal, thus making our society a better and happier place in which to live.

Allow me to amplify. It is insufficient merely to help our undergraduates assimilate a liberal education with human values in our Judeo-Christian tradition. It is insufficient merely to guide them in developing a healthy formation of their personality and to synthesize their personal faith in the context of our American culture. In addition to educating our students intellectually, socially, culturally, morally, and spiritually, and showing them how to live well-integrated lives, one of the remaining purposes of our educational enterprise is to help our students become *more effective leaders in society*; to mold them to use their knowledge and expertise to serve and to lead others living and working in their communities. As Jesuit and lay faculty and administrators working in close collaboration, we must keep our educational aims clear and distinct as we prepare our students for the kind of world in which they will live. We must prepare them not simply to survive in that world, but to be an effective presence in it; that is, to play an active role in helping to transform its values, attitudes, and behaviors.

One of the most important goals of our educational enterprise, which we faculty and administrators need to focus on continually, is to help our undergraduates become more effective leaders in American society. There is a leadership crisis in the United States today. We need to help fill this leadership vacuum.

Is it not our obligation as educators to stir the minds and feelings of our students to consider how they should live in our society, to challenge them to take an ethically-based firm stance against injustice and hypocrisy, to become affirmative builders of a better society? How can we cultivate our students' potential to actualize their adventurous, creative abilities to make certain that their fellow brothers' and sisters' highest priority needs are being served? The very essence of leadership, going out ahead to show others the way, is derived from more than our students' basic personality traits and educational experience of academic studies.

A hallmark of a leader is that of pointing out problems and finding solutions to them. A leader has a goal and always knows what it is. They can articulate it. The leader manifests a certainty and purpose to others who may have difficulty themselves in achieving the goal. We need to foster leadership in our students by our own modeling of leadership and by acquainting our students with historical models of Christian courage and leadership. In the words of the Second Vatican Council:

> In every group or nation, there is an ever-increasing number of men and women who are conscious that they themselves are the artisans and authors of the culture of their community. Throughout the world there is a similar growth in the combined sense of independence and responsibility. Such a development is of paramount importance for the spiritual and moral maturity of the human race. This truth grows clearer if we consider how the world is becoming unified and how we have the duty to build a better world based upon truth and justice. Thus we are witnesses of the birth of a new humanism, one in which

man is defined first of all by his responsibility toward his brothers and toward history.[2]

How can we, therefore, put into proper perspective our undergraduates' desire to live good, happy, and productive lives in terms of material possessions, security, and status? How can we help them need to stretch, to reach beyond these objectives and realize more altruistic, overarching goals — to strive to make big dreams become a reality?

All of us in the academic community need not look far to see all kinds of injustice: political infringement on our basic human rights such as racism, sexism, and ageism; the arms race threatening a nuclear nightmare; the mindless exhaustion of our natural resources and the pollution of our environment; economic injustices such as hunger, unemployment, and inflation, and collective injustice in the Third World.

VISIONS AND VALUES

How well do we prepare our students to cope with the world as it is and challenge them to lead, to do something about its problems? Education is a means to shape a vision of the world to be renewed. A vision guides us in our decisions. A vision enables us to open our minds and spirits to possible creative — even dangerous — responses to ameliorate the human dimensions of the quality of life. Values are the motivating forces that propel us to make sound ethical decisions. Values are the signposts that measure a civilization's progress to make the world a better place in which to live. We need to ask ourselves — faculty and administrators — what are *our visions and values*? Are they compatible with the basic thrust of Jesuit goals and ideals of higher education? If so, to what extent do we instill, nurture, and cultivate these same visions and values in our undergraduates so that they, as potential leaders, can live and work in their careers and vocations to eradicate injustices in the world and to make it a more humane world?

At the heart of any American Jesuit college or university are its students, staff, faculty, and administrators, and the Judeo-Christian principles, ethics, values, and beliefs by which they all choose to shape their lives. At its very center lies the conviction that there is a wisdom carried within the intellectual tradition of the church. One of the many functions of a Jesuit college or university is to appropriate consciously those traditions, as well as to criticize and to develop them. The Catholic tradition is, in part, intellectual. It created universities in order to continue the goal of *fides quaerens intellectum*. It is our shared responsibility as members of a Jesuit academic community to help our students to discipline and to enrich their minds in order to think clearly about that which is new, critical, and technological. Our students are called to a truly responsible life of the mind. However, we must first clarify our own intellectual perspectives in order that we may better help our students.

We must all be committed to pursue truth together and to share this truth with each other and with our students. Our talents, interests, and experiences should provide our students with a strong curriculum that systematically offers the methods of analysis, criticism, and eventual appropriation of knowledge. We must continually find better ways to prepare our students vocationally and professionally to lead in our American society a life to which they will bring their God-given talents and expertise, and thus help influence and affect positively those whom they, in turn, will serve.

We live in a period in which we and our students experience varying degrees of disorientation. We find ourselves confused about long-cherished beliefs, ethical values, and standards of personal and communal behavior. Several elements in our American society are either hostile to our Judeo-Christian tradition or indifferent to it, or offer us powerfully convincing attractions in competing directions. We are forever being challenged to reflect, analyze, and act appropriately. All of us share the responsibility of maintaining and developing the intellectual standards and goals of Jesuit higher education. But we can do this only by immersing ourselves in the new generation. This requires us to face present problems in American society and to find renewed forms of solving these problems in order to answer the needs of men and women in the world, and to push forward, in cooperation with the creative Spirit, "to renew the face of the earth."

TODAY'S EDUCATIONAL CHALLENGES

It is not easy during a four-year undergraduate curriculum to equip students with all the knowledge and skills they will need to enter fully into their chosen vocations. The overwhelming changes in our society continue today to accelerate. The futurist, Alvin Toffler,[3] has illustrated the staggering rapidity of change by translating the last 50,000 years into 800 lifetimes. He noted that of those

800 lifetimes, only 70 could communicate with their descendants through the medium of the written word; only the last eight lifetimes ever saw a printed word; only the last four were able to measure time with any precision; only the last two used an electric motor; and only during the 800th lifetime were most of the material goods that we use in our daily lives developed. And most shocking, Toffler predicts that more technological progress will be made during the 801st lifetime than during all the lifetimes of the previous 800.

No period of human history has witnessed similar political, social, economic, or cultural changes. Yet we are committed by our common profession to help society think through its problems and to help our students to sort things out in the midst of this exciting yet confusing period. We may even find ourselves hard pressed to stay abreast of what is happening. However, we have an advantage in this situation because our Judeo-Christian tradition gives us a perspective lacking in those who think that everything worthwhile was invented only yesterday. There is no shortcut to wisdom and no substitute for it.

On October 24, 1984, *The Chronicle of Higher Education* published a report from a study group established by the National Institute of Education. The report was on the "Conditions of Excellence in Higher Education." The panel of educators noted:

> We thus conclude that the best preparation for the future is not narrow training for a specific job, but rather an education that will enable students to adapt to a changing world. Successful adaptation to change requires the ability to think critically, to synthesize large quantities of new information, and to master the language skills (critical reading, effective composition, clear speech, and careful listening) that are the fuel of thought. Adaptation to change requires that one draw on history and on the experience of other nations, and that one apply the theories and methods of empirical investigation. It requires a disposition toward lifelong learning and the ability to partake of and contribute to the richness of culture and citizenship of our nation. . . . We know that a liberal education curriculum will not and cannot be the same for students of all levels of ability, ages, and interests. But we are convinced that what should distinguish the baccalaureate degree from more specialized credentials is the broad learning that lies behind it. An increase in liberal education requirements is one way to guarantee that comprehensiveness. But simply adding requirements — or offering students a larger set of liberal arts courses from which to select — does not achieve one of the principal

aims of liberal education, the ability to integrate what one has learned in different disciplines. What happens too often when liberal education requirements are increased is fragmentation, as departmental politics comes to overwhelm learning objectives.[4]

Within five weeks, *The Chronicle of Higher Education* (November 28, 1984) also published a report entitled, "To Reclaim a Legacy,"[5] written by Dr. William J. Bennett, formerly chairman of the National Endowment for the Humanities, and now Secretary of Education. Dr. Bennett laments the present state of the humanities in American colleges and universities. He places much of the blame for the widespread decline in the study of the humanities on academic administrators and faculty members. His, as well as the earlier report, gives not only the "warning signals" for the future of undergraduate education, but also challenges all of us to examine our own views, attitudes, and biases toward liberal arts and undergraduate education as well as our curricula and outcomes of our undergraduates.

Bennett, for example, argues that we have become too preoccupied with "basic skills" to the detriment of classical models. There are, however, certain bedrock skills that every educated person today needs simply to get along in the socio-cultural context of the United States: English language skills for one, so that they can receive and give information clearly, concisely, and coherently. Foreign language skills are also essential in our shrinking world. Most Americans are supercilious and obviously ignorant in their conviction that they need not learn another language nor would it benefit them to appreciate another culture. Modern transportation and electronic communication have produced faster, more effective and efficient means to acquire, analyze, and synthesize greater amounts of data. Mathematics and science are other bedrock skills that educated persons need in a world increasingly dependent on computers, automation, and high technology.

Certain ignorances are unacceptable in our times. According to a recent *U.S. News and World Report*,[6] 52 million American adults are functionally incompetent at computation, 44 million at solving problems, 34 million at reading and 26 million at writing. In our world that is growing increasingly complex every day, this is simply unacceptable. It is no secret that our national achievement scores in all these areas have been declining for more than twenty years. For example, student performance on 11 of 15 major Subject Area Tests on the Graduate Record Examination has declined between 1964 and 1982. The sharpest declines occurred in the subjects requiring high verbal skills.

COLLEGIALITY

Our Jesuit and Catholic perspective of education at all levels arises out of the deeply rooted conviction that the life of intelligence must make an indispensable contribution to the spiritual life. We must all have a stronger commitment to long-range projects that deal with the crushing problems facing our nation and our world. We must help our students face head-on issues such as social justice, personal and communal ethical behavior, integration of values and beliefs. The very nature of the Jesuit *collegium* is to witness. Recall the Latin derivation of the word *collegium* — "a group of persons or associates (that is, 'colleagues') who are appointed to gather together in order to pursue a common purpose or to accomplish certain goals." We are all delegated to become scholars, and by the very fact that we have been appointed to teach in the *collegium artium et scientiarium*, we become committed to the task of pursuing truth together with our colleagues and to share this truth with each other and with our students. We give testimony and present evidence in our profession as educators to seek and present the truth. We are, therefore, missioned with this awesome duty to communicate and convince our students of the truth, and we are to do this in a spirit of unity and fellowship. The *collegium* witnesses in action and in atmosphere.

The atmosphere of a college of arts and sciences may be hard to define or to describe, yet it is singularly important. The spirit of its administrators, faculty, staff, and students all contribute to it. Either there is warmth, charity, contentment, and understanding, or there is coldness and disinterest. Either there is enthusiasm, eagerness, and fellowship, or an air of matter-of-factness, routine, and suspicion, or, worse yet, indifference toward one another. I hope there is a fundamentally healthy atmosphere in all our Jesuit undergraduate colleges. It should be apparent in the spirit of care and concern among our students and among ourselves.

I firmly believe that we can all develop this spirit during the coming academic years in the 1990s. I also hope that the academic leadership, policies, decisions, and curriculum of all of our twenty-eight Jesuit institutions of higher learning in the United States will continue to be compatible with the spirit, objectives, values, and vision of St. Ignatius Loyola.

8 / In Oratione Directa: Philosophy in the Jesuit Liberal Arts Curriculum in the United States

Joseph A. Tetlow, S.J.

PHILOSOPHY continues at the heart of the Jesuit liberal arts curriculum, not because it makes final sense of the content of other disciplines, not because it midwifes each student's intellectual and moral integration, and not because it forms the intellectual basis for theology. Philosophy is de jure at the heart of the Jesuit liberal arts curriculum because more than any other discipline it can provoke the intellectual conversion of the conventional thinker to principled reflection. This function of philosophy requires faculty members who are themselves intellectually converted, which means in our day that they are convinced of the general truth of some system of philosophy, but content with the pluralism of philosophy itself and of the Catholic philosophy department, and persistent in their questioning and quest. Finally, if philosophy is de facto going to be at the heart of the Jesuit liberal arts curriculum, it will be taught by men and women who hope to elicit in others what the arduous, exhilarating experience of intellect and valuing has brought to be in themselves.

Perhaps it will be useful, in handling these suggestions, to use the framework of functional specialties that Bernard J. F. Lonergan devised in his *Method in Theology*. He divides the theological enterprise into eight specialties: research, interpretation, history, dialectic, foundations, doctrine, systematics, and communications. Using the framework is troublesome for two reasons: first, Lonergan was dealing with theology, not philosophy, and an obvious and considerable number of accommodations need to be made, which I cannot make here; and secondly, the framework fits my material loosely and might prove rather a distraction than a help. However, I am not dealing with philosophy itself, only with philosophy in education, and in one kind of education at that; and having even a loose framework will give a sense of progression if not an illusion of order in a mass of material that no one has ordered as yet. So I have chosen to use it because it will underscore precisely those points that I consider most central in this discussion.

IN ORATIONE OBLIQUA: WHAT THEY USED TO SAY

The functional specialties are divided in half, and the first half concern matters *in oratione obliqua* — what "they say." This suggests that I talk about the history of teaching philosophy in American Jesuit institutions, and about the history of philosophy as an element in Jesuit education itself.

So I begin with the functional specialty that Lonergan puts first: research. I ask: What has the role of philosophy been in the American Jesuit curriculum? I should tell you that fresh, or even explicit, thinking on this matter, except to repeat the Renaissance conviction that philosophy is the handmaid of theology and of itself forms the whole thinking person to critical thought and accurate judgment, is relatively recent. It was only twenty-three years ago that the question of "The Role of Philosophy and Theology as Academic Disciplines and Their Integration with the Moral, Religious, and Spiritual Life of the Jesuit College Student" was ripe enough to be digested at a workshop of the Jesuit Education Association (FitzGerald, 1980). Fifteen years before that, in 1948, Robert Henle thought that the problem of philosophy in the liberal arts college was a problem of preparing enough and good enough Jesuits to teach the subject (Henle, 1948), and most Jesuits were arguing immediately after World War II only about the reduction of the number of hours given by the curriculum to philosophy.

Jesuit education in America had not always been crowned by philosophy, and its very beginnings were steeped in a kind of academical controversy. When Catholic higher education consisted of just two institutions, their leaders quarreled over philosophy. Early in the 1800s, John Carroll saw introduced into Georgetown's curriculum a course in philosophy. At just the same time, Leonard Neale introduced a preparatory course into St. Mary's Seminary in

Baltimore. When each heard of what the other had done, both fired off letters. Carroll contended that St. Mary's was a seminary, not a college, and needed no classical course. Father Neale countered that Georgetown was a college, not a seminary, and needed no philosophy (Daley, 1957). The two were mollified by an increase in their respective enrollments.

The truth is that Georgetown was hardly a college in 1835, when its staff tried to implement the *Ratio Studiorum* of 1832. Before then, the only students who had studied any philosophy at all were those who stayed around after completing the baccalaureate. In that extra year, they studied some logic, physics, and metaphysics, and received a master's degree. But after 1835, Georgetown lengthened the baccalaureate curriculum to six years, and in the last year put in some philosophy. That became a paradigm, and it introduced systematic philosophy into the American Catholic college, where it was to remain.

But how did Jesuit schools get from a couple of courses in senior year to twenty-four or more credits during three or four years? Some details of the story are fairly pertinent to our concern with the place of philosophy in the curriculum, and involve several developments in American education as a whole: emergence of the "moral philosophy" movement, of the high school, of the commercial course, and of the various professions.

FOUR DEVELOPMENTS IN AMERICAN COLLEGES

First, moral philosophy. During the eighteenth century, those parts of philosophy prior to metaphysics kept exfoliating into physics, chemistry, astronomy, and mathematics, and into what we know as the "behavioral sciences" — economics, sociology, psychology, and political science. During the last half of the century, as we rebelled and became a nation, denominational colleges in the country dropped more and more of the theology they had always taught, replacing it with a single course in senior year. That course was called "moral philosophy."

The foremost historian of the curriculum, Frederick Rudolph, believes that this course moved "into a kind of ascendancy over the curriculum as a whole," usurping the function of logic, divinity, and metaphysics, and became "a kind of capstone course that was wonderfully reassuring in its insistence on the unity of knowledge and the benevolence of God" (Rudolph, 1977, p. 39). This course was often taught by the man with the greatest authority in the institution, the president. It was at least as often taught by a dolt; no denomination has a corner on dullness (Smith, 1956).

By the time Georgetown was under way, this "moral philosophy course" had become a fixture. Thus, in 1813, President Timothy Dwight of Yale was mesmerizing the seniors with a course of lectures and discussions that began with logic and rhetoric, moved through Locke on human understanding and through a catechism, and ended with the reasonableness of faith in Christ. Dwight always ended with "the big question," such as whether humanity is moving toward perfectibility, whether war is good, whether the soul is demonstrably immortal (Rudolph, 1977). Again, from 1836 to 1872, Mark Hopkins sat seniors on the other end of a philosophical log and did the same, starting in physiology and ending in divine providence.

For their part, the Jesuits did not trust any individual that far, and clung to systematic philosophy. Obviously, they had trouble getting their subject into the collegiate curriculum, and in this difficulty they found unexpected help in an educational development quite outside their control: the high school.

For a century before Georgetown's curricular innovation, academies had been teaching everything from crocheting to bookkeeping, but in 1821, not long before the innovation, an institution appeared in Boston called a "high school." It was this institution that gradually took more and more of the studies that had once belonged to "college" — Latin and Greek, writing and history, fiction and poetry. By the 1880s, more students were in high school than in academies (partly because rural education was in such poor shape), and this put a peculiar pressure on Jesuit schools. Their baccalaureate degrees were being considered high school degrees (Burrowes, 1915). Thus, in 1902, the great canon-lawyer-to-be, Timothy Bouscaren, finished his baccalaureate at St. Xavier in Cincinnati and began at Yale as a freshman. Something had to be done, and "the St. Louis plan" led the way at the turn of the century into dividing the old six- or seven-year curriculum into two curricula of four years each. By the end of World War I, all twenty-five Jesuit colleges had made the change (Power, 1958).

The division was serendipitous and played directly into the hands of the Jesuits, who wanted to have a good deal more philosophy in the curriculum than they had had before. No one has written this history yet, but by the early years of this century, as I shall say presently, every collegian in a Jesuit school was receiving a complete course in scholastic philosophy, unless his science prevented his taking one or another course. The courses were by this time in English, which brings me to the third development.

This development began as the introduction, into what were hoped to be strictly classical schools, of "commercial courses," as Jesuits chose the American school they found most amenable. The development, it can be noted, simply dismantled the neat and orderly progression from beginning Latin grammar to final proof that the doctrine of the Trinity does not insult reason.

About "commercial courses." The College of the Holy Cross was unique in announcing from the very start, in 1843, a commercial course, but it was like the rest of the Jesuit colleges in resisting pressure from Jesuit superiors to continue only the classical education. The provincial thought Holy Cross's course "humbugging, but *ne quid nimis*," and it was his kind of pressure that brought the Jesuits gradually to introduce into this commercial course the teaching of systematic philosophy (Power, 1958, p. 270). As Jesuit colleges were founded or developed during the second half of the nineteenth century, they all went the way of Creighton University, which "tried to arrange and apply its course in such a way as to be helpful to those who can profit by it" (Dowling, 1903, p. 223). That is, they began offering business, accounting, chemical engineering, and the like, in English. The Jesuits' idea of what their "course" was, however, included a lot of philosophy, in orderly succession.

This brings me to the fourth larger development in American education, which I will have to handle even more summarily than the first three. From the Civil War on, Jesuits watched other colleges introduce departments of economics, sociology, political science, and the like. They watched schools introduce the idea of electives, and they watched schools begin using a business model to count the amount of learning a student accomplished and to give credit for it. Jesuit colleges responded to these interrelated changes with what can charitably be called "great deliberation." But where changes in other schools eventuated in the elimination of philosophy from the curriculum (except as an elective or a minuscule requirement in general culture), the Jesuits resolutely retained philosophy.

They retained more than philosophy, of course, not taking very kindly to the idea of "electives." But in the mind of two of the best historians of this educational development, they knew what they were about. J. S. Brubacher and W. Rudy argue that the debate over electives involved German versus English ideals, faculty psychology versus experimental philosophy, practical versus liberal learning, and lots more. But they conclude that the deepest question was: "Should college be predominantly secular or religious in orientation?" (Brubacher and Rudy, 1968, p. 96).

Is the debate about electives over yet?

Jesuit colleges changed what they required, only very gradually allowing electives. By 1900, what they required added up to what we came to call the "core curriculum." This curriculum in 1904 required, by Matthew Sullivan's count: Latin, Greek, and English, two to four years (that is, at least one hour of class each day); mathematics, one to four years; religion, four years; elocution, four years; philosophy, two years or sometimes only a single year.

Even as we who make such distinctions among disciplines hear this list, we need to remember that these material divisions function in a formal unity, for the Jesuits who taught could still insist on the unity of all knowledge. What Rudolph says of American colleges a century earlier is still true of Jesuit colleges in 1900: "Latin grammar *could* be a course of ethics in disguise" (Rudolph, 1977, p. 43). Jesuits were different to this extent: they wore no disguise.

AN INTERPRETATION: WHY SCHOLASTICISM?

I have now brought us to the establishment of the core curriculum, and to the place in it of philosophy. At this point, I should go to Lonergan's second functional specialty, interpretation, and ask what kind of philosophy the Jesuits kept in their curriculum.

Why did the Jesuit cling to scholasticism so tightly? The reasons are so well known as to be boring, but perhaps the attempt to put them in a few sentences is brash enough to be amusing. The first reason lies in the *Ratio Studiorum* itself.

As John O'Malley has pointed out, the *Ratio* of 1599 called for three years of philosophy, completely well ordered, to be taught from the texts of Aristotle themselves, preferably in Greek. But by the middle of the seventeenth century, the standard in Jesuit colleges was "five years' study of languages, followed usually by two years of work in the advanced arts subjects, philosophy conjoined with mathematical and physical sciences" (Farrell, 1938, p. vii). That is the curriculum Jesuits taught European boys like Descartes and Calderón. What they taught boys in the colonies, only God knows, and probably George Ganss.

You remember that the Jesuits, with many other religious groups, were suppressed at the end of the eighteenth century. When they were restored in 1814, they turned promptly to reestablishing their educational empire and its *Ratio*. But they lacked two philosophical abilities that the founding Jesuits had had in abundance. First, they were not in a position to go back to the original texts of Aristotle (or even of Thomas). Aristotle, in 1832, was not the source of the philosophical enterprise; he was the possession of antiquarians. And secondly, Jesuits reemerged into a church fighting for its internal cohesion and notably on the defensive. The pope was not safe even in Rome. Consequently, these men were not in a position (even if they were of the caliber to do it) to take the philosophy at hand and apply it to the concrete problems the way, for instance, Suárez had applied it to the question of the course of political power, and others to questions of lending money at interest, the slave trade, and regicide.

The Jesuits therefore expunged every mention of Aristotle from the *Ratio* that they published in 1832. They perhaps showed that they were wiser than we might think by never giving a formal approval and a binding force to this new *Ratio* of 1832. What they did do, emphatically, was to embrace the scholasticism current in their day, a scholasticism at second or third remove from its deepest sources, and tinged with rationalism.

The thing about it is that it was safe — I mean, religiously. As William Wade pointed out, the *Ratio* of 1599 had stated two reasons for studying philosophy: it prepared the mind for theology and it helped students give glory to the God of this orderly universe. Jesuits added this reason when they wrote the *Ratio* of 1832: to give persons the weapons and tools they needed to defend themselves against the errors of innovators. Wade concluded that the Jesuits "considered philosophy primarily as a means of refuting the errors that opposed the faith of their students" (Wade, 1942, p. 197).

Why did Jesuits cling to scholasticism? Wade argued that it was apologetics, and his opinion is certainly confirmed by the churchly context in which they kept making their decision: the battle against modernism. This needs no interpretation and it will be enough to just recall the main lines of the story.

A HISTORY OF ERROR AND CORRECTIVES

This is Lonergan's third functional specialty: history. This particular history is about a carrot and a stick.

Along with all other Catholics, Jesuits felt the stick first when, in 1864, Pius IX published the *Syllabus of Errors*. Jesuits were certainly at least chary of the errors of their British confrere George Tyrrell, who questioned some of the basic tenets of scholasticism. They then perceived the carrot, when Leo XIII published *Aeterni Patris* in 1879. He encouraged a return to Thomism and to Thomas himself, and gave a tremendous impetous to scholasticism.

If any American Jesuit felt tempted to think that these were European concerns only, he would also have felt the lash of papal wrath on his possible or futurible errors when Leo XIII condemned the *phantôme hérésie* that he chose to name "Americanism." The Jesuits and all American Catholics — this is the accepted wisdom on the matter — responded to this vague swatch of error with an ultramontanism strong enough to leap several mountain ranges and an ocean, too. Why not? At home was virulent nativism and hate.

All of this kept Catholic philosophers from being in touch with philosophical development in the world around them. Not that they were ignorant, necessarily, of what was being said and proclaimed. Rather, they were not free to find in Kant, Kierkegaard, or even Orestes Bronson, sympathetic companions in the quest for truth. Incredibly, they even suspected John Henry Newman — all that business about kinds of assent and about doctrines evolving — in spite of the fact that Leo XIII had made Newman a cardinal in the same year he issued *Aeterni Patris*.

Now, about Jesuit colleges. Between the *Syllabus* of 1864 and *Lamentabili* of 1907, Jesuits founded forty percent of their current colleges and universities. They also gave final shape to a curriculum in which they lectured to their juniors and seniors five days a week, at least once a day, on systematic philosophy. They were teaching a philosophy that enjoyed an "impressive unity and solidity" in the post-*Pascendi* period (Newman, 1980, p. 273). Until the very last American Jesuit college was launched at Wheeling, West Virginia, in 1954, Jesuits were teaching all or practically all the courses of philosophy in their schools — another impressive unity and solidity. At Santa Clara as late as the early 1960s, Julian Foster witnessed "a general homogeneity of viewpoint" (Foster, 1967, p. 166). In general, through the 1920s and 1930s, Jesuits were very content with this homogeneously held viewpoint. "Our undergraduate philosophy still remains on the level of elementary introduction to and popularization of philosophy," Hunter Guthrie wrote in 1940. "That is not too unsatisfactory, provided we are popularizing the right philosophy" (Guthrie, 1940, p. 40).

Jesuits were sure they were and we ought to underscore the differentness Jesuit colleges experienced before World War II with a sentence written by Philip Gleason:

> To an age whose education was secular, scientific, and technical in spirit, particularized in vision, flexible in approach, vocational in aim, and democratic in social orientation, the Jesuits thus opposed a system that was religious, literary, and humanistic in spirit, synthetic in vision, rigid in approach, liberal in aim, and elitist in social orientation [Gleason, 1967, p. 46].

Here is the curriculum, stated in the highest and lowest number of credit hours among the 25 institutions open in 1945: philosophy, 28 to 15; theology, 16 to 8; English, 12; modern languages, 16 to 12; mathematics, 12 to 6; history, 12 to 6; science, 8; speech 2 (Maline, 1955).

World War II marked the dramatic change from this curriculum to where we are today. It brought about two definitive changes in the way philosophy functions in our colleges.

First, because it turned loose an enormous increase in enrollment in our colleges, it made impossible the ideal that Jesuits, completely trained in scholasticism, teach all the philosophy. By the end of the Vietnam era, that "general homogeneity of viewpoint" that Foster noted was simply dissipated. One of the deepest consequences of that is the dissociation of all other disciplines than philosophy and theology from the single, unified worldview (or mindset, or vision) that had been mediated by great amounts of philosophy in the curriculum. Hence, the amount was reduced and reduced to its current sliver of 6 or 9 hours (O'Brien, 1942).

But mid-century brought another change in the homogeneity of philosophical viewpoint in our colleges. The Jesuits themselves abandoned scholasticism as the unique philosophy in their colleges (McInerny, 1965; Donceel, 1966). In the 1930s and 1940s, Foster wrote of Jesuits, "a few instructors tried to offer an objective presentation [of the philosophical alternatives of Thomism], although the student was seldom left long in doubt about what his teacher considered to be the correct view on any question" (Foster, 1967, p. 166). By mid-century, William Wade and others at St. Louis had gone back to Aristotle himself. Donald Gelpi was writing in Cambridge about Jonathan Edwards and Ralph Waldo Emerson, and Joseph O'Hare at Fordham, about Kant. Many were discovering an exhilarating philosophical impetus in their fellow Jesuit, Teilhard de Chardin, and others in Heidegger, Marcel, Scheler, and Sartre. If

Petrarch talked about Saint Socrates, some Jesuits sounded as though the church would soon canonize at least Heidegger and perhaps Blondel.

Here, then, is the condition of the philosophy departments today: consciously and deliberately "Catholic" in the fields and ideologies represented, and determinedly pluralistic. I should really note in passing how differently independent and state schools' philosophy departments have developed. Jay Newman puts it this way: "While the Catholic colleges in North America have been broadening their curriculum, the secular colleges, responding to the increasing professionalization of academic philosophy, have narrowed the scope of theirs" (Newman, 1980, p. 277).

The consequences to what philosophy can do in the curriculum are notable. We are in a time when collegians face a crisis in the development of values, when they urgently need concrete philosophizing (I mean, on issues and events). But, as Newman points out about non-Catholic institutions, "academic philosophers can no longer hide the fact that the philosophy to which they are committed has become increasingly technical, turgid, sterile, and 'irrelevant'" (Newman, 1980, p. 277). Just recently, John Wilson listed seven possible purposes for teaching philosophy in college: critical thinking, formal logic, conceptual analysis, ideological instruction, sociological instruction (namely, the comprehension of how society works), the history of philosophy, and the enlargement of general experience, or "finding a faith to live by" (Wilson, 1982, p. 194). As far as I could tell, he did not think it made much difference which one a faculty chose.

Another philosopher defends these two propositions on the role of philosophy in higher education: "Philosophy is the heart of liberal education. Philosophy is and has been a metadiscipline — that is, a discipline which exists only as a criticism of or commentary upon other disciplines" (Turnbull, 1979, p. 24). My guess is that you have to be a philosopher to believe that today's student would eagerly enter into the criticism or commentary upon his business courses or history major as the heart of his liberal education.

I have to say that I sense discouragement when the best advice given to departments of philosophy is that "it is common-sensical . . . to require some courses in philosophy in liberal arts curricula" because of the need to expose students "to the *idea* of and reflection upon language and culture" (Adams, 1979, p. 11).

Abraham Heschel somewhere, a quarter century ago, chided

philosophers for "the failure of philosophic nerve," the nerve to keep searching for the truth, instead of turning aside to fool around with models of logic or to fondle grammar. Well, in our pluralistic departments of philosophy are men and women searching for the truth, if that is not too optimistic a belief. If it is too optimistic, at least this much is true: Jesuit colleges have deliberately chosen pluralism, and that means that we intend to do philosophy as a dialectic among systems and ways of philosophizing.

Here is the end of our history, and here is Lonergan's fourth functional specialty: dialectic. I will go through this only briefly.

Dialectic is dialog with the past and in the present. First, Lonergan points out that theology "has to do with the concrete, the dynamic, and the contradictory, and so finds abundant materials in the history of Christian movements" (Lonergan, 1972, p. 129). Well, philosophers are in the same situation, and philosophers in Jesuit college departments surely find themselves cheek-by-jowl (is that a sexist image?) with scholastics, existentialists, phenomenologists, analysts, and the occasional Marxist. If they are serious thinkers, they find *that* a greater philosophical challenge than being surrounded by horses of the same color — which would occasion another kind of challenge and competitive horse race. Further, they are teaching the same students, and that alone ought to put them in dialog with one another over current problems and conflicts. They all reach their own conclusions. Lonergan continues:

> Comparing them will bring to light just where differences are irreducible, where they are complementary and could be brought together within a larger whole, where finally they can be regarded as successive stages in a single process of development.

I have come now to the end of *oratio obliqua* and begun direct discourse, *oratio directa*. I have also finished the first half of Lonergan's functional specialties and am in a position to say where, as I see the matter, they belong in the curriculum. I believe that the philosophers of any Jesuit college ought themselves to pursue and teach to their majors matters that fall within the first four functional specialties: research into philosophical sources, interpretation of those sources in themselves and for our day, the history of philosophy, and the method of arriving at the truth of controversies (as well as some of those truths, I might add). These matters, the faculty ought to teach to majors, to those among students who are turned on to the philosophical enterprise, have the necessary (and necessarily great) endowments for success in it, and can find a general education through philosophy. I personally believe that such young men and women are very rare.

But these specialties are specialties *in oratione obliqua*. In our culture and time, collegians mature in a culture without coherent public discourse, in which values are incessantly trivialized, and in which pluralism of viewpoint is bewildering. I suggest, therefore, that what today's student needs is philosophy done *in oratione directa*.

FOUNDATION: THE INTELLECTUAL CONVERSION

I believe that dialog among faculty members who work out of differing systems is the basis of philosophy's function in the liberal arts common curriculum (and in the major, too, but I take that as manifest from what will be said). The reason I say this is that I believe that intellectual conversion is the specific aim of philosophy in the Jesuit curriculum, and the possibility of achieving that aim is immensely enhanced by faculty members in a pluralistic faculty, in dialog among themselves.

I need to say what I mean by intellectual conversion. "Conversion, as lived," Lonergan says of religious conversion, "affects all of a man's conscious and intentional operations. It directs his gaze, pervades his imagination, releases the symbols that penetrate to the depths of his psyche. It enriches his understanding, guides his judgments, reinforces his decisions" (Lonergan, 1972, p. 131). Philosophical conversion — in a cave on a riverbank — is similar.

We surely go through something like that when we move from the naive assertion of what we see as unchallengeable fact to a more nuanced affirmation of what we know is reformable statement. We *learn* to doubt and to question. We need to grow out of affirmation based more on emotional needs to affirmation based on information. We *un-learn* prejudice. We can grow, if we have the time and occasion, from asserting what we believe without reference to any underlying system to asserting beliefs with reference to our way of arriving at them and confirming them. We *grow* to critical thinking. Finally, we can even reach the point at which we are aware that we have chosen among systems of truths and that we have used certain criteria for reaching our choice among available systems. We *learn* systematic thinking.

Donald Gelpi has worked out eight stages in this process from naive dicta to nuanced, systematic affirmation (Gelpi, 1978). As you reflect on any one of his stages, you can see that a person at that stage would not readily comprehend truths that belong to later stages. For instance, a freshman at Santa Clara once brought up an atheistic speaker short by asking him how, if he did not believe in God, did he account for Adam and Eve? (Foster, 1967, p. 165). What would that mind do with the assertion that "A person should study philosophy for its own sake"? To use a current idiom, it would not compute.

I do not know how we would gauge where, in their course of intellectual maturation, our students might be. I do know that they will move along from stage to stage as long as they are in discourse with minds that go in front of them. I do not know whether we can hope that any given student would reach any given level of maturation — whether the level of reasoned assertion, reflected-upon and systematic affirmation, or awareness of systematic thinking.

But I think that this steady conversion from less reasonable to more reasonable discourse, from more merely particular to more basically universal thinking, is the product before anything else of philosophy in the common curriculum. Other disciplines may suffice, of course; that is why we still give the title "doctor of philosophy" to all scholars far enough advanced in their discipline. And if my assertion seems cute, the reason is that so few Ph.D.s are in the least concerned about the philosophical basis of their learning and affirming and valuing.

I argue that philosophers cannot *not* go through conversion, or perhaps conversions, if they are serious about the profession of philosophy. Perhaps I am overoptimistic.

I further argue that intellectual conversion is a good way to understand what Jesuit higher education, from the *Ratio* of 1599 on, has been aiming at.

Conversion is what happened to Matteo Ricci during his course at the Roman College, so that even after he had steeped himself in Chinese learning and culture, he continued to envision and evaluate in Aristotelian terms and symbols. He thought the Chinese could not be good warriors, for instance, because to his eye the walls that fortified their cities had not been built according to "geometrical principles."

Conversion is what happened to Timothy Bouscaren two and a half centuries later in Cincinnati, so that neither Yale nor the study of law shook the scholastic cast of his mind and argument, apparent in the important things that he wrote.

Conversion was the aim for every Jesuit scholastic going through studies before Vatican II, and its true success gave substance to the popular belief that all Jesuits sound alike.

Finally, conversion is what the Jesuits of philosophy departments hoped for and aimed at in their students. "Gradually the student should realize," Thomas Fitzgerald wrote in 1962, "that he is heir to a growing, living body of truth which has developed within a tradition stemming from Plato and Aristotle. He should arrive at a solid core of certitudes which have been personally experienced and grasped" (Fitzgerald, 1962, p. 96). Why not recognize that as an intellectual conversion, or at least as the beginnings of one? A man or woman is invited into the world of systematic thinking and accepts the invitation. They find there the possibility of conviction on other than emotional or dogmatic grounds, the recognition of their own fallibility. They find there a new confidence in their own ability to think and discern. That is conversion.

In 1954, George Ganss reminded Jesuits of the complex but clear purposes of Jesuit colleges in his St. Ignatius' Idea of a Jesuit University. Ganss took issue with Robert Maynard Hutchins, who maintained that the only aim of the university is the pursuit of intellectual virtues, contending that a true university — and certainly Jesuit institutions — are also aimed at pursuing the moral virtues and certain specific social purposes. In this conviction he was not just updating an old conviction, he was only a little bit ahead of the Carnegie Commission, which discovered that the college that imagined that it had no influence on the morals of its students was seriously misled (Carnegie, 1977). The "specific end of a Jesuit university is at least threefold: directly and deliberately to cultivate the intellectual, moral, and theological virtues, in order that the student may practice them in private and social improvement" (Ganss, 1955, p. 26). I think one way of understanding what Ganss intended in the philosophy curriculum is to understand that he is calling for more than the prudence and critical thinking Hutchins hoped for. He is calling for commitment and enactment as the result of specifically intellectual growth.

Finally, Barry McGannon argued in 1965 that "integration" was the aim of a liberal education in a changing world. He argued that the student must integrate his learning to reach what Philip Phenix described as "meaning" (McGannon, 1965, p. 83; Phenix, 1964). If Viktor Frankl is correct, the calm possession of "meaning" is the outcome of a process whose intellectual moment can properly be called conversion (Frankl, 1969).

I do not mean to force Fitzgerald, Ganss, and McGannon to my way of thinking, but I think that they fit with many other Jesuits. Several score of them gathered at Loyola University in Los Angeles in 1962 to discuss the role of philosophy and theology in Jesuit education (FitzGerald, 1984, p. 156). They concluded that philosophy tends to inculcate five dispositions: taking the critical view, accepting the spiritual dimensions of human life, achieving a measure of intellectual confidence and maturity, achieving an openness of mind and an intellectual humility and charity, and this fifth one: "Since the introduction of philosophical thinking occurs in college at the same time as the awakening of the student's powers of higher reason, philosophy has the natural function of guiding his reason to an understanding of himself in history, so that he can make a reasoned choice for God and give a fundamental orientation to his life" (*Statement of Positions*, p. 251). Those Jesuits may have been optimistic about the totality of students' conversion, but they surely intended to include an intellectual conversion.

I contend that those purposes — Ganss's, McGannon's, the Jesuits' in Los Angeles — however enunciated, required a staff of philosophers who were themselves already converted to a specific philosophical way of thinking. I maintain that that continues true. Thus, the members of a department of philosophy necessarily spend their time laboring toward a statement of the fundamentals of human knowing, meaning, valuing, and explaining. They embody what Lonergan refers to as conversion in its communal moment, "with its own cultural, institutional, and doctrinal dimensions" (Lonergan, 1972, p. 131).

A DOCTRINE IN PHILOSOPHY

This brings me to Lonergan's sixth functional specialty, the elaboration of doctrine. I plan to handle it and the last two very briefly.

Fifty years ago, Jesuits who taught philosophy did not have to elaborate doctrine. They passed along an elaborate doctrine.

Today, the members of a philosophy department are in no position to formulate a doctrine to which the department subscribes. We have enough trouble deciding when Monday morning will begin. Are we, then, without "doctrine" in our departments?

I suggest not. Our doctrine is a dynamic set of affirmations and commitments that allow a genuine pursuit — in fact, encourage and support a genuine pursuit — of the truth in the milieu of pluralism. I say "dynamic," because I doubt that assertions and commitments can readily be put into coherent essays and proclamations, though the effort would be tremendously fruitful and useful. Instead, by merely pursuing serious questions, for their students and among themselves, the department is embodying the furthest reaches of intellectual maturity: the systematic search for meaning and the searching critique of each system of meaning.

I suggest that this "doctrine" is the inevitable outgrowth of choices we have made — Jesuit and every colleague — in shaping today's philosophy departments. For myself, I am as content with it as Hunter Guthrie was with the doctrines of Maréchal and Scheeben.

FINALLY, A SYSTEM

Lonergan makes systematics his seventh functional specialty. Obviously, none of us thinks that we are going to find a new system of philosophy that will dominate all others and become our new orthodoxy. But why could we not find a way of teaching philosophy identifiable as the eighteenth- and nineteenth-century "moral philosophy"?

Candidly, as far as my information goes, I think that we have a good start on it. We have departments that are more than ordinarily "catholic" and pluralistic. We have faculty members who are serious about wanting to comprehend the "educational philosophy" of our twenty-eight institutions — or, even better, who want to contribute to its creation and enlivening. We have students who have taken the first steps in intellectual conversion by choosing institutions that are distinctive and convey a sense of purpose and meaning. If those students come to us convinced that all they want in life is a good job and lots of money — can we not think of that as (among very many other things) intellectual immaturity? How far toward the truth can a person go who is convinced that money and security will bring happiness?

How we are to teach these students philosophy brings me to Lonergan's final functional specialty, and to the end of my ideas.

COMMUNICATIONS AND CURRICULAR DESIGN

Lonergan's eighth functional specialty is communications. In higher education, this means curricular design, about which I should like to suggest that every design I have heard of for teaching philosophy and for provoking philosophizing seems to have its usefulness. And in our colleges, students find an enormous variety of methods: introductory courses, the history of philosophy, problematics, great thinkers, courses in functional specialties, great books. How does a faculty select among these?

I suggest this basic principle: a faculty of philosophy should expect to teach, principally to philosophy majors, the first four functional specialties, *in oratione obliqua*: research, interpretation, history, and dialectic. Majors are taught what "they said." But in the common curriculum, the faculty should take whatever means is most useful to teach *in oratione directa*. I mention the most obvious: reflections on desperate problems like nuclear arms, abortion, lying, and human inequities among nations. By teaching on such topics what they themselves have concluded through systematic reflection and a sophisticated application of the theory of criteria, they are most likely to provoke their students into similar reflection. That is philosophizing, and it is the way to invite others to intellectual conversion (Ozar, 1978).

Philosophers teach foundational truths as they perceive them, working within a system that each has chosen for themself, unfolding a kind of "philosophical doctrine" in full awareness that other doctrines are in the immediate air. They are careful not to suggest that they are teaching the irrefutable truth, or to suggest that what they teach is merely likely. Nor do they propagandize, an activity appropriate to more immature teachers. Hence, in the core curriculum belong these functional specialties: foundations, doctrine, systematics, and communications.

I should like to say in closing that I do not underestimate the speculative problems that this scheme conceals. But I say that the dynamic contained in the scheme is eminently worth continuing in our colleges, where I think it has already begun, and that the dynamic is not impossible to realize in at least some useful ways.

References

Adams, E. M. "Philosophical Education as Cultural Criticism." *Teaching Philosophy*, 3:1 (Spring 1979) 1–11.
Adelmann, Frederick J., S.J. "Philosophy in the Jesuit College." *Jesuit Education Quarterly*, 23:3 (January 1961) 151–56.
Brubacher, J. S., and W. Rudy. *Higher Education in Transition: A History of*

JESUIT HIGHER EDUCATION

American Colleges and Universities. New York: Harper & Row, 1968.

Burrowes, A. J., S.J. Letter dated August 9, 1915, Course of Studies for the Colleges of the Missouri Province of the Society of Jesus. St. Louis, privately printed.

Carnegie Commission. Missions of the College Curriculum. San Francisco: Jossey-Bass, 1977.

Daley, John M., S.J. Georgetown University: Origin and Early Years. Washington, D.C.: Georgetown University, 1957.

Donahue, John W., S.J. Jesuit Education: An Essay on the Foundations of an Idea. New York: Fordham University Press, 1963.

Donceel, J., S.J. "Philosophy in the Catholic University." America, 115 (September 24, 1966) 33–331.

Dowling, M. P., S. J. Creighton University: Reminiscences of the First Twenty-Five Years. Omaha: Burley Printing Co., 1903.

Farrell, Allan P., S.J. The Jesuit Code of Liberal Education. Milwaukee: Bruce, 1938.

FitzGerald, Paul A. The Governance of Jesuit Colleges in the United States. University of Notre Dame Press, 1984.

Fitzgerald, Thomas R., S.J. "The Humanities and the Jesuit Liberal Arts College." Jesuit Educational Quarterly, 25 (October 2, 1962) 90–102.

Foster, Julian. "Some Effects of Jesuit Education." The Shape of Catholic Higher Education, Robert Hassenger, ed. University of Chicago Press, 1967.

Frankl, Viktor E. The Will to Meaning. New York: World Publishing, 1969.

Ganss, George E., S.J. St. Ignatius' Idea of a Jesuit University. Milwaukee: Marquette University Press, 1954.

_____. "St. Ignatius and Jesuit Education." Jesuit Educational Quarterly, 18:1 (June 1955) 17–32.

Gelpi, Donald L., S.J. Experiencing God: A Theology of Human Emergence. New York: Paulist, 1978.

Gleason, Philip. "A Historical Perspective." The Shape of Catholic Higher Education, Robert Hassenger, ed. University of Chicago Press, 1967.

Guthrie, Hunter, S.J. "The Field of Philosophy in the Jesuit College." Jesuit Educational Quarterly, 3:1 (December 1940) 40–43.

Hamilton, Raphael N., S.J. The Story of Maruqette University. Milwaukee: Marquette University, 1953.

Hassel, David J., S.J. City of Wisdom: A Christian Vision of the American University. Chicago: Loyola University Press, 1983.

Hassenger, Robert, ed. The Shape of Catholic Higher Education in America. University of Chicago Press, 1967.

Henle, Robert J., S.J. "A Commentary on the 'Moral, Religious, and Spiritual Formation of the Jesuit Student.'" Jesuit Educational Quarterly, 26:1 (June 1963) 5–14.

_____. "The Problem of Philosophy in the Liberal Arts College." Jesuit Educational Quarterly, 11:3 (June 1949) 113–27.

Hill, Walter H., S.J. Historical Sketch of the St. Louis University. St. Louis: Patrick Fox, 1879.

Kahane, Howard. Logic and Contemporary Rhetoric: The Use of Reason in Everyday Life, 3rd edition. Belmont, Cal.: Wadsworth, 1980.

Lonergan, Bernard J. F., S.J. *Method in Theology*. New York: Herder and Herder, 1972.

Maline, Julian, S.J. "The Status Quo of Jesuit Curricula." *Proceedings*, Jesuit Education Association Meeting of Deans, Santa Clara, 1955. Andrew C. Smith, S.J. ed. Private circulation.

McGannon, J. Barry, S.J. "Liberal Education for a *Changing* World: Integration and the Curriculum." *Jesuit Educational Quarterly*, 28:2 (October 1965) 80–97.

_____, Bernard J. Cooke, S.J., and George P. Klubertanz, S.J. *Christian Wisdom and Christian Formation: Theology, Philosophy, and the Catholic College Student*. New York: Sheed and Ward, 1964.

McGucken, William J., S.J. *The Jesuits and Education*. Milwaukee: Bruce, 1932.

McInerny, Ralph, S.J. "Thomism in an Age of Renewal." *America*, 113 (September 11, 1965) 358–60.

Muller, Herman J., S.J. *The University of Detroit 1877–1977*. University of Detroit, 1976.

Newman, Jay. "The Teaching of Philosophy in Catholic Colleges." *Teaching Philosophy*, 3:3 (Spring 1930) 271–81.

O'Brien, John A., S.J. "Philosophy at Dunkerque." *Jesuit Educational Quarterly*, 5:1 (June 1942) 90–98.

Ozar, David T. "Teaching Philosophy and Teaching Values." *Teaching Philosophy*, 2:3–4, (1978) 237–45.

Phenix, Philip H. *Realms of Meaning; A Philosophy of the Curriculum for General Education*. New York: McGraw-Hill, 1964.

Power, Edward J. *Catholic Higher Education in America*. New York: Appleton-Century Crofts, 1972.

_____. *A History of Catholic Higher Education in the United States*. Milwaukee: Bruce, 1958.

Rudolph, Frederick. *The American College and University*. New York: Knopf, 1962.

_____. *Curriculum: A History of the Undergraduate Course of Study Since 1636*. San Francisco: Jossey-Bass, 1977.

Smith, Wilson. *Professors and Public Ethics: Studies of Northern Moral Philosophers Before the Civil War*. Ithaca, N.Y.: Cornell University Press, 1956.

"Statement of Positions," from Jesuit Education Association Workshop, Los Angeles, 1962. *Jesuit Educational Quarterly*, 25:4 (March 1963) 243–64.

Sullivan, Matthew G., S.J. "The Influence on Curriculum of Jesuit Traditions." *Proceedings*, Jesuit Education Association Meeting of Deans, Santa Clara, 1955. S.J., ed. Andrew C. Smith, Private Circulation.

Turnbull, Robert G. "The Role of Philosophy in Higher Education." *Teaching Philosophy*, 3:1 (Spring 1979) 23–35.

Vesey, Laurence R. *The Emergence of the American University*. University of Chicago Press, 1965.

Wade, William L., S.J. "The Function of Philosophy in Jesuit Colleges." *Jesuit Educational Quarterly*, 4:4 (March 1942) 192–206.

Wilson, John. "Teaching Philosophy." *Teaching Philosophy*, 5:3 (July 1982) 193–99.

9 / The Jesuit Experience with Graduate Education and Education for the Professions

J. A. Panuska, S.J.

IT is most fitting that we should reflect on Jesuit graduate and professional education at Saint Louis University. This university awarded its first Master's degree in 1834.[1] This and subsequent master's degrees went to those with bachelor's degrees who pursued two additional years of literary studies. Such was the consistent policy and practice of institutions at the time.

In tracing the historical evolution of American Jesuit colleges and universities, one cannot help recognizing the formative contributions to graduate education by Saint Louis University, especially by several individuals associated with it, most notably James B. Macelwane, S.J., and Alphonse M. Schwitalla, S.J. Indeed, when the Society of Jesus concentrated its educational forces to achieve parity with other American institutions in the 1930s, it chose St. Louis University as one of its centers of graduate study.[2]

The history of Jesuit graduate and professional education is mirrored in the history of Saint Louis University — an institution whose evolution reflects the general pattern of development of American higher education as well.

A HISTORICAL TRADITION

The American system of higher education emerged in its modern form between the 1860s and the turn of the century. Its structural development was largely influenced by the German model with its emphases on rigorous scholarly research and scientific specialization.[3] The principal effect of the German influence was manifested in the development of the graduate school, which did not replace the college, but was added to it as a seat of higher-level study. The graduate school that trained students for the doctoral degree was an improved version of the German university research institute.

The American university system, although based on actually or potentially equivalent units, was in fact a highly differentiated system. The differentiation was open and recognized, and even differences in quality were admitted and tolerated. However, the differentiation of functions (unlike that of quality) took place mainly *within* institutions, not *between* them.

One of the principal assumptions that guided this transformation of American higher education was that advanced education needed to be specialized, and that specialized study was necessary for a professional career. The study of specialized disciplines in Germany and in the mature English universities came to be regarded, in many cases, as the way to obtain an education that would qualify the student to become part of the intellectual elite. Only the acquisition of deep knowledge in a single field and observing at close range a professor exploring the frontiers of knowledge was considered advanced education.

Increased specialization paved the way for a change in the concept of professionalism. Prior to the nineteenth century, the rationale for basing professional privilege almost exclusively on classical learning was twofold. First, the ability to master Greek and Latin and to interpret classical texts was considered (with some justification) the best available gauge of intellectual ability. Secondly, classical learning had been the main repository of scientific knowledge. The untouchable status of classical learning, however, began to crumble with the rise of modern chemistry, biology, physics, and astronomy. Inevitably, scientific knowledge based on empirical research replaced classical learning as a test of superior intellectual ability. This occurred first among the European centers of learning, and then, as the influence of scientists and scholars returning from Europe began to be felt, at American colleges as well.

German-trained scientists and scholars envisioned universities as institutions engaged primarily in disciplinary and selected professional studies, especially in medicine and law. University presidents, however, were pragmatic persons intent on finding and creating a demand for higher education to advance the standing of their own colleges. Education for the professions was a goal acceptable to both scholars and presidents. It was acceptable to scholars because, according to the German model, professional training had to consist primarily of study and research in the basic disciplines, and it was acceptable to presidents because the demand for professional training was widespread and expected to grow. It was a market easy to develop, for there were unused facilities for advanced professional training in the United States but, at the time, those who desired such training had to go to Europe.

Education for the professions became one of the most distinctive and influential of the innovations of American higher education. The success of the modernized liberal arts course, and the expansion of higher education, aided the success of the graduate school. Teachers in the arts and sciences had to be trained for up-to-date undergraduate liberal arts programs, and the demand for such teachers spurred the growth of graduate schools. In the humanities and social sciences, and to a somewhat lesser extent in the natural sciences, Ph.D. programs developed as professional training programs for teachers in colleges and universities.

The integration of research and teaching meant that students of arts and sciences were taught preferably by competent, professionally trained researcher-teachers. There was one framework for the training of professional research workers — namely, the graduate school, especially that of the arts and sciences. The liberal arts college served as another framework for teaching these disciplines as a background for, or introduction to, further professional studies, or as a means of general education. The graduate school became a professional school for researchers in which apprenticeship was an integral part of the training. In the liberal arts course, research served as a background for a didactic complement to studies.

A similar relationship emerged between research, teaching, and practical training in the professional schools. First professional degrees had been, and still are, highly vocational and practical. Training at the master's level may have been slightly more research-oriented, but only in doctoral level programs has professional training been invariably integrated with research.

Gradually, the training of future civil servants, men and women in business, politicians, and aspirants to the elite professions came to be regarded as no less important a mission than the training of scientists and scholars. The "professionalization" of the occupations led to the development of both basic disciplinary and problem-oriented research focused on a given professional field and a Ph.D. program based on such research. This conception of professions combined the logic of the German academic system with the British tradition that regarded professional training as the acquisition of a high degree of competence in a technically complex field.

THE JESUIT CONTRIBUTION TO AMERICAN GRADUATE EDUCATION

To suggest that there is little that is unique in form about the Jesuit or Catholic experience with graduate and professional studies is not to disparage these institutions. Rather, it is meant to suggest simply that they developed alongside their counterparts in American higher education.

The basic rationale for Jesuit institutions to engage in graduate and professional education is the same one that underlies the Society of Jesus' general efforts in education. It should be remembered that the humanistic tradition that has characterized undergraduate education contained a very definite and dynamic reform thrust. The humanists believed that the right education would produce a better person and that social improvement would follow. This coupled with the need to serve an often excluded and growing Catholic population augured the growth of the impressive system of Jesuit institutions we find today.

The dramatic growth of Jesuit graduate and professional education is evidenced by its contemporary size and breadth. In the fall of 1983, some fifty thousand students were enrolled in the graduate or professional programs offered by twenty-seven of the twenty-eight Jesuit institutions. This represented almost a third of all students enrolled in Jesuit colleges and universities. In addition, a substantial number of undergraduates are enrolled in First Professional programs, such as nursing and physical therapy.[4]

At Jesuit institutions, there are twenty-one schools of business offering an extensive array of graduate degree programs. There are nine schools of education, thirteen law schools, four medical schools, five dental schools, six engineering schools, nine nursing schools, and four schools of social work. Our listing of graduate programs almost spans the alphabet from accounting to world history. Doctoral degrees are awarded in such diverse fields as chemistry and criminal justice, economics and education, English and engineering, mathematics and microbiology, sociology and student personnel. It is truly an impressive list.

More impressive is the list of achievements related to the unique service provided by these programs in their own communities. Allow me to illustrate this point with an example from my own experience. When I assumed the presidency of the University of Scranton in 1982, I was struck by the strong service commitment to the region, which the university expressed in its "goal statement." I have come to understand that the university over the years had quite consciously adapted itself to meet the educational needs of its community. Because there is no four-year public institution in our immediate area, the University of Scranton has come to assume certain responsibilities normally associated with the public system. This required scrupulous attention to cost so that high tuition would not become a barrier in a community that has experienced serious economic hardship — and still does. It also required the development of a curriculum that was broadly professional and preprofessional at the undergraduate level. We could not be a Williams College at Scranton, even if we had its endowment and resources. It would not fit our situation. At the graduate level, our curriculum had to be shaped by the largely service-oriented local economy. Now, 65 percent of our students are from outside the region, but the formative influence of this beginning is still there. The genesis of our programs lies in a sensitive adaptation to the vital needs of the region.

A CONTINUING MISSION

Simply to assert that Jesuit graduate and professional education has developed in a sympathetic way with American higher education, or that it is successful because of its breadth or adaptability, is not quite enough, because it does not deal with the question of mission. What are we about in these enterprises? And how do we expect to accomplish our ends?

The church has been committed to the intellectual apostolate for a long while. This commitment was strongly affirmed by the Holy Father, John Paul II:

> The Catholic university or college must train young persons of outstanding knowledge who have made a personal synthesis between faith and culture, who will be capable and willing to assume tasks in the service of the community.[5]

He speaks of a community where there is a sincere commitment to scientific research and study joined with a commitment to authentic Christian religion.

The Jesuits' own general congregations, especially the thirty-first, affirmed the society's historical commitment to the international apostolate of higher education. In the thirty-first General Congregation, under "Training of Scholastics," specific reference is made to those destined for scientific research, teaching the secular sciences, special training, doctoral degrees, and the development of eminent scholars.[6] The thirty-first General Congregation also emphasized scholarly research and teaching, especially in the sacred sciences.

In the thirty-second General Congregation, which I was privileged to attend, there is special mention of supporting Jesuits who are working in scholarly research, in publishing, and in other forms of the apostolate. In the document, "Our Mission Today," the question is raised about how the Society can fulfill the dual mission of faith and justice in its various corporate apostolates, including education:

> Are we ready to give ourselves to the demanding and serious study of theology, philosophy, and the human sciences, which are ever more necessary if we are to understand and try to resolve the problems of the world? To be involved in the world in this way is essential if we are to share our faith and our hope, and thus preach a gospel that will respond to the needs and aspirations of our contemporaries.[7]

Two years after the thirty-second General Congregation, Pedro Arrupe, S.J., enunciated his full support for the intellectual apostolate in a letter to the Society of Jesus:

> [It] is clear that the Society as a body could not do justice to the intellectual dimension attaching to our key apostolic options unless a sufficient number of its members are committed with a special priority to research, to science, and, more broadly, to an apostolate that is explicitly intellectual. And further, what better means do we have, in many cases, for carrying out these tasks, than well-organized centers, universities, colleges, research institutes, periodicals. . . .[8]

If a university contributes to the general purposes of education as outlined in *The Constitutions* referred to earlier and if it helps groups to a life of greater wisdom, charity, and service, we can be proud of our association with it.

We cannot claim to be unique — but that type of activity is certainly Jesuit. In a significant way, professional and graduate school programs shape society's leaders. They really do, in many different fields and in society at large. And that, too, is in the best tradition of Jesuit education.

Talking of really Jesuit graduate-school education does not make it happen. We need, even in the graduate school and in the professional school, sufficient dialogue and reflection so that there can be some integration of purpose and some interaction between disciplines, so that theology is not an island but is a part of an intellectual excitement that is touching every part of the system.

We also need in the graduate and professional school one of the distinguishing features of Jesuit education: namely, the personal emphasis characteristic of our undergraduate Jesuit schools. We are well aware that the graduate student or the professional student is very often an individual in genuine need of personal attention. These students generally lack campus housing; they do not have the support of peer relationships that can be formed in the undergraduate campus. They are very often hard pressed for money. They can be at a point where they feel they should be independent of their families. They are often separated from their families for the first time. They often still need to be broadened in their vision of the world. Some come into our colleges without having very much in terms of theological training. Many graduate students come without having adequate cultural training or exposure as well. They are moving into a world that should become more and more specialized, which fewer and fewer persons are going to understand. So the chances of loneliness will likely increase. Definitely, they are also quite likely to find a lack of satisfaction in their own home parishes, if they are Catholic — or also, if they are Protestant or Jewish — in their places of worship. We should try at least to think about how we can help them to grow in the totality of their being as they grow in their profession. So, simply put, campus ministry still has a role in graduate education and in professional education. Counseling still has a role, and general educational activities still have a role. And we cannot simply transfer what is done at the undergraduate level to these older and more mature students. The problem requires a good deal of serious thought. It is often neglected, I fear.

Now I should like to summarize some of my thoughts about why I think a Jesuit presence in graduate education and professional schools is important.

First, in *graduate school.* I am a great believer in undergraduate education and I believe that, whether we can define it or not, most of our Jesuit colleges have a truly special spirit. There is something unique that goes on in this believing community, in this interrelationship — the attention given to students. And the existence of graduate programs strengthens the undergraduate effort. That is the least we can say for it. We do not get frozen intellectually too early, because graduate studies tend to stretch us more. They keep us in touch with primary sources. The presence of graduate students and graduate courses can have an overall very positive effect on the general environment of an institution. That is extremely important. Even to offer courses to advanced undergraduates, to which they would not ordinarily have access, is wonderful; but I am thinking more about the general attitude of persons who are engaged in research and who are thinking with knowledge as it is advanced.

The presence of graduate programs applies pressure on the administration to do certain things that tend to be neglected because they are costly, but which graduate schools and programs need, such as better library facilities. We are far more likely to have a very poor library in a school that has no graduate programs.

Professional education often does provide a very special service, perfect or not, to a particular group of persons who would not be getting that service elsewhere. And it always somehow links a believing community with professions, and it can reinforce the faith, the understanding, and the integration of knowledge of professional persons who are very influential in our society.

There are some things that really apply to both graduate education and professional schools. Both give the school and the church special credibility in the educational, intellectual worlds. Both can satisfy needs, especially in areas where we are not in competition. Both help us meet our responsibility to share in the development of new knowledge for the good of humanity. The presence of a graduate program, although not essential, really encourages this development.

And if there is an interaction among faculties, the chances for an integration among disciplines with a believing community are greatly enhanced. That is truly important for the development of an enlightened society. Isolation (personal and institutional), I believe, is one of the greatest of all destroyers. It diminishes the quality of life. Graduate schools and professional schools give us a special opportunity to influence systems that have greatest effect on the way our society lives out its obligation to justice.

These are not easy times for graduate schools or professional

schools. There are a number of threats. Generally, there is a declining enrollment and a declining interest in graduate schools. That has
multiple deleterious effects. There is difficulty in creating interactions among faculties, interactions that are important to the achievement of the general objectives of colleges and universities.

It is very difficult to maintain cost-effective program, although law
may be one of the few exceptions. Services are always hard to keep
out of deficit. As a college president, I look for cost-effective programs, but I realize that not every unit has to be cost-effective. And
in the homeostasis of the entire system, institutions have to make
some sacrifices. The institution cannot be isolated; it has to look at
its local community, and indeed it has to look at a much broader
geographical spectrum than that.

There are a number of problems that come with cost-effec-
tiveness. We tend to overuse graduate students, for example. That
is a very bad sign. Using them too often as instructors is not good
training for them and it does not provide good education for others.
There is difficulty in maintaining meaningful religious, ethical, and
moral awareness within the schools because of the tremendous
programatic pressures of accrediting agencies.

Too often, I think, some graduate programs are maintained when
they should be dissolved. That can be a response to overprotective
faculty pressures. Sometimes there is a sense of pride in the institution or a conservatism that is unreasonable. It takes a lot of courage
to eliminate a graduate program that is no longer achieving a
needed purpose, or whose quality is no longer doing honor to the
institution or helping the individuals in it. But we hang on. I always
admire the administrators and faculty committees willing to make
tough decisions that affect the overall programmatic quality of an
institution.

We must continually examine our schools' departments and programs with freedom and with honesty. Not everything has to be
perfect. We often have to stretch where there is need. But we have
to be critical.

When one faces a question of mission and apostolate, whether it
be personal or institutional, one cannot follow simple logical lines. I
learned that as provincial. A leader cannot plan without a contextual
framework or without a great understanding of the abilities and
interests of those entrusted to his or her supervision. To my mind,
persons and organizations accomplish most in areas where there is
talent and personal enthusiasm. As a teacher, I always felt that one
of the best things I could do was to arouse the interest and enthu-

siasm of students to such a heightened degree that they would go beyond me and not just limit themselves to my notes or my references. If I could encourage a student to go to original literature, I would be delighted, especially if I had not recommended the specific literature.

Following that sort of philosophy, I think it is more important to know what our talents are for certain graduate and professional areas, and what enthusiasm we feel for that mission, than it is to know how we got there, or whether or not we should be there in terms of service and need.

In conclusion, in my opinion, professional and graduate education are very important components of any educational system that hopes to touch the modern world. I used the term "system" rather than "institution" because not *each* institution need be engaged in this for the attainment of its educational mission, but the broader system *must*. And there are systems within systems. I am thinking of a university like St. Louis University, or Georgetown, or Fordham, or Scranton (all are systems), and I am thinking of the broader Jesuit system. Our system does this, and I think it should continue to do so. And our efforts will be special to the extent that we are uniquely concerned about the integration of knowledge, even in our older professional and graduate students, and to the extent that participants in this enterprise share in the Ignatian vision of loving service.

10 / Humanizing the Campus Environment to Promote Student Development

Charles C. Schroeder

IN less than three decades, the whole landscape of American higher education changed dramatically — enrollments doubled; financial aid increased by 6,000 percent; and federal regulations provided increased access for minorities, the handicapped, and other special populations. Not surprisingly, Jesuit institutions experienced the full impact of these changes. Institutions that were once characterized by very homogeneous student bodies and faculty are now larger, quite heterogeneous, and increasingly complex. In an attempt to respond to these changes, Jesuit institutions designed a variety of specialized academic programs and student services. Although many programs addressed the diverse needs and preferences of students, the heavy emphasis on specialization has often resulted in isolated and fragmented approaches to promoting student development.

Just as higher education has experienced monumental changes in recent years, the field of student personnel work has also changed, shifting its emphasis from controlling students to serving students, to the current emphasis on helping students develop. Although originally the concept of "student development" was rather ambiguous, in recent years research has led to a dramatic proliferation of theories and process models for describing psycho-social, affective and cognitive dimensions of college students' development. Such theorists as Erik Erickson, Arthur Chickering, William Perry, Law-

134

rence Kohlberg, among others, have provided provocative insights for describing and understanding the nature of student development during college years. This presentation focuses on relationships between aspects of the campus environment and dimensions of student development.

I begin by drawing on a parable used by Jesus. Before sharing this parable, however, it is important to indicate why Jesus chose parables to illustrate his point. Parables, like all kinds of stories, are attractive to us. They can often sweeten a bitter truth. The parables were not designed to comfort and console — they challenge us to radically change our perspectives, ordering our lives along unfamiliar lines. They are not meant to be interpreted to conform to our old polite ideas about what is good and acceptable. They lead us into a new arena, an arena where we must critically examine who we are, what we believe, and why we behave the way we do. They ask us to leave behind familiar, comfortable patterns and pioneer a new existence.

I selected the parable of the farmer sowing seed to illustrate the major points in my presentation. It is drawn from Matthew 12:1–9, and reads as follows:

> A farmer was sowing grain in his field. As he scattered the seed across the ground, some fell beside a hardened path and the birds came and ate it. And some fell on rocky soil where there was little depth of earth; the plants sprang up quickly enough in the shallow soil; but the hot sun soon scorched them and they withered and died for they had so little root. Other seeds fell among thorns and the thorns choked out the tender blades. But some fell on good soil, and produced a crop that was thirty, sixty, and even a hundred times as much as he planted. If you have ears, listen.

A number of lessons can be learned from this parable. First, the seeds that fell in areas where the soil was rocky and shallow eventually wilted and died. This occurred because the environment was much too rigid — it lacked appropriate nutrients and the security usually afforded seeds in deep furrows. Secondly, the seeds that fell among thorns had a similar fate. Their growth was constricted because of the ceaseless struggle competing for limited resources with the more powerful thorns. Finally, the seeds that fell on good earth eventually prospered. The deep, rich soil provided optimum conditions for their growth — appropriate amounts of nutrients, security, and stimulation — all *balanced* in accord with the unique requirements of the seeds.

The parable is obviously describing the relationship between the seed and the seeds' milieu. Let me examine this relationship with regard to a college or university setting. Naturally, a college or university has its own unique ecology: there are significant relationships between its personnel, organizations, space, functions, and so on — each is related to the other and to the whole. This notion has been expressed as an equation by the noted psychologist, Kurt Lewin (1936):

$$[B = f(P \times E)]$$

Behavior is a function of the interaction between person and environment. In considering this interactionist perspective, most educators usually focus on only one variable in the equation — the person. Considerable energy is devoted to gathering information on student aptitudes, abilities, needs, and interests almost independently of their interaction with various environmental conditions. For example, how often do faculty and staff consider the significance of residential settings, peer group influences, classroom environments, architectural arrangements, and personality types in influencing academic choices, performance, and persistence? What unique needs and preferences are exhibited by such special student populations as minorities, internationals, athletes, returning adults, high-risk, gifted — and how are these affected by various environmental conditions? How many students are like the seeds that fell on a hardened path, in the shallow soil, or among the thorns? How many spend their time and energy trying to adapt, to adjust, or to cope with environments that are too harsh, too challenging and, hence, too overwhelming? How many cease to prevail, not because they are defective, but because the campus environment can sometimes create inhumane conditions for them — conditions that actually foster their dissatisfaction, poor performance, ineffective functioning, and high attrition. Clearly, if there is a "bad fit" between the student and the campus, the burden of change usually falls directly on the student. Such a viewpoint is perhaps best characterized by saying, "if the shoe doesn't fit, there must be something wrong with the foot." If one assumes that the deficient factor is the student, then efforts may be unintentionally targeted at helping students adjust to a defective and inhumane campus environment.

Let me return for a moment to the parable of the seeds. Let me use an analogy of a carefully tended garden to suggest a new perspective for our educational efforts. Knowledgeable and committed gardeners know a great deal about seed. They also know that various seeds need specific growth-enhancing conditions at certain times in their development. A knowledgeable gardener attempts to provide a balance between these various conditions in order to promote growth. The campus environment perspective suggests a similar role for educators. This perspective attempts to describe *what ecology is most appropriate for certain types of students at certain times during their college experience.* This theme can be illustrated by modifying Lewin's equation to read:

$$SD = \frac{f(P \times E)}{c/s}$$

Student development is a function of person/environment interaction mediated by the challenge/support ratio. Theories of student development, be they psycho-social, cognitive, or topological, all have one thing in common — they view development as facilitated by a dynamic balance between challenge and support. William Perry (1970) refers to this as "cognitive conflict". Rudolph Moos (1976) uses the term "optimally incongruent environments." Feldman and Newcomb (1969) advocate that students' growth and development is a result of confronting a "series of not-too-threatening discontinuities." Hence, the developmental and environmental literature strongly suggests that a key element in student development is the balance in an environment between elements of challenge and support. Challenge is often the product of the degree and intensity of diversity and the degree of freedom in an environment, whereas support results from the degree of structure and personal atmosphere in the environment. If an environment is oversupportive, students may be satisfied but not adequately challenged to grow. In an environment that is overchallenging, students may be so overwhelmed and overstimulated that development will not occur. Therefore, a *balance of the elements of support and challenge is necessary for student development.* To design environments that facilitate the development of students, the relative degrees of challenge and support characteristic of a specific setting and a specific student population must first be assessed. This is where the value of the interactionist equation is realized because such an assessment would focus on the following:

1. "The person(s)" — basic needs, preferred styles, and developmental levels.
2. "The environment" — social climate, architectural features,

administrative policies and procedures, and so on.
3. "challenge/support" — relative degrees of diversity, freedom, structure, and personalism.

Now that we have a tool — an equation — for humanizing campus environments, let me use these concepts to address typical problems that students encounter on our campuses. In particular, let me focus on sources of challenge and support that influence students' experience in various settings.

Residence Hall Settings

Let me begin by using the interactionist perspective to focus on the quality of students' lives in residence halls. Using our equation — student development is a function of person/environment interaction mediated by relative degrees of challenge and support — let us start with the person.

Most residence halls are inhabited by traditional students ranging in age from 17 to 21. According to Arthur Chickering (1969), most are struggling with such developmental tasks as managing emotions, establishing competence — social, academic, and interpersonal; achieving more autonomy; solidifying a personal identity; and clarifying purposes. With regard to their cognitive development levels, William Perry's (1970) research suggests that the majority can be described as dualists — they function most effectively in environments with low to moderate degrees of diversity and freedom, and high degrees of structure and personalism.

Now, let me take a few moments to describe the typical residence hall environment. Think about the residence halls on a typical campus. Can they be characterized as dense, crowded, stimulating, unpredictable, noisy, unpleasant, chaotic, and institutional in atmosphere? Have authorities ever been confronted by students who complain about their inability to sleep and study, who do not like their roommate, and who desire to be released from their housing contract? How would one characterize the architecture of residence facilities? What about the size of the rooms — Are they spacious, or do they resemble prison cells? What about the decor — tastefully decorated in earth tones, or institutional green? If facilities are similar to others across the country, they represent what Robert Sommer (1974) calls "hard architecture" — architecture that is "impervious to human imprint." An excellent example of hard architecture appears on the inside front cover of a national housing journal.

This advertisement, entitled, "The Student-Proof Lamp," reads something like this:

> So tough it may be the last lamp you will ever buy! All connections threaded together, vise tightened, and epoxied. A hammer blow may dent the metal but won't chip the baked enamel finish. Resilient molded fiber shade, won't break even if tossed off the school roof [*Journal of College and University Student Housing*, 1985].

The design assumptions behind the "student-proof lamp" are similar to assumptions used in the design, construction, and maintenance of residence halls: inasmuch as students are basically hostile and destructive, harden up the architecture! And as gardeners, we take our seeds and throw them into these cold, impersonal concrete and steel structures and say, "grow, dammit!" If by some chance they begin to wilt, we encourage them to seek counseling or the advise of a resident adviser.

Let me turn our attention to another major dimension of the residence hall environment — the social milieu, particularly roommate and floormate characteristics. Can you imagine how it feels to be assigned to a 10' × 12' room with another person who is *totally different* from you in basic needs and interpersonal styles? Or, to be placed on a hallway where you have very little in common with your floormates? Research consistently demonstrates that student dissatisfaction with roommates and floormates is usually the result of students' inability to accommodate style differences in tight spaces. As a result of this diversity, the environment is often too stimulating, complex, and unpredictable. Inasmuch as students feel limited degrees of control, dominance, and influence, they often devote considerable time and energy trying to cope with the overwhelming nature of the environment. Many students pay an extremely high adaptation cost in terms of personal goals, physical and mental well-being, and academic performance.

The preceding process illustrates a method of utilizing the variables in the interactionist equation to analyze residence hall settings. If the analysis reveals an oversupportive environment, educational efforts would focus on increasing relative degrees of challenge. On the other hand, if the analysis suggests an overwhelmingly challenging environment, an increase in the relative degrees of support would be appropriate. On many campuses, most residence halls are overchallenging spaces because of the following factors: density of persons assigned to floors; heterogeneity of student characteristics; the physical design of buildings — in particular, small cell-like rooms, built-in furniture, and institutional decor — and low student/ staff ratios. What strategies could be developed to achieve a *better balance* of challenge and support with regard to this particular setting?

First, efforts should be directed at decreasing the negative effect of too much diversity and stimulation in the environment. This can be accomplished through increasing the degree of homogeneity among student characteristics. By assigning room and floormates on the basis of some commonality — such as similar academic aspirations, personality traits, special interests, or a combination of all three — friendships and a sense of community would emerge in a natural fashion. There is a wealth of empirical evidence to support this strategy. For example, students assigned to homogeneous living units on the basis of similar personality types (as measured by the Myers-Briggs Type Indicator) and common fields of study, perceive their environment as more supportive, emphasizing greater academic achievement and intellectuality, and providing more student influence and innovation than students assigned to heterogeneous units. In addition, students in the homogeneous units achieved significantly higher grades, reported more stable friendship patterns in their units, described themselves as more content and intellectual, experienced less negative effect, drank less, made fewer visits to the psychological services center, and persisted in their curriculum at a rate 50 percent higher than those students in the traditional units (Schroeder and Belmonte, 1979). In addition to homogeneous groupings, small, self-supporting residential groups significantly increased students' feelings of security, well-being, and involvement. Small groups actually offer more opportunities for student development, because as group size increases, opportunities for meaningful involvement and participation decrease. Finally, a better balance between challenge and support could be achieved by encouraging students to structure their physical environment through a process of room and hallway personalization. To overcome the challenges associated with enforced sociability, lack of privacy, and few opportunities for solitude, students should be encouraged to rearrange furniture, build sleeping lofts, and in general, soften the negative effects of hard architecture through painting and decorating their spaces. Although students cannot be given a legal deed to their residence hall space, encouraging them to modify their physical setting in accord with their needs will foster a sense of psychological ownership. Consequently, retention is enhanced while hostile interaction, damages, and vandalism are substantially reduced.

Classroom Settings

As previously stated, higher education has experienced dramatic changes during the past thirty years. Not only have institutions changed but, equally important, students have changed. The interactionist perspective can be very useful in creating effective classroom settings for today's "new students" — students with much different characteristics from students of the 1960s.

Faculty members nationwide agree that today's students are different. These students do not stage protests or disrupt institutional activities; they dress neatly and seem more polite, more serious. Yet somehow, the gap between students and faculty may be wider than it was in the 1960s: Where are the ideals, the dreams? Where are the students eager to talk all night about moral or philosophic issues? Faculty members are sometimes heard to complain, "All these students want is the diploma — they don't care about learning anything."

Who are these "new students"? What things do they do well or poorly? What do they want and expect from college? How do they approach the learning process? Finally, do they represent a serious threat to the traditional goals of liberal learning?

Although once a minority on most campuses, new students represent a majority today. They come to our campuses expecting, and often demanding, a heavy emphasis on vocational training and the development of practical skills directly related to the world of work. Because they see education as a means to a better life, they are not interested in learning for learning's sake. To be sure, they often do not expect, or even want, the traditional academic experience. Not only do these new students expect vocational training, they also expect a significant amount of personal attention from faculty, administrators, and peers.

How do these new students approach the learning process? Research evidence provided by Patricia Cross (1976) suggests the following learning-style characteristics: new students are motivated primarily by extrinsic rewards. They have difficulty with complex concepts and ambiguity, are less independent in thought and judgment, feel particularly uncomfortable with abstract ideas, and are more dependent on the wishes of those in authority. Compared to their more traditional predecessors, they are more passive, have less tolerance for diversity, and are more dependent on immediate gratification. They prefer highly structured situations and like to have things explained rather than figuring them out by themselves. Think about these characteristics for a moment — uncomfortable with abstract ideas, difficulty with complex concepts and ambiguity, less independent in thought and judgment, more passive, less tolerance for diversity. Might this suggest that the basic characteristics of "new students" are diametrically opposed to those of the "old faculty"?

Although faculty meetings on most campuses are usually quite unpredictable and chaotic, one common faculty concern is routinely raised. Invariably, a faculty member will make the following statement: "What's *wrong* with our students is that they simply don't score high enough on the SAT — if we can only get students with higher Board scores, we would have a much better academic environment!" This intriguing assertion impelled me to explore the relationship between new-student characteristics, learning styles, and performance on various aptitude tests. Although the relationship is somewhat speculative, there are a number of similarities between the characteristics of new students as described by Cross, and students entering Saint Louis University from 1981 to the present. During this period, my colleagues and I administered the Myers-Briggs Type Indicator to entering freshmen — a total of 1,200 completed the Instrument. The results indicate that approximately 60 percent of our students prefer what the MBTI calls the sensing mode of perceiving, compared to 40 percent who prefer the intuitive mode. Sensors prefer direct, concrete experiences, moderate to high degrees of structure, linear learning and explanations about why a task is assigned. In general, sensing types prefer the concrete, the practical, and the immediate. They focus their perceptions primarily on the physical world. Contrast these learning styles with those of intuitives. They are generally global learners who prefer to focus their perceptions on imaginative possibilities rather than on concrete realities. Intuitives love the world of concepts, ideas, and abstractions — characteristics that are measured all too well by the SAT, MAT, GRE, and other standardized aptitude instruments. In investigating the relationship between preferred learning styles and scores on the SAT verbal and quantitative, our research revealed, not surprisingly, that sensing types scored 47 points lower than intuitives on the SAT verbal test and 52 points lower on the quantitative test. Although it might be assumed that these differences indicate different intelligence levels, the evidence does not support this hypothesis. In general, sensing students tend to do just as well as intuitive students on aptitude tests that are *not* timed. Sensors usually take longer to read the questions, often going over them several times, where intuitives tend to respond immediately. The difference in scores seems to be related to the way they take tests, not to intelligence. So, what my faculty colleagues might really be suggesting when they assert, "What we need are students with higher Board scores" might be translated "What we need are students who are more like us".

Obviously, a growth-enhancing classroom setting would take into account the differences in learner characteristics and how they relate to various aspects of the classroom experience. New students prefer structure and personalism, whereas faculty members usually value freedom and diversity. Because of these differences, a great deal of potential for disappointment and disillusionment exists for students and faculty alike. In order to create an effective classroom setting, faculty might initially provide high degrees of structure, small amounts of diversity, and high degrees of personalism in order to respond to the unique needs of these "new students." In suggesting this strategy, I am not advocating that faculty teach thirty different ways. I am, however, suggesting that if faculty members want to ensure content mastery, skill acquisition, and increases in cognitive complexity, there must be a better "fit" between student learner characteristics and instructional methodologies. Initially, such a fit might be produced more effectively by grouping students according to preferred learning styles, and assigning them to faculty with similar teaching styles. In addition, faculty can create different testing procedures, assignments, and projects that appeal to various learner characteristics. Such an approach could create a more humane classroom setting — one that responds effectively to the diverse learner characteristics of today's "new students."

Retention Programs

Before concluding, I will make a few remarks concerning campus retention strategies. The literature consistently suggests that retention is a function of the social and academic integration of students with the campus environment. This integration process is especially important for freshmen during their first six weeks on campus. To be sure, the quality of students' experiences during the first six weeks often determines whether they stay or leave.

By using an interactionist perspective, the University of Notre Dame designed a unique program through marshaling campus resources and focusing them on the quality of freshman educational experience. By recognizing the unique needs and predictable transitions of freshmen, staff created programs and services that effectively respond to these needs and preferences. The result — *the attrition rate is less than one percent*. Obviously, the folks at Notre Dame are pretty good gardeners!

The Notre Dame program is marked by the following critical features. First, staff "front-load" resources — the best teachers are assigned introductory courses. Now this approach alone sets them apart from most colleges and universities where many faculty members avoid introductory courses like the plague. In addition to "front loading" their best teachers, Notre Dame also assigns their most effective advisers and counselors to work with freshmen. Finally, their program provides additional support systems that are effectively integrated to meet the special needs of freshmen. The results seem to suggest that faculty and staff at Notre Dame have designed an ecologically balanced and humanized environment.

CONCLUDING REMARKS

Let me go back to the parable of the farmer sowing grain. Jesus used parables not to comfort, but to challenge. Parables were designed to shake us up, to make us question what we are doing and whether we are really effective in our efforts. On many campuses, staff are often captives of trial and error approaches to student development. Staff efforts are usually focused on only one variable in the ecological equation — the individual. Only recently have staff come to appreciate Donald Blocher's (1974) assertion that "developmental processes do not just happen, but rather must be purposely triggered and carefully nurtured by the environment if full potential for growth is to be reached" (p. 361). The ecological perspective impels us to understand the interactions of all components of the campus environment — the relationship of each to all others and to the whole — and to plan ways that our campus resources can be marshaled to insure student development outcomes.

Such an understanding must start with a systematic approach to assessing both student and environmental characteristics, and interaction between the two. This does not necessarily require highly sophisticated research and evaluation skills. On the contrary, we are often guilty in our research efforts of generating trivial hypotheses and then amassing great methodological arsenals to test them. To paraphrase Maslow, what is not worth doing, is not worth doing well! The critical issue is to determine what is worth knowing about our students and their interactions with the campus environment?

Next, it is extremely important to recognize that student development does not occur in a vacuum — it is the responsibility of every member of the campus community. The greatest threat to student development on most campuses is overspecialization — not only in the student affairs arena, but also in the academic sector. Although members of academe have always had difficulty speaking a common language, our overemphasis on specialization has led to increased fragmentation and alienation. This situation significantly limits our ability to truly impact the personal development of our students, and hence fulfill the Jesuit vision of intellectual and spiritual growth in the context of a true community.

Finally, the approach advocated throughout my presentation is that educators should become managers of the campus environment. To some educators, the idea of environmental management may conjure up visions of an Orwellian "big brother" who tries to control our every move, or a "giant, impersonal computer." After all, you may say, is not *environmental management* just fancy words for manipulation? Is not its goal behavioral change through the manipulation of the environment?

Obviously, I do not use the term that way. Manipulation is defined as the deliberate attempt to change the behavior of others without their knowledge and consent, regardless of whether such behavioral change is good or ill. I am certainly not advocating such an approach for educators. What I am advocating is a collaborative effort between faculty, students, and administrators in designing settings that *facilitate the learning process both in and outside the classroom.* As we recognize the inhumane conditions the college environment can sometimes create for students, are we not ethically obligated to make some effort to change them? There is no possibility of remaining uninvolved. The lesson that ecology teaches us is that we all make an ecological impact — whether we try to or not. The question is not, then, *whether* to manage, but *how.* I am suggesting that, like good gardeners, we not only need a thorough knowledge about the characteristics of seeds, but we also must design conditions to help them grow and develop.

References

Blocher, D. "Toward an Ecology of Student Development." *Personnel and Guidance Journal,* 52 (1974) 360–65.

Chickering, A. *Education and Identity.* San Francisco: Jossey-Bass, 1969.

Cross, K. *Accent on Learning.* San Francisco: Jossey-Bass, 1976.

Feldman, K., and Necomb, T. *The Impact of College on Students.* San Francisco: Jossey-Bass, 1969.

Journal of College and University Student Housing, volume 15, number 2, Winter 1985.

Lewin, K. *Principles of Typological Psychology.* New York: McGraw-Hill, 1936.

Moos, R. *The Human Context: Environmental Determinants of Behavior.* New York: Wiley Interscience, 1976.

Perry, W. *Intellectual and Ethical Development in the College Years.* New York: Holt, Rinehart and Winston, 1970.

Schroeder, C., and Belmonte, A. "The Influence of Residential Environment on Prepharmacy Student Achievement and Satisfaction." *American Journal of Pharmaceutical Education,* 43 (1979) 16–19.

Sommer, R. *Tight Spaces: Hard Architecture and How to Humanize It.* Englewood Cliffs, N.J.: Prentice-Hall, 1974.

11 / The Role of Campus Ministry in a Jesuit College or University

Donald Sutton, S.J.

THERE is a long history to the development of the educational setting that we now identify as a college or a university. The educational process has not always been organized in the manner in which we know it now. Educational institutions in their present form have evolved because of the increasing value placed on learning for more and more of the population, which therefore necessitated structures that might make it possible. It is an institution that once did not exist and came into being because of certain perceived needs and certain values. That same statement might be made about one of the most recent developments *within* the setting of higher education in Catholic colleges and universities — namely, the specialization known as campus ministry.

Saint Louis University is over 170 years old. The first mention of a campus minister in a university bulletin occurs in 1970. Somehow, the university managed to function well for all those years without having a special department or group of persons identified as campus ministry. How did they do it?

In the earlier years of our institutions, a higher percentage of the students were Catholic than we find in them today and a relatively greater percentage of those teaching and working within the university were Jesuit priests and brothers. Campus ministry was taken care of by *everyone*. In more recent years, the growing pluralism of the student body and of the faculty and staff, coupled with the decrease in numbers of Jesuits, made it necessary to specialize. In effect, we move from a kind of "implicit" campus ministry to a more

147

"explicit" campus ministry. As the number of Jesuits in the academic areas of the university grew smaller (and as those remaining in these areas grew older), it became necessary for them to limit their involvement outside the academic arena to some extent — and so it became necessary for someone to be specifically designated within the university to provide some of the services and programs formerly done by many: and an "explicit" campus ministry was born.

This "explicit" campus ministry serves, to some degree, the same function its predecessor, the "implicit ministry," served: to enable persons to know the love of God, to save their souls, and to serve others for the greater glory of God. But being a new specialization or department, it does things differently, and has to work to "credentialize" and "professionalize" itself, and it needs to be professional and it needs to have credibility if it is to work effectively within a higher educational setting. For campus ministry is intended, not just for the students alone, but for the *whole* university community. It is a ministry to students, faculty, staff, alumni, parents, and families in some cases too. Campus ministry at Saint Louis University has sponsored retreats for groups of faculty, for example, to acquaint them with Ignatian spirituality and its role as a foundation for the identity of the university. Campus ministers do counseling with families and students at times of stress or difficulty. After the murder of one of our students, for example, campus ministry became involved with the mother of the deceased student and to some degree with his fiancée. Campus ministry sponsors a dinner to recognize the contributions of the support staff of the university to the good of the whole university community. All these things reflect the belief that this ministry is to the *whole* community, not only to the students.

The tasks of campus ministry are multifaceted. One dimension of campus ministry is the directly pastoral; another dimension is educational. *Both* of these dimensions of campus ministry at a Jesuit institution should reflect the spirituality of Ignatius of Loyola. Major treatises have been written to define and describe and explain that spirituality. It is often referred to as a "world-affirming" spirituality. I like to say it is a spirituality that produces in those who live it three definite characteristics: they are *open*, they are *optimistic*, and they are *other-centered*. Why I choose those three would be the subject of another paper, but it is enough to say that somehow the work of campus ministry, in both its educational and its pastoral dimensions, must reflect the vision, the mind-set, the spirituality found in the *Spiritual Exercises*.

That worldview (or better, I suppose, "God-view") is obviously going to color the retreat work of a Jesuit campus ministry team. The *Exercises* are a decision-making experience, designed to take about thirty days and designed to be done in a one-on-one situation, with a director and a person being directed. Seldom if ever is that the case with what is done under the rubric of retreats on Jesuit campuses today. But nonetheless, those involved in retreat work must be familiar enough (I'd like to say "imbued with") the spirituality of Ignatius, so that whatever *form* is used as a retreat vehicle, the spirit may be colored with the vision contained in the *Spiritual Exercises*. Using the 19th Annotation form of the *Exercises* has also been valuable on some of our campuses.

Counseling is another pastoral activity of campus ministry. In a complex and highly specialized setting such as a university, with a well-trained and competent counseling center, it is important that campus ministers know and understand their role and their own limitations in dealing with students' problems. There are appropriate problems: students dealing with guilt, students dealing with issues of religious or faith development, questions of life direction and vocation, questions of values and value clarification, crisis intervention. Because of the place of campus ministry in the residence halls, campus ministry can be front-line referral agents, along with the housing staff, to the counseling center. They, as well as academic departments, in turn, refer persons to campus ministry. The line between pastoral counseling and therapy is sometimes a difficult one to discern, but campus ministry and counseling need to work together to remain alert and sensitive to the differences between them and to those areas in which they can work together.

Obviously, the liturgical life of the university community comes under the heading of the pastoral function of campus ministry. It is important to offer the university community the opportunity to pray together, and to do it well, according to the directives of the church and also according to norms of good taste and good liturgy. But even in this area, we begin to bridge the gap (or perhaps blur the distinction) between the work of campus ministry as pastoral and its work as educational. In liturgy, for example, by involving students in the preparation and planning of the liturgical celebrations of the university community, they can be guided in the development of an understanding of what constitutes good liturgy, they can be helped to develop the skills necessary to execute good liturgy, they can be encouraged in becoming leaders in organizing and planning good liturgy. All these are "transferable skills," which they can use in areas other than liturgy — even in areas other than the religious arena.

Campus ministry becomes Ignatian when the campus ministers themselves understand the pastoral and educational ideals of Ignatius. These are found (at least implicitly) in the *Exercises* and in part 4 of the *Constitutions*. Fr. Robert Newton, in an interesting monograph, *Reflections on the Educational Principles of the Spiritual Exercises*, elucidates some of these principles:

> Jesuit education is *student-centered*. Its goal is to produce an *independent learner* who internalizes the skills of learning and eventually is able to act without the support of the formal educational environment. The educational process is *adapted to the individual*, and to the extent possible, responds to his abilities, needs, and interests, Jesuit education emphasizes the *self-activity of the student* and attempts to make him (or her) the primary agent in the learning situation. The goal of the teacher is to decrease while the student increases in the direction of her or his own learning.
>
> Jesuit education is characterized by *structure and flexibility*. The structure always includes a definite statement of objectives and systematic procedures for evaluation and accountability, for constant reflection on how to improve performance.[1]

What might this look like in an activity sponsored by campus ministry? Let me try to make it more concrete. Campus ministry at Saint Louis University sponsors an annual food drive. Its most obvious goal is to raise money to support various programs and agencies involved in feeding those without adequate resources. In every phase of that food drive, students are involved in the planning as well as the execution of projects designed to raise money. The students who elect to engage in the 50-hour vigil of prayer and fasting have an opportunity at the beginning to pray together and to hear some reflections on the place of fasting with prayer in the Christian tradition. During the 50-hour vigil, they come together to share their own reflections on the experience of being hungry. A deliberate, conscious effort is made by the campus ministry staff to help students with the many implications of the experience they are undergoing. In SLUCAP (Saint Louis University Community Action Program), students are encouraged to take initiative in the various placements where they work, and then come together to pray and reflect on their experience and what long-range meaning it might have in their lives.

Enabling students to be active in living out their Christianity, in a personalized way, taking each person where he or she is now, within some structure that is yet flexible: these ideas should undergird the programing of a campus ministry department in a Jesuit university or college.

Michael Buckley, S.J., sees one of the primary functions of campus ministry in a Jesuit institution as what he calls "*nurturing the culture*," the Christian, Jesuit culture of the university or college.[2] If you look to sociology for elements of culture, you find that culture is defined by a common, shared history, a shared language, and a common value system, and common goals. In the past, that commonality existed by dint of membership in the Society of Jesus by a large percentage of those on the faculty and in the administration. Almost everyone knew what AMDG meant, where its origins were to be found.

During orientation, I ask students who Loyola was, and I get some very strange answers! Now that this thing called "Jesuit culture" is not so readily possessed by the majority of persons in the institution, I think deliberate efforts must be made to share it with everyone, to give it away, so to speak, so that everyone may feel fuller ownership of the institution by understanding and possessing its history and heritage, as well as the history, heritage, and "jargon" of the Society of Jesus. By sharing this heritage, by discussing the value system of the *Exercises*, more and more persons can be drawn into a sense of belonging to the university family. Individuals can be helped to see their part and their worth — and helped to understand that their value and their contribution to the university community is most certainly not *diminished* because they are not Jesuit or Roman Catholic. Buckley makes the point that varying traditions are not just tolerated but are *essential* for the good of the community of higher education. By our definition of ourselves as a community committed to the search for truth, we are not meant to be a *closed* community. We are meant to be open to knowledge in its many facets and many forms, and to many traditions as they have formulated and expressed truth in their search for it. Once this was considered impossible in the religious sphere, but the expressions of Vatican II have helped us to see that truth, even religious truth, is to be found in many places. Buckley says that the good news of Jesus Christ must be related to *all* cultures. Valid faith can stand *in front of* and *with* all knowledge. In an address to the presidents of Catholic colleges and universities in 1979, Pope John Paul II said:

> . . . the church needs the university; if it is to speak a credible faith to the world today, it must do it in the university; it must be in the university.

So it is our diversity, not our uniformity, that makes us valuable in the service of faith.

What does all this say about campus ministry and campus ministers? Well, if campus ministry is to be a respected department of an academic community, the department members, the campus ministers, must be able to stand shoulder-to-shoulder with everyone else in the academic community. They must be as well informed, as well educated (and I might add, *as well paid*), as the other members of the academic community. They must be educated theologically, skilled in counseling, aware of the world around them, sophisticated about the complexity of life in a university or college setting, knowledgeable (preferably in a personally experienced way) about Ignatian spirituality, committed to a well-articulated value system that informs and enlivens their personal lives. These are very high standards. Such qualities and characteristics are necessary if the campus ministry staff is to carry out the functions I have named: if they are to teach, to pastor, to nurture the Jesuit identity of the college or university community. And they are necessary to carry out one other dimension of Christian work: that is, if they are to be prophetic for the community of which they are a part.

Campus ministry must be able to challenge the university community, to ask it what it is doing vis-à-vis the truth, to call it to reflect upon its goals and its commitments, its expenditures and its resources and their use. Campus ministry needs to be able to ask the students and the faculty and the administration to reflect on what it is doing with the truth, when and how does (in Ignatian language) the truth move into the "service of the gospel and the neighbor"? Does your possession of, your comprehension of, your understanding of truth help *anyone*? Someone has to be helping the community, reminding the community, in a gentle yet persistent and persuasive way, that we are not here for ourselves primarily or for ourselves alone. Fr. Arrupe, the former superior general of the Society of Jesus, said we are to become *persons for others*, an apt and popular expression for the kind of awareness of and service of others demanded by the gospel. Campus ministry can do this in its programing with students but it must also do this for the university community as a whole — for it is meant to minister to the whole community. Everyone, from board member to administrator to faculty and staff and alumni, must be called to reflect upon the direction and goal of her or his own life in the light of the revelation of Jesus Christ.

I should like to conclude by offering two caveats to those who do campus ministry in Jesuit institutions of higher learning. First, campus ministers must be aware, if they are to be true to Ignatian spirituality, that their work is *not* the *only*, nor is it always the *most* religious work being done on a campus. We in campus ministry are not "holier than thou" who are in other departments. Nor is it necessarily in the activities and programing of campus ministry that students will most readily find the Lord or grow in holiness. There is something about the openness to God ("finding God in *all* things") of genuine Ignatian spirituality — the notion that God really *is* found everywhere and that God really *is* served in many, diverse ways — that is a challenge to campus ministry and its work. It is important that we not allow it to seem to students (or to any member of the university community) that what we do is better than what someone else is doing. In point of fact, for some students, it may be far better (the *magis*) to play on the volleyball team than to serve a meal in a soup kitchen if in playing volleyball the student learns more about working as a team member and more about the value of different talents and abilities being used in a cooperative fashion and about the value of exercise and good health. Campus ministry must develop for itself and help the entire community develop a vision as universal in scope as the vision of Ignatius when it comes to finding God's will and serving God.

And finally, although campus ministry has come into being in a very explicit sense where formerly it was more implicit in the university community, I do not want to leave you with the impression that I think *only* campus ministry is called upon to minister in and to the university community. In my view of church, we are all called upon to minister to one another; it is the result of our call as Christians in baptism. It may well be that for campus ministry the most important task of all is to deepen in each member of the university community an awareness of the ramifications of that universal call of the baptized: the call to ministry and service.

References

Buckley, Michael J., S.J. "Jesuit, Catholic Higher Education: Some Introductory, Tentative Theses." Unpublished.
Newton, Robert R., S.J. *Reflections on the Educational Principles of the Spiritual Exercises*. Washington, D.C.: Jesuit Secondary Education Association, 1977.

12 / St. Ignatius and Jesuit Higher Education

George E. Ganss, S.J.

URING some forty years of academic interest in the Jesuit educational tradition and its underlying philosophy, I have been curious about this question: What has been the cement that has held together the bricks and stones making up that tradition throughout these four centuries of educational changes? And steadily I have become more and more convinced of this answer: that cement was, not chiefly the Plan of Studies (*Ratio Studiorum*) of 1599, the impression given by many books on the history of education, but rather part 4 of St. Ignatius's *Constitutions of the Society of Jesus*, which were published forty years earlier, in 1558.

The *Ratio* or Plan of Studies was indeed a great document for its purposes in its own era. Yet it dealt chiefly with matters external, such as the branches of study, their organization in the curriculum, or the administration of a school. Consequently, it devoted very little of its space to the larger values to which Ignatius had pointed those studies, and which the *Ratio* presupposed rather than stated or expounded. But in part 4 of his *Constitutions*, Ignatius himself clearly articulated the dynamic and perennial principles by which he guided his educational practices.

Hence, changing the metaphor of cement to another that Ignatius himself used often in other contexts, this statement can be made: the *Ratio* produced the body of the Jesuit educational tradition from 1599 to 1773, but part 4 of the *Constitutions* infused the soul, that animating spirit or tenor of thought that made these schools successful and distinctive from 1545 into the 1980s.

It is along this line that I shall reflect sketchily on three headings: (1) Ignatius's worldview, (2) his application of it to Jesuit higher education in the 1550s, and (3) our own application of it to American Jesuit colleges and universities in the vastly changed circumstances of the 1980s and beyond.

IGNATIUS'S WORLDVIEW

To add precision to my previous statement, the spirit or tenor of thought that animated the Jesuit educational tradition came, not from part 4 alone, but from what part 4 expressed and applied — namely, Ignatius's own worldview, or vision, or outlook on God, humankind, and the universe, or *paideia*, or *Weltanschauung*, or whatever other such word anyone prefers. However, to understand that part 4 aright, we must view it first in its context of the other nine parts or chapters of his *Constitutions*; and then further still, we must view those *Constitutions* themselves within their larger context, which was Ignatius's frame of reference: his worldview that took in God, the universe and human beings with their place and function within it.

That worldview arose in Ignatius's deep conversion experience at Loyola and Manresa from 1521 to 1523. During it he was guided by God, largely through mystical experiences, to an outlook unusually inspirational for personal sanctification and for servive to his fellow men and women. His vision took in all things as coming from God and then serving as means or stepping stones by which men and women can achieve the chief purpose of their lives, eternal happiness in loving God and being loved by God. All those things, therefore, are worthy of study, because of both their own inherent value and of that aspect of their being simultaneously stepping stones toward happiness with God. This does not diminish their value, but supplements it. Ignatius's worldview was one focused squarely on the central marvel or "mystery" in God's revelation: God's plan for the creation and redemption of humankind, and then for their eventual beatification or glorification in heaven. Ignatius found himself eager to communicate that divine plan, for it made life meaningful for both time and eternity.

Hence in everything he did or wrote for the rest of his life, Ignatius was drawing from and applying that worldview. While composing his *Spiritual Exercises*, for example, he was applying it toward aiding individuals to discern how they could best achieve personal fulfillment by serving God and their fellow humans. While composing his *Constitutions*, he was applying it to the foundation, government, and inspiration of an apostolic religious institute. And in part 4 of those *Constitutions* he was applying it to the Jesuits teaching or administrating in the concrete circumstances of the thirty-three colleges or universities he had opened before he died in 1556.

In multitudinous ways, some clear and direct and others so subtle as to be discoverable only by analysis, that outlook of his permeated the Jesuit schools from 1545 onward. Furthermore, once the *Exercises* had been published in 1548 and the *Constitutions* in 1558, each small book exerted an influence on the other in regard to its interpretation and application in practice. All Jesuit teachers, for example, had been trained through the *Exercises*. Thus the *Exercises* influenced these teachers in all their dealings with students — for example, in counseling or administering the sacraments. The *Constitutions*, in turn, aided them in applying Ignatius's worldview, in terms of large guiding educational principles clearly articulated, to the structures, curriculum, and other activities in the school. They also enabled these teachers to see more profoundly that one and the same spirit or tenor of thought animated both these documents. Both books taken together became the channel through which Ignatius's worldview permeated the Jesuit schools from 1545 onward. It is what gave teachers and staff a set of values of which they were deeply convinced, and were, therefore, consciously or subconsciously eager to communicate to their students.

APPLICATION OF HIS WORLDVIEW TO SIXTEENTH-CENTURY JESUIT HIGHER EDUCATION

In an attentive reading of part 4 we can observe Ignatius's mind at work in applying his worldview to his schools. Consequently, that part also presents his chief educational ideals, aims, and prescriptions for the schools of that day. From some fourteen objectives,[1] which he tried to make characteristics of his schools, I shall touch only on six key samples.

1. "The end of the Society and of its studies is to aid our fellowmen to the knowledge and love of God and to the salvation of their souls."[2] This deals with the ultimate end, to which other activities are means. The various other branches of study have their own

autonomous ends, but they are also stepping stones to higher purposes.

2. Students should strive to attain excellence in mastering their fields of study, both sacred and secular.[3] This deals with the proximate and specific end of the teachers' or students' studying — that is, mastery of the subject matter and the skills it entails.

3. Ignatius's chapter 12 of part 4, mirroring his esteem for the "manner of Paris," the *modus Parisiensis*, presented a curriculum for orderly advance from humanities into philosophy and then theology. By a little analysis we easily see that the overall goal of the curriculum as a whole was the communication of Ignatius's worldview — that is, the offering of the theistic outlook on life to students, who had the free will to accept it and guide their life by it. Students, it was hoped, would grow continually in ability to give a studied and well-grounded reason for the faith that was in them and for the morals they were called on to practice. Further, every branch in the curriculum and every faculty in the university was expected to throw its own proper light upon that overall goal. Thus that goal was the integrating factor that synthesized all the elements in the university into a unity. The studies in humanities, philosophy, and theology gave students a comprehensive synthesis, a framework of reference into which they could fit everything else in life. Taken together, these studies were intended to form students into the good Christian, and the studies in medicine or law, for example, were to make the good Christian a competent physician or lawyer.

4. Theology was to be regarded as the most important branch in the university,[4] because the light that theology gives is the chief means of imparting the carefully reasoned Christian worldview, and then of integrating the other branches of study into it.

5. The Society of Jesus hoped by means of education to pour capable and influential leaders into the social order, in numbers large enough to leaven it effectively for good.[5]

It was by these and his other educational principles, clearly articulated, that Ignatius gave to the teachers, administrators, and students in his schools the values and goals that sprang from his worldview, and that in turn became the values they desired to share with their fellow men and women.

APPLICATION OF THE IGNATIAN VISION TO JESUIT HIGHER EDUCATION
TODAY

Can that worldview of Ignatius and its resultant educational
principles still infuse their dynamic spirit into an American Jesuit
college or university today? All of us think that they can, at least to a
considerable extent. All the studies and activities to that end can be
attached to that worldview somewhat like spokes to the hub of a
wheel. All of them, too, receive a reinforced strength and cooperative unity through their being attached to that hub.

But to carry this work forward, and to avoid discouragement, it is
very important to keep this key fact in mind: the circumstances amid
which these Ignatian objectives are to be pursued today are vastly
changed from those of Ignatius's own era. Hence our task must be a
creative one, the discovering and perfecting of new means to
achieve those objectives to the extent possible in our own circumstances. This involves recognition that principles and statements in
Ignatius's *Constitutions*, which were legal precepts in the 1550s,
must today be converted into inspirational principles willingly em-
braced as challenges and opportunities. A few examples, proposed
as bases for further discussion, are the following.

In Ignatius's days his schools were relatively small (for example,
60 students in Venice; 800 in Billom, France; 900 in Coimbra, Por-
tugal), and almost all the teachers were Jesuits. In our days, the
universities are large, and only a small minority of the personnel can
be Jesuits. In the 1500s, except in missionary countries, virtually all
the students were Catholic. In the 1980s and beyond, we Jesuits
sincerely welcome students, professors, and staff members of many
faiths as our colleagues with whom we hold many interests in
common, and happily too we are living in an era of strong ecumenism. In his era, all the teachers, staff, and students were men; in
ours both men and women are students; they complement one
another and cooperate in the multitudinous ways God intended
when God made both male and female. In Ignatius's times he and
his fellow Jesuit superiors could and did conceive his *Constitutions* as
legal precepts binding the all-Jesuit faculty. But the Jesuit superiors
of our times are not trying to enforce them as laws (except perhaps
for a few matters utterly basic if the school is to remain Catholic).
Instead, these officials are working by articulation of the Ignatian
vision and by persuasion, aware that imposition of such precepts is
no longer possible in our new circumstances. Moreover, this proce-
dure has received official approval by the incorporation of the Jesuit

communities as separate from the colleges or universities. The task of the Jesuit community is to keep the Ignatian educational principles alive in the schools by articulating them clearly and by exemplifying them in practice.

Things will never go back to what they were in Ignatius's era, or even to what they were twenty-five years ago. How, then, to speak realistically, can a university be kept so genuinely Jesuit and distinctively Catholic that it wins patronage from students and their parents, and additional financial support from multiple other sources? Chiefly, it seems to me, by a cooperative partnership between Jesuits and lay professors, administrators, and staff members who care. That is, these interested persons who have an informed and even documented knowledge of the Ignatian vision and the consequent educational ideals that have always animated Jesuit schools, who see their importance for imparting a meaningful life to our students for here and hereafter — these persons will have to dialog continually in creatively working out the means to achieve those ideals today. In such dialoguing, they will regard Ignatius's educational *Constitutions* not as binding laws, but rather as sources of guiding light and inspiration; as having about the same function for a university community that the *Spiritual Exercises* have for an individual who makes them in their genuine manner.

Ignatius and his colleagues never achieved their educational ideals 100 percent. They always wanted to do more, but always also they met obstacles and troubles. Nevertheless, he and they kept doggedly at work, achieving their ideals to the extent possible in their circumstances. So let us too keep on working toward achieving them to the extent possible in our times. We shall accomplish, not everything we want to, but truly much.

These reflections, I hope, have shown some of the reasons for the statement I made at the start, and that can now be repeated with some enrichment. The cement that has held together the bricks and stones composing the Jesuit educational system has been, and still is, the theistic worldview of Ignatius, along with the synthesis of educational principles he drew from it when he was applying it to his schools in part 4 of his *Constitutions*. That vision, which has functioned with so much success from 1545 until now, even amid the last three decades with their welter of opinions and changes — that same vision can continue successfully to guide and inspire us in the 1980s and beyond.

13 / Jesuit Higher Education Worldwide

James W. Sauvé, S.J.

I am going to ask readers to consider a topic not yet discussed in this volume. I want to bring you beyond the borders of the United States, and ask you to consider the international dimension of Jesuit university education.

My presentation has two very distinct parts. The first is to give you information about where some of the other Jesuit universities are to be found, and what they are like: to demonstrate, therefore, that the Jesuit university apostolate is truly international. The second is to suggest that greater contact among these Jesuit universities located in different parts of the world could help each one of the institutions individually to accomplish the task we have been treating in these chapters: how to face the challenges that the immediate future is going to present to all of us.

THE WORLDWIDE JESUIT UNIVERSITY APOSTOLATE[1]

A description of the worldwide collection of Jesuit universities could be very brief: I could simply say that there are 183 Jesuit postsecondary institutions, which enroll approximately 450,000 students. However, a statement given that simply hides the very wide diversity that exists among these institutions. To begin to appreciate this diversity, a few more details will be necessary. I shall try to give you these without turning this part of the presentation into a long list of names and numbers.

160

Jesuit university institutions can be divided into five broad categories. The first are the universities themselves: institutions that resemble the colleges and universities you are familiar with here in the United States. In this category, the United States predominates: of the 59 Jesuit universities in the world, 28 are the ones you know here, and the entire rest of the world has the other 31: 14 are in Latin America, 9 in East Asia, 1 in the Middle East, and 7 in Europe. (Europe includes the Gregorian University, which was called the Roman College until this century; this was the first Jesuit university, and St. Ignatius wanted it to be the model for all the others.) These institutions educate about 385,000 students: 185,000 here in the United States, and 200,000 in the rest of the world.

The second category consists of university colleges that are a part of a larger private or government university. Although free in many areas, they are dependent on the parent university for such things as curriculum requirements and degree requirements. It is the English pattern of university structure, and institutions of this type are to be found throughout what was once the British empire. The Society of Jesus is responsible for 24 university colleges: one in England (Campion Hall at Oxford), 3 in Canada, 17 in India, and one each in Belize, Bhutan, and Zambia. A few of the colleges have as many as 4,000 students, but most are much smaller than that; the total number of students in the entire group of 24 university colleges is about 34,000.

A third category will group together a variety of different types of specialized institutions, all of them professional schools of one type or another: schools of engineering, or music, or business, or education. Jesuits are responsible for 7 professional schools in Spain, 3 in France, 5 in South America, 19 in India, and one each in Belgium and Japan. There are 36 institutions in all, with about 20,000 students.

The fourth group is a category unknown in the United States, but quite important in those parts of the world where, for various historical reasons, nearly all university education is under government sponsorship. These are also called university colleges, but you might be more inclined to call them university residence halls. They are indeed residences for students, but not necessarily for students attending a single university. More important, they are far more than places for students to sleep, eat, and study, though these facilities are certainly provided. They exist in order to offer a combination of academic tutoring, personality formation, and opportunities for growth as a Christian. They are, therefore, a means by which the Society of Jesus attempts to achieve the goals of a Jesuit university in those situations where we do not actually have our own universities. Five Jesuit university colleges are to be found in Australia, another 7 in East Asian countries such as Hong Kong, Singapore, Thailand, and Malaysia, 6 in Spain, and another 9 in other European countries.

To complete the list, we need to include 37 schools of philosophy and theology. They were originally established for the formation of students preparing to become priests, but today are admitting growing numbers of lay students. Though the number of lay students is not large, these schools add 6,000 to the total number of students in Jesuit postsecondary institutions.

Geographically, of the collection of 183 institutions that I have just described, 36 are in the United States and Canada, 24 in Latin America, 53 in Europe, 41 in India, 24 in East Asia, 5 in Africa, and 1 in the Near East. The exact type of institution varies, and depends on local needs, local traditions, and historical circumstances; the dedication and commitment of the Society of Jesus to university education is worldwide, adapting itself to the specific conditions of each individual country.

With such a wide diversity of individual situations, it is not easy to describe the institutions themselves in any detail. Though university life is, in many ways, the same throughout the world, a few generalizations may help you to appreciate some characteristics that make them different from institutions you are familiar with.

The first remark that may be surprising to an American audience is that, in most parts of the world, there is no attempt to recruit students — because there is no need to do so! This is especially true in the Third World, where many more young persons are trying to be admitted to universities than there are places available for them. In some of these countries, the number of students that a school is allowed to accept is decided by the government, even for private schools. In a few countries the government also determines which student attends which university and, occasionally, even assigns textbooks and teachers.

In most Latin American countries, there is very little financial support of any kind from the government, and there is no tradition there of development or fund-raising. Our Jesuit universities must sustain themselves on the tuition they receive from students and, in order to avoid becoming schools for the rich in countries where it is the poor who are most in need of an education, tuition is kept as low as possible. The result is that the institutions tend to be rather large;

for the same economic reasons, both faculty members and students are, in general, part-time.

In spite of the obvious difficulties that this situation creates, Jesuit universities in Latin America have a significant influence within their respective countries because, within the limitations of the country, they tend to be among the best and most famous institutions. This is especially true in small countries such as Nicaragua or Guatemala, but it is also true in countries such as Colombia and Brazil.

To give only one other example of a quite different situation, let me turn to India. Government support, even of our Jesuit university colleges, is relatively generous: in the Indian Constitution, minority groups receive special privileges, and Christians are a small minority in India. Government support, as often happens, brings with it government control. There is limited autonomy, therefore, but there is still a significant Jesuit influence in the Indian world of university education and, in more recent years, there has been a growing sense that it is not the ability to determine curriculum or degree requirements that makes a college Jesuit so much as the spirit or climate of the campus as it pervades all university activities.

University education in India is relatively recent, and our Jesuit university colleges are going through a growth process that is somewhat similar to the one Catholic university education in the United States went through earlier in this century: a search for identity, a certain priority given to heightened quality in teaching and research, in selection of both professors and students. India, finally, is one of the very few countries in the world where the number of Jesuit institutions continues to grow. Five new Jesuit high schools and two new university colleges have recently been opened, and more are being planned.

INTERNATIONAL COOPERATION

With this brief description of the international dimension of the collection of Jesuit universities as a background, I want to turn to the second part of my remarks: the possibilities for greater contact on an international level.

A great deal of contact already exists, and it is important to recognize this. To name only a few of the most obvious types of contact at the international level, there are programs for faculty exchange, international student programs, and exchange of written materials. There are a few cases of university "twinning" such as that between Xavier University in Cincinnati and Xavier University in Bogotá, Colombia. But the model that I have in mind and wish to propose to you, though it is perhaps only a dream, could lead to something much broader and perhaps more productive. The model comes from our Jesuit history.

In these chapters, many writers have referred to the *Ratio Studiorum*. The *Ratio* is universally recognized to be the foundation document of Jesuit education; but the real importance of the *Ratio*, at least for me, lies not so much in the document itself as in the process that led to its publication in final form in 1599.

With the dramatic increase in both the number and the size of Jesuit schools toward the end of the sixteenth century, the superiors of the Society of Jesus who succeeded St. Ignatius repeated with greater and greater insistence the Ignatian principle that these institutions could preserve their inspiration and quality only through a constant interchange among them of ideas and experiences; the decision to create a document common to all the schools intensified this process. There were regular meetings, frequent mailings, continual exchanges of all types — including an exchange of faculty among schools at a rate and level that would be impractical today.

The concrete result, the *Ratio Studiorum* itself, is a plan of studies that gives rather minute details about the way administrators are to administer, teachers are to teach, and students are to behave. It was the interchange leading to the final publication of the *Ratio* that was the single most important factor in creating a common vision. It has been said that the *Ratio* created the first real educational *system* that the world has ever known; to the extent that this is true, it is the common vision that unified the schools into a system much more than the external fact that they were all applying the rules set down in the *Ratio*. And it is the common vision that truly created the Jesuit tradition in education.

The *Ratio* was never intended to be a static document; interchange was meant to continue, and this interchange was to lead to changes and revisions of rules. Unfortunately, it did not happen; the need was not felt in the first decades after 1599 and when, in the nineteenth century, efforts were finally begun to undertake a complete revision of the *Ratio*, it was too late: the combination of government educational directives and local educational traditions made any attempt at a uniform set of regulations for all Jesuit schools impossible. Gradually, in the course of the twentieth century, the regulations have been abandoned.

I have no desire to revive these efforts to create a new *Ratio Studiorum*; but I have a great desire to revive the common spirit that led to the *Ratio* and, I am convinced, is still individually alive today in each Jesuit institution. I believe that we have, in recent years, put too much stress on the uniqueness or the distinctiveness of each individual institution and focused our attention on the differences that separate us. It is time to pay greater attention to the basic vision we have in common, to the ideas we can share, to the ways in which we can learn from one another and can enrich one another.

This is not in any sense a loss of individual autonomy; it is not a way of regaining some sort of outside control of individual institutions. Moreover, lest I be misunderstood, I am not advocating some sort of an aid program for poorer countries — one in which, for example, the universities in the United States would be asked to help those in Latin America, whether financially or in any other way. What I am trying to describe as my dream is a common sharing, a common exchange, which would enrich each of the institutions involved by learning from the others.

The difficulties are obvious, whether in language and culture, or in government restrictions and educational traditions. But they do not make the project impossible; as I have already indicated, there are already many areas in which exchange is already a reality. I will end by suggesting a few other possibilities.

The first has to do with identity and the educational community. The chapter by Father Ganss speaks about the collaborative efforts of lay persons and Jesuits in the university today in the United States. The same search is going on throughout the world: Jesuit institutions are looking for ways to create an educational community in which Jesuits and lay persons can share a common sense of mission. At national meetings in the United States, such as the meetings of the Association of Jesuit Colleges and Universities or the meetings of the Jesuit community superiors, there has been an increasing exchange of experiences — what individual institutions have been doing to promote this educational community. I would suggest that the exchange be extended to the international level: that we help one another by studying the seminars, summer programs, faculty orientation programs, and other initiatives being tried in other parts of the world, to see if there is some way in which we can profit from them; and I suggest that we share with others the experiences being gained in the United States. The Jesuit high schools are already doing this, and with great success. The Jesuit universities could begin to do something along similar lines.

The second area is external to the university itself, and has to do with some of the vital concerns of our day: peace and justice, the world economy, the search for a society that will more effectively promote and defend human dignity. The university does not deal with these problems directly, by involvement in politics; but it does play an important role in this area by its influence on culture, on the world of ideas. And culture today is, in many respects, worldwide: peace and economic stability, to take the two most obvious examples, depend on worldwide factors of interdependence.

I would suggest that Jesuit universities can assist one another in this interdependent world, and learn more about one another in the process. In the struggle for peace, Americans may be able to learn from those in European countries who have seen the destruction of war in their own countries and who continue to live with the threat of a war that could begin on their borders. And Americans have much to learn about justice from the struggles going on in Latin America. The American experience of democracy, on the other hand, can assist other nations, such as Spain or Argentina, where democracy is still young and fragile. And the independence of the private school system of the United States could become a model for many countries. Such examples could be multiplied, and could provide topics for a common research effort in which each scholar would contribute the specific experience and expertise of his or her own country and traditions.

There is talk everywhere today about the global village — about the need for greater international cooperation and greater international understanding. And Jesuits have, for many years, noted that we already have an international network of schools, at both the high school and the university level, which could promote such cooperation and understanding. The time has come to take this seriously, to recover our sense of an international system that has more than statistical interest and historical importance. In spite of our worldwide system of communication and transportation, there are many ways in which it is more difficult to do this today than it was in the sixteenth century. But it also far more essential than it was then.

Interchange is best brought about through personal contact. For that reason, a meeting is being planned in Rome for November 1985, whose theme will be somewhat similar to the theme for this meeting.[2] We will look at the things that we have in common, to see whether it is possible to have more interchanges of the type that I have been talking about. But only the university presidents will be there. My dream cannot become a reality through the presidents alone, and it cannot be the work of one meeting. I would urge you to continue to hold meetings of the type we are presently concluding, looking for the possibilities of interchange at both the national and international levels. I would further urge you to undertake an ongoing discussion of the topic — a discussion to involve as many members of the university community as possible. And, finally, I urge you to be imaginative, to continue to build on the inspiration that has been ignited during this meeting here in St. Louis.

14 / Jesuit Education and Social Justice in Theory and Practice

John F. Kavanaugh, S.J.

ORIGINALLY, the title of this essay was to be "Jesuit Education and Social Action or Relevance," but I have taken the liberty of changing it. Why? Partly due to the suspicion that the words "social relevance" or "action" are freighted with ambiguity, indefiniteness, vagueness, or even diffidence — the very qualities that often seem to mark our understanding and our commitment in this area.

The original title was also something of an affliction, even before writing began, because "relevance" drips with the taste of trendiness. And the word "action," clean and powerful as it is, is often set in opposition to the deliberateness and meditative distance required in seeking truth.

Moreover we have all been warned of the bankruptcy of "activism" and some of us may even be keenly aware of the pejorative weight of being called "activist."

The words "relevance" and "activism," however, do carry some valuable and important intentions. "Social relevance" actually indicates and acknowledges the relationship between education and our social, political, and economic realities — as well as all the ways that human exchange is ordered within them. The note of "action," moreover, provides us with the reminder that education has a dialectical impact upon the entire network of human behaviors and practices.

Jesuit education, if it is to be real, will both influence and be influenced by the socio-political order and the lived concrete praxis of the persons educated and educating.

168

The upshot of these preliminary remarks is that I wished to keep the intent, but change the wording of the title. Let it be: "Jesuit Education and Social Justice in Theory and Practice."

Even this title, however, will need some definitional constraints; for in such a short paper I will not be able to examine many areas that fall within the wide spectrum of social concern. For example:

1. a university's relationship to the local community and national consensus. This area touches upon the issues of housing, displacement of local tenants, hiring, urban development, investment portfolios and corporate proxy resolutions, investments related to a militarized economy, and the role of research and development in establishing dependencies that might possibly restrict free inquiry.

2. just relationships within the university community itself. This area includes the issues of labor organizations, teachers' unions, decision-making procedures, the setting of priorities, negotions concerning tenure and salaries.

3. concerns of justice within the educational profession. Here might be confronted the manipulation and exploitation (economic, sexual, psychological, or otherwise) of students, the ideologizing of class lectures, the failure to fulfill contractual promises — by perfunctory teaching, neglect of professional development, and negligence in keeping minimal hours of work.

These would all be important considerations from the viewpoint of justice, but I prefer, at the risk of neglecting these particular issues, to examine Jesuit education and social justice from a higher altitude, where I will be able to address the overarching question: What are the conditions for the possibility of even asking the above questions concerning justice in the community, the university, and in one's personal life? Indeed, why is there a problem of justice in the first place? Why should we be just? And what difference would any of our answers make?

Whence comes the concern for justice? Is it intrinsic to any education that would call itself humane, especially one lodged in the Judeo-Christian tradition, and even more so, embodied in the spirituality and mission of the Society of Jesus?

And what is the future of such a concern? Especially in a "postenlightenment" age of deconstruction, of the "decentered" self, and of a prevailing scepticism concerning the effectiveness of rationality?

The philosophical tradition of the Catholic and Jesuit university is central to any discussion concerning the foundations for social justice. Even so "non-Jesuit," non-Christian, and non-traditional a thinker as Herbert Marcuse had been convinced, before his death, of the position that one cannot logically support commitment to justice at all, without an objective universal moral law grounded in the dignity of human persons:

> The doctrine of the right of resistance has always asserted that appealing to the right of resistance is an appeal to a higher law, which has universal validity, that is, which goes beyond the self-defined right and privilege of a particular group. And there really is a close connection between the right of resistance and natural law. Now you will say that such a universal higher law simply does not exist. I believe that it does exist. Today we no longer call it natural law, but I believe that if we say today that what justifies us in resisting the system is more than the relative interest of a specific group and more than something that we ourselves have defined, we can demonstrate this. If we appeal to humanity's right to peace, to humanity's right to abolish exploitation and oppression, we are not talking about self-defined, special group interests, but rather and in fact interests demonstrable as universal rights. That is why we can and should lay claim today to the right of resistance as more than a relative right.[1]

Similarly, but from a quite different academic context, the late Abraham Maslow, after decades of psychological research and theory, concluded that philosophical anthropology is centrally important in elaborating one's politics, economics, philosophy of education, therapeutic model, or system of ethics and value:

> When the philosophy of man (his nature, his goals, his potentialities, his fulfillment) changes, then everything changes, not only the philosophy of politics, of economics, of ethics and values, of interpersonal relations and of history itself, but also the philosophy of education, of psychotheraphy, and of personal growth, the theory of how to help men become what they can and deeply need to become.[2]

I refer to these two thinkers from different academic fields because they confirm from their own perspectives my conviction that men and women cannot substantiate and maintain a commitment to justice or rights without an understanding of human personhood and the foundations of human dignity.

Marcuse knew quite well that civil disobedience and the challenge to unjust orders could not be justified without some grounding in an objective theory of intrinsic human rights. So also, Maslow was insistent that one's view of human nature was the ultimate foundation of culture, education, therapy, and behavior.

This recognition, of course, brings us to the philosophic enterprise — for at the very heart of philosophy one finds the impulse for
justice, whether it is in the confrontation with Thrasymachus in
Plato's *Republic*, or the earliest desires of Descartes to be an ethical
person, or in the awe of Kant in the presence of the moral law.

The issues of human identity and value — central to the issue of
justice — generate every authentic philosophic impulse and they
have never been successfully surpressed or purged from philosophical discourse. There have been many pronouncements of "mean-
inglessness," "decenteredness," logical inappropriateness, and various revolutions promising some form or other of the "end of
humankind." But the questions remain.

Who and what am I? And what am I to do? Identity and responsible action. These questions generate not only the search for human
integrity; they are the prerequisites of ethics. Without them, the
issue of justice would never emerge. Without them, the issue of
human value would not arise. And without these questions in some
way grounding a theory of human value and dignity, there could
never be a basis for moral outrage.

Why be just?

Why is it an abomination that persons are terrorized, that children
are incinerated? Why is it a profound disorder that we could con-
template extinquishing ourselves and our future? Why is the slaugh-
ter of innocents — whether it be in abortion clinics or in the dust of
Ethiopia, or in the deadly poisoned beds of central India — an
outrage?

The mission of philosophy — not withstanding all the protesta-
tions of Anglo-American game playing and logical gymnastics, all
the attempts to portray rational inquiry as the procurer of power or
the clown of cultural amusement — is inextricably bound to these
questions, which gird the very problematic of justice.

Each year I ask my students a number of questions based upon a
Heinrich Himmler speech to his generals at Posen:

> "I want to talk to you quite frankly on a very grave matter. Among
> ourselves it should be mentioned quite frankly, and yet we will never
> speak of it publicly. . . . I mean, the elimination of the Jewish race
> . . . . Most of you must know what it means when 100 corpses are
> lying side by side, or 500, or 1000. To have stuck it out and at the same
> time . . . to have remained decent fellows, that is what has made us
> hard. This is a page of glory in our history which has never been
> written and is never to be written."

QUESTION: Where do you stand on ethics and the philosophy of the human person? Is genocide right if you are sincere? If 80% of a nation thinks it is permissible? If a law approves it? If it would end all our troubles? Is this a relative issue? Or just an "emotional" unresolvable issue? Why not?[3]

Over the last twenty years there has been an increasing majority of students who reveal a startling absence of intellectual conviction and commitment. There may be a depth of *feeling* that genocide is wrong, but it is overwhelmed by a moral relativism, a deterministic helplessness. Students believe in the U.N. Declaration of Human Rights, but they do not know why. They think that "all persons are created equal . . . endowed with inalienable rights," but they cannot for the life of them come up with reasons to support the claim.

Our culture entertains romantic vestiges of human dignity. It can still move us in our television shows, thrill us at the movies, and gratify us in the rhetoric of skilled politicians. But in the regnant theory of many academic disciplines, in social and political practice (embodied in our governmental and international policies and behaviors) and in the lived experience of culturally conditioned lost interiority and fragmented relationship, our encountering of human value and irreplaceability is diminished.[4]

The philosophical arena — as well as the religious and spiritual arenas — is a testing ground of the great struggles over human identity. In the philosophical ambient of Christian and Jesuit traditions — at their best — that identity is revealed in the fact that I as a human person am endowed with the ability to know and question myself and discover myself as an inalienable center of consciousness and action. I am capable, by my human endowments, of entering into self-consciously responsible relationship to myself and my world. I am free.

The very intelligibility of education rests upon the often unarticulated conviction that human beings are capable of an emancipation brought about by the labor of self-understanding, leading to a consequent self-possession and a crowning self-determination or commitment.

It is this philosophical insight that is equally (1) the foundation of human dignity, (2) the basis of human irreplaceability, and (3) the objective grounds for moral outrage at any enterprise that would reduce the human person to a mere commodity, a dead object, or an instrumentality.

If our educational efforts have helped form a scientist, a public official, a physician, or a businessperson who does not know these truths and does not live out of them; if we have educated someone who believes that persons are expendable in the name of public pressure or political exigency; if we have educated a man or woman who thinks that human worth is a function of value "placed" upon them by others rather than an intrinsic endowment, we have not formed an educated person. We have created a menace.

Human dignity and emancipation are at the genesis of all authentic education, wherein the truth of human personhood elaborated in literature, science, professions, art, and discourse yields a greater and richer range of human freedom. Education is the cultural and institutional embodiment of the Aristotelian principle that desire and choice follow upon cognition: if one enlarges the range of knowledge, one expands the capacity for self-appropriation and the depth of human commitment.

Thus, propaganda, prejudice, authoritarianism, and all forms of thought-control are put under assault in the act of educating a human being. The great project of education — which is that of human self-understanding in all its forms — is a project of human emancipation. It is also, in that very fact, an affirmation of human dignity.

The meaning and purpose of education is justice itself. Human dignity is its premise. Human freedom is its goal.

We might look at education as a liberating transfer of ownership: out of the grip of fear and ignorance, so well portrayed in Plato's illusion-bound cave of cultural ideology, our humanity is taken into our own hands as persons endowed with self-understanding and self-determination.

Authentic education, whether it be in Russia or the United States, in Brazil or Poland, will consequently be an ever-present force of subversion calling into question any dominion that is not at the service of human interest and the affirmation of human personhood.

But the philosophical foundations of human dignity and justice — grounded in the common discourse of reflective humanism — are, for a person of Christian faith, only the beginning. With a profound faith in the reality and revelation of Christ, all humane philosophies are radicalized. For the Gospels are a revelation of the transcendent value of even the least human being — not only made in the image and likeness of God, but reconstituted in the eternal Word made historical flesh.

The irreplaceable value of the human person as an earthly embodiment of a personal God is expressed in our freely uttered, self-defining words: "I believe, I hope, I love." Our capacities to fallibly and humanly possess ourselves empower us to give ourselves away in covenant and commitment. Each of us in this sense is utterly unique. And all of us, so humanly endowed, are utterly equal.

Although this mystery of human value can be found in numerous themes and texts of scripture and Judeo-Christian traditions, it appears preeminently in the twenty-fifth chapter of the Gospel of Matthew.

Here we find articulated a theological and christological foundation for the intrinsic connection between human dignity and belief in Jesus. By equating himself with the "least" human person, Jesus Christ says, in effect, "this is my body" — consecrating all human flesh. Not even Marx in his most outraged indictments of human injustice uttered such a radicalizing vision of humanity and of justice.

Justice issues are no longer issues merely of political balance, competitive group interest, and legal prudence. They are issues of faith. They are issues of love. Housing, food, clothing, prison, and distribution of wealth are not some merely liberal programatic. In the Last Judgment scene of Matthew 25, they are the very criteria against which the final moral evaluation of men and women will be made.

Human dignity and the justice required by it is the glory of God in time — intrinsic to the salvation of souls. This is central to our understanding of the Pauline epistles and the writings of the school of John. It penetrates the sermons of Chrysostom and Ambrose, inspires the great reform movements of the mendicants, and inhabits the mighty educational and health agencies of social transformation.

As human educators, as Christians, as collaborators in the Jesuit tradition, we have no tradition or future outside this realm of justice. The truth of the inviolable dignity of the human person is the basis of our educational mission.

And it is a truth that is incarnate, historical, embodied in praxis.

The commitment to human dignity is not merely speculative. It must be concrete. It pulls us into the economic order (that is why investment policies must be of moral significance to us.) It touches our internal institutional relationships (this is why policies concerning salaries, research, and development are morally germaine) and it informs our individual sense of professional integrity and respect for students.

Social justice is affirmed by an educational institution's fidelity to its own great humane traditions, by its being open to the ever-radicalizing message of the gospel, and by its provision for a lived ambient of social praxis. Justice, moreover, is enhanced by the commitment of an institution to the world of moral discourse. And it is justice that is served when the corporate effort of a university community is directed to the reconstitution of the person as the center and telos of all human affairs.

But all of this is proclamation. The final and crucial question before us is: what to do. And in this context, it is best for me to answer for myself as a member of a university in a particular academic profession.

It is really rather simple. As a teacher and writer at a Jesuit institution of higher learning, I can no longer look upon my own labors as career management or as isolated efforts in my own field. Rather, I will hold before me our corporate traditions of Christian humanism — not because they are traditional, but because they are true and because they are crucial to any advocacy for human rights.

And as a collaborator in a community of scholars, I invite you to do the same: whether we speak of the passion of Pascal or Einstein, or interpret the catastrophic tests of history or read the texts of nature and cosmos, or heal and arbitrate the great wounds of humanity, or encounter the human spirit in Shakespeare, Dostoevsky, the Qur'ān *The Divine Comedy*, or *Rabindranath Tagore*.

If we do not enlist ourselves in the reconstruction of the person in the postmodern world, if we allow our students to pass through our environment and be unable to challenge unspeakable crimes against humanity, then we will be little other than accessories to historical terrorism.

Let our philosophy and theology, our sciences and arts, our professions be unashamedly true to their originating impulse: a devotion to humanity — its inherent dignity, its capacity for freedom, its high destiny.

The theory and practice of justice can intensify the focus not only of an institution, but of an individual's life. If such focusing is permitted, both individual and institution embark upon the noblest of undertakings: forming and informing men and women of passion and intellect — persons who indeed are not menaces to society, but are most assuredly dangerous to any system or ideology that would degrade the only acceptable earthly image of God.

Notes

Notes to Introduction

1. Reverend Theodore Hesburgh, C.S.C., *The Hesburgh Papers: Higher Values in Higher Education*, (Kansas City: Adrews and McMell, Inc., 1979), p. 43.

2. David J. Hassel, *City of Wisdom: A Christian Vision of the University*, (Chicago: Loyola University Press, 1983), p. 63.

3. John W. Donohue, S.J., *Jesuit Education:An Essay on the Foundations of Its Idea* (N.Y.: Fordham University Press, 1963), p. 16.

4. Remarks delivered by Pope John Paul II, October 6, 1979 at the Catholic University of America.

5. Reverend Edmund G. Ryan, S.J., "Pressure of Jesuit Higher Education — Remaining Healthy and Distinctive,"*Association of Jesuit Colleges and Universities Conference*, (Boston, 1981), p. 23.

6. John W. Donohue, S.J., *Jesuit Education An Essay on the Foundations of Its Idea* (N.Y.: Fordham University Press, 1963), p. 16.

7. Father Arrupe, "Jesuit-Lay Collaboration in Higher Education," speech delivered at St. Joseph's College, July, 1978.

Notes to Chapter 1

1. The following were the studies most useful to me: William A. Bangert, S.J., *A History of the Society of Jesus* (St. Louis: The Institute of Jesuit Sources, 1972); Miguel Batllori, *Cultura e Finanze: Studi sulla storia dei Gesuiti da s. Ignazio al Vaticano II* (Rome: Edizioni di Storia e Letteratura, 1983); Gian Paolo Brizzi, ed., *La "Ratio studiorum:" Modelli culturali e pratiche educative dei Gesuiti in Italia tra Cinque e Seicento* (Rome: Bulzoni Editore, 1981); L. W. B. Brockliss, *French Higher Education in the Seventeenth and Eighteenth Centuries: A Cultural History* (Oxford: Oxford University Press, 1987); François Charmot, S.J., *La pédagogie des jésuites: Ses principes, son actualité* (Paris: Edition Spes, 1951); Gabriel Codina Mir, S.J., *Aux sources de la pédagogie des jésuites: Le "modus parisiensis"* (Rome: Institutum Historicum Societatis Jesu, 1968); Marie-Madeleine Compère, *Du collège au lycée: 1500–1850, géneologie de l'enseignement secondaire français* (Paris: Gallimard, 1985); idem, *L'éducation en France du XVIᵉ au XVIIIᵉ siècle* (Paris: Societé d'éducation d'enseignement supérieure, ca.1976); François de Dainville, S.J., *La naissance de l'Humanisme moderne* (Paris: Beauchesne et ses fils, 1940); idem, *L'éducation des jésuites (XVIᵉ–XVIIIᵉ siècles)*, Marie-Madeleine Compère, ed. (Paris: Les éditions de

minuit, 1978); John W. Donohue, S.J., *Jesuit Education: An Essay on the Foundations of Its Idea* (New York: Fordham University Press, 1963); Marc Fumaroli, *L'âge de l'éloquence: Rhétorique et "res literaria" de la Renaissance au seuil de l'époque classique* (Geneva: Droz, 1980); George E. Ganss, S.J., *Saint Ignatius' Idea of a Jesuit University* (Milwaukee: Marquette University Press, 1954); Nigel Griffen, "Miguel Venegas and the Sixteenth-Century Jesuit School Drama," *Modern Language Review*, 68 (1973) 796–806; J.-B. Herman, S.J., *La pédagogie des jésuites au XVIe siècle: Ses sources, ses caractéristiques* (Louvain: Bureaux du Recueil, 1914); Pedro Leturia, S.J., "Perchè la Compagnia di Gesù divenne un Ordine insegnante," *Gregorianum*, 21 (1940) 350–82; Ladislaus Lukács, S.J., "De prima Societatis Ratione studiorum sancto Francisco Borgia praeposito generali constituta (1565–1569)," *Archivum Historicum Societatis Jesu*, 27 (1958) 209–32; Mabel Lundberg, *Jesuitisiche Anthropologie und Erziehungslehre in der Frühzeit des Ordens (ca.1540–ca.1650)* (Uppsala: Universitas Upsaliensis, 1966); Anita Mancia, "La controversia con i Protestanti e i programmi degli studi teologici nella Compagnia di Gesù," *Archivum Historicum Societatis Jesu*, 54 (1985) 3–43; Pierre Mesnard, "La pédagogie des jésuites (1548–1762)," in *Les grands pédagogues*, J. Chateau, ed. (Paris: Presses Universitaires, 1956), 45–107; John W. Padberg, S.J., *Colleges in Controversy: The Jesuit Schools in France from Revival to Suppression, 1815–1880* (Cambridge: Harvard University Press, 1969); Dennis E. Pate, *Jerónimo Nadal and the Early Development of the Society of Jesus* (Ann Arbor: University Microfilms International, 1983); Mario Scaduto, S.J., "Alle origini della pedagogia dei gesuiti," *Civiltà Cattolica* (1976), 1:451–62; Aldo Scaglione, *The Liberal Arts and the Jesuit College System* (Baltimore: Johns Hopkins University Press, 1986); André Schimberg, *L'éducation morale dans les collèges de la Compagnie de Jésus en France sous l'Ancien Regime (XVIe, XVIIe, XVIIIe siècles)* (Paris: H. Champion, 1913); Robert Schwickerath, S.J., *Jesuit Education: Its History and Principles*, 2nd ed. (St. Louis: B. Herder, 1904); Jean-Marie Valentin, *Le théâtre des jésuites dans les pays de langue allemande (1554–1680)*, 3 vols. (Bern, Frankfurt, Las Vegas, 1978); idem, "Gegenreformation und Literatur: das Jesuitendrama im Dienste der religiösen und moralischen Erziehung," *Historisches Jahrbuch*, 100 (1980) 240–56. The bibliography on the subject is considerable. For further titles, see the pertinent sections in László Polgár, S.J., *Bibliographie sur l'histoire de la Compagnie de Jésus, 1960–1980*, 3 vols. now in print (Rome: Institutum Historicum Societatis Jesu, 1981–83).

2. The best study is still H.-I. Marrou's, *A History of Education in Antiquity* (New York: New American Library, 1964). See also his *Saint Augustin et la fin de la culture antique*, 4th ed., rev. (Paris: Editions E. de Boccard, 1958).

3. There are many studies of this phenomenon. The standard work is still Hastings Rashdall's, *The Universities of Europe in the Middle Ages*, rev. ed., F. M. Powicke and A. B. Emden, 3 vols. (Oxford: Oxford University Press, 1936). See also Charles Homer Haskins, *The Rise of the Universities* (Ithaca: Cornell University Press, 1957), and John W. Baldwin, *The Scholastic Culture of the Middle Ages, 1000–1300*, (Lexington, Mass.: Heath, 1971).

4. Thomas Kuhn, *The Structure of Scientific Revolutions*, 2nd ed. (University of Chicago Press, 1970). See also Garry Guting, ed., *Paradigms and Revolutions* (University of Notre Dame Press, 1980).

5. Few studies treat of the internal dynamism and aims of the scholastic

system. See, however, the pertinent sections of Walter J. Ong, S.J., *Ramus, Method, and the Decay of Dialogue* (Cambridge: Harvard University Press, 1958). See also M.-D. Chenu, O.P., *Towards Understanding Saint Thomas* (Chicago: Regnery, 1964), esp. pp. 79–99; idem, *La théologie comme science au XIIIe siècle* (Paris: Vrin, 1957); idem, *La théologie au douzième siècle* (Paris: Vrin, 1957); J. de Ghellinck, S.J., *Le mouvement théologique du XIIe siècle* (Paris: Desclée de Brouwer, 1948); Ulrich Kopf, *Die Anfänge der theologischen Wissenschaften im 13. Jahrhundert* (Tübingen: Mohr, 1974); Brian E. Daley, S.J., "Boethius' Theological Tracts and Early Byzantine Scholasticism," *Mediaeval Studies*, 46 (1984) 158–91.

6. *S. T.*, I, 1, 4: *Magis tamen est* [sacra doctrina] *speculativa quam practica, quia principalius agit de rebus divinis quam de actibus humanis.*

7. For a historiographical review of this issue, see my "Catholic Reform," in *Reformation Europe: A Guide to Research*, Steven Ozment, ed. (St. Louis: Center for Reformation Research, 1982), pp. 297–319.

8. See, e.g., Bernard Cook, *Ministry to Word and Sacraments: History and Theology* (Philadelphia: Fortress, 1976), pp. 297–98, where it is described principally in relation to catechetics.

9. See his "The Schools of Christian Doctrine in Sixteenth-Century Italy," *Church History*, 53 (1984) 319–31; also, "Borromeo and the Schools of Christian Doctrine," forthcoming in the volume of studies on St. Charles edited by John M. Headley, *San Carlo Borromeo: Catholic Reform and Ecclesiastical Politics in the Second Half of the Sixteenth Century*; and also, "Schools, Seminaries, and Catechetical Instruction," in *Catholicism in Early Modern Europe: A Guide to Research*, John W. O'Malley, ed. (St. Louis: Center for Reformation Research, 1988). See also E. Mangenot, "Catechisme," in *Dictionnaire de théologie catholique*, 2:1895–1968.

10. The standard work is still William Harrison Woodward's, *Vittorino da Feltre and Other Humanist Educators*, first published in 1897. See the edition with a foreword by Eugene F. Rice, Jr. (New York: Columbia University Press, 1963). On the complex problem of Renaissance humanism, see Paul Oskar Kristeller, *Renaissance Thought: The Classic, Scholastic, and Humanist Strains* (New York: Harper and Row, 1961); idem, *Renaissance Thought II: Papers on Humanism and the Arts* (New York: Harper and Row, 1965); idem, *Renaissance Thought and Its Sources* (New York: Columbia University Press, 1979); Paul F. Grendler, "The Concept of Humanist in Cinquecento Italy," in *Renaissance Studies in Honor of Hans Baron*, Anthony Molho and John A. Tedeschi, eds. (De Kalb: Northern Illinois University Press, 1971), pp. 447–63; Marie Boas Hall, et al., *Il Rinascimento: Interpretazioni e problemi* (Rome-Bari: Laterza, 1979). Still useful is the pamphlet by William J. Bouwsma, "The Interpretation of Renaissance Humanism," 2nd ed., Publication Number 18, Service Center for Teachers of History (Washington: American Historical Association, 1959).

11. See Woodward, *Da Feltre*; Anthony Grafton and Lisa Jardine, *From Humanism to the Humanities: Education and Liberal Arts in Fifteenth- and Sixteenth-Century Europe* (Cambridge: Harvard University Press, 1986), esp. pp. 1–28; and Robert Black, "Humanism and Education in Renaissance Arezzo," in *I Tatti Studies: Essays in the Renaissance*, Louise George Clubb, ed., vol. 2 (Florence: Villa I Tatti, 1987), pp. 171–237.

12. See Grafton and Jardine, *From Humanism*.

13. On the ancient roots of humanistic education, see the references in note 2, above. On mutations in the medieval period, see Pierre Riché, *Education and Culture in the Barbarian West: From the Sixth through the Eighth Century* (Columbia: University of South Carolina Press, 1978); Jean Leclercq, *The Love of Learning and the Desire for God* (New York: New American Library, 1962); and especially R. R. Bolgar, *The Classical Heritage and Its Beneficiaries: From the Carolingian Age to the End of the Renaissance* (New York: Harper and Row, 1964).

14. See Paul Oskar Kristeller, *Medieval Aspects of Renaissance Learning: Three Essays*, Edward P. Mahoney, ed. and trans. (Durham: Duke University Press, 1974), and my own *Praise and Blame in Renaissance Rome: Rhetoric, Doctrine, and Reform in the Sacred Orators of the Papal Court, c.1450–1521* (Durham: Duke University Press, 1979).

15. See Codina Mir, *Aux sources* (note 1, above), pp. 53–99. On the earlier phenomenon in Italy, see Grafton and Jardine, *From Humanism*, pp. 58–98.

16. On the opposition and interaction, see, e.g., Ong, *Ramus*, pp. 53–59, 92–130 (note 5, above).

17. Bolgar, *Classical Heritage*, p. 255.

18. See, e.g., Craig R. Thompson, "Better Teachers than Scotus or Aquinas," in *Medieval and Renaissance Studies*, John L. Lievsay, ed. (Durham: Duke University Press, 1968), pp. 114–45.

19. Quoted in Donahue, *Jesuit Education*, p. 186 (note 1, above).

20. I will use the standard edition of the *Ratio* of 1599 edited by G. M. Pachtler, S.J., with a German translation, in *Monumenta Germaniae Paedagogica* (Berlin: A. Hofmann, 1887), 2:234–481, henceforth simply *Ratio*. Selections from the Latin text, along with related documents, are also found in T. Corcoran, S.J., *Renatae Litterae saeculo a Chr. XVI in scholis Societatis Jesu stabilitae* (Dublin: University College, 1927). The most recent English translation is by Allan P. Farrell, S.J., *The Jesuit Ratio Studiorum of 1599* (Washington: Conference of Major Superiors of Jesuits, 1970). For the evolution of the *Ratio*, see the new critical editions of the pertinent texts, now up to 1580, by Ladislaus Lukács, S.J., *Monumenta Historica Societatis Jesu* (Rome: Institutum Historicum Societatis Jesu, 1965–81), vols. 92, 107, 108, 124. On the practical implementation of the *Ratio*, see now Brizzi, "*Ratio studiorum*" and Scaglione, *Liberal Arts* (note 1, above).

21. *Aux sources* (note 1, above).

22. On this issue, see de Dainville, *La naissance*, pp. 57–69 (note 1, above), and especially Marc Fumaroli, "Définition et description: Scholastique et rhétorique chez les jésuites des XVIᵉ et XVIIᵉ siècles," *Travaux de Linguistique et de Littérature*, 18 (1980) 37–48. Fumaroli has written the most comprehensive study of the impact of Jesuit rhetoricians on French culture in the late sixteenth and seventeenth centuries, *L'âge de l'éloquence* (note 1, above).

23. See Batllori, *Cultura*, p. 178 (note 1, above).

24. I here use the translation from *Erasmus and His Age: Selected Letters of Desiderius Erasmus*, Hans J. Hillerbrand, ed. (New York: Harper and Row, 1970), p. 23. This is letter #64 in the critical edition by P. S. Allen. For a comprehensive presentation of Erasmus's understanding of the relationship among piety, theology, and ministry, see my Introduction to vol. 66 of the *Collected Works of Erasmus* (University of Toronto Press, 1988), pp. ix–li.

25. On Erasmus's influence on early Jesuit education, see the Introduc-

180   NOTES TO PAGES 19–26

tion by J. K. Sowards in vol. 25 of the *Collected Works of Erasmus* (University of Toronto Press, 1985), pp. l–li; A. H. T. Levi, "Erasmus, the Early Jesuits, and the Classics," in *Classical Influences on European Culture A.D. 1500–1700*, R. R. Bolgar, ed. (Cambridge: Cambridge University Press, 1976), pp. 223–38; Irmgard Bezzel, "Erasmusdrücke des 16. Jahrhunderts in bayerischen Jesuitenbibliotheken," in *Das Verhältnis der Humanisten zum Buch*, Fritz Krafft and Dieter Wuttke, eds. (Boldt: Deutsche Forschungsgemeindshaft, 1977), pp. 145–62. Saint Ignatius' antipathy to Erasmus has surely been exaggerated; see, e.g., John Olin, *Six Essays on Erasmus* (New York: Fordham University Press, 1979), pp. 75–92.

26. See *Ratio*, pp. 234–36.
27. See ibid., and pp. 294–300.
28. See the edition, ibid., pp. 67–72.
29. See ibid., p. 300 (#1 and #5).
30. Quoted in Codina Mir, *Aux sources*, p. 282 (note 1 above).
31. See *Ratio*, especially p. 286 (#1–#3).
32. Quoted in Codina Mir, *Aux sources*, p. 282 (note 1 above).
33. See *Ratio*, p. 288 (#7).
34. See ibid., pp. 300–8.
35. See, e.g., Juan de Polanco's letter, May 21, 1547, *Monumenta Ignatiana: Epistolae et Instructiones*, 12 vols. (Madrid: G. Lopez del Horno, 1903–11), 1:522.
36. See *Ratio*, p. 268.
37. For the fundamental document on the "faith and justice" issue, see *Documents of the 31st and 32nd General Congregations of the Society of Jesus* (St. Louis: The Institute of Jesuit Sources, 1977), pp. 411–38.
38. See *The New York Times*, November 26, 1984, pp. 1, 20.
39. As far as I know, there has been no attempt to study this question, which somewhat resembles the one studied by Gerald Strauss in his *Luther's House of Learning: Indoctrination of the Young in the German Reformation* (Baltimore: Johns Hopkins University Press, 1978).
40. See, e.g., Aquinas, *S.T.*, I, l, 8: . . . *gratia non tolit naturam sed perficit.*
41. Part 4, chap. 14 [464]. On Thomism in fifteenth- and sixteenth-century Rome, see my "The Feast of Thomas Aquinas in Renaissance Rome: A Neglected Document and Its Import," *Rivista di Storia della Chiesa in Italia*, 35 (1981) 1–27.
42. See, e.g., *Ratio*, p. 414.
43. The words are spoken by Nephalius in "The Godly Feast" (*Convivium religiosum*), in *Opera omnia* (Amsterdam: North Holland Publishing Company, 1972), I/3:254. See *Ten Colloquies of Erasmus*, Craig R. Thompson, ed. and trans. (New York: Liberal Arts Press, 1957), p. 158.
44. Quoted in de Dainville, *La naissance*, p. 223 (note 1, above).

Notes to Chapter 2

1. *AJCU-JSEA 1984–85 Directory.* This — and other statistical data — may also be found in the *Fact Files* series published by the Association of Jesuit Colleges and Universities since 1977.

2. Paul A. FitzGerald, S.J., *The Governance of Jesuit Colleges in the United States, 1920–1970* (University of Notre Dame Press, 1984), p. 3.

3. Ibid., p. 47.

4. *AJCU Fact File #125* (October 1, 1984) and *Fact File #128* (October 25, 1984). A bound set of *Fact Files* (1977–1983) may be found in the AJCU Archives (hereafter referred to as A.A.)

5. John Tracy Ellis, "American Catholics and the Intellectual Life," *Thought*, 30:118, September 1955.

6. Arthur A. North, S.J., "Why is the American Catholic Graduate School Failing to Develop Catholic Intellectualism?" *Bulletin, National Catholic Educational Association*, 1/1 (August 1956), Proceedings and Addresses, 53rd Annual Meeting, p. 179.

7. FitzGerald, *Governance*, p. 74.

8. A list of Jesuits in doctoral studies is published annually by the Jesuit Conference. The latest summary (November 1984) is published in *AJCU Higher Education Report*, 8:3 (December 1984) p. 9.

9. *Tilton v. Richardson*, 403 U.S. 672 (1971) and *Roemer v. Board of Public Works*, 426 U.S. 736 (1976).

10. John J. McGrath, *Catholic Institutions in the United States: Canonical and Civil Law Status* (Washington, D.C.: Catholic University of America Press, 1968) and Ruth Cessna, "John J. McGrath: The Mask of Divestiture and Disaffiliation," 1971, A.A.

11. The primary reason for locating the AJCU in Washington and enlisting the full-time services of a federal relations expert (Joseph Kane) was because of a desired focus on public policy as an apostolic work. Other church-related colleges have had lesser presences in Washington; AJCU has the longest continuous record of shaping public policy — e.g., student aid, civil rights, research assistance, building grants and loans — of any church-related group. No other Catholic college or university group maintains a Washington office. Rather, they are represented by the Association of Catholic Colleges and Universities (ACCU) of which AJCU is a member.

12. This movement has been outlined in "The Jesuit Purpose in Education — an Institutional Description" by William McInnes, S.J., which was presented at Loyola College, Maryland, March 26, 1981, and is contained in A.A.

13. William C. McInnes, S.J., "Jesuit Higher Education: Gaps in the Narrative," The Third Rev. Charles F. Donovan, S.J., Lecture, delivered at Boston College, March 1982; A.A.

14. Bruce F. Biever, S.J., and Thomas M. Gannon, S.J., eds., *General Survey of the Society of Jesus, North American Assistancy* (Chicago: National Office of Pastoral Research, 1969), p. 11.

15. Ibid., p. 120.

16. Ibid., p. 71.

17. *Project 1: The Jesuit Apostolate of Education in the United States*, 6 Volumes (Washington, D.C.: Jesuit Conference, 1974–75).

18. "The Jesuit Mission in Higher Education: Letter from the American Provincials" (Washington, D.C.: Jesuit Conference, 1978), p. 10.

19. The Jesuit Conference produced "The Context of Our Ministries: Working Papers" in 1981 with the hope expressed by Fr. James Connor, S.J., president of the conference, "that at this time they receive a thoughtful

reading from each of you [6,000 Jesuits]." Two of the papers discuss education. Others review politics, the economy, the people, social issues, the international dimension, science and technology, criminal justice, communications, church life. The publication has been little used — or even referred to — since that time.

20. "The Catholic University in the Modern World," *College Newsletter*, National Catholic Education Association, 35:3, March 1973.

21. Ibid., p. 2.

22. Obviously Jesuit education is one form of Catholic education. But is there something distinctive (though not often articulated) that sets it apart from Dominican, Franciscan, or diocesan educational systems? The advantage of exploration of this topic rests not so much in being able to find the unique lodestone of the system, but in the very exercise of exploration. Our problem is not that we do not have one clear answer, but that we have not engaged in systematic, serious thought.

23. *JEA Denver Workshop on Jesuit Universities and Colleges: Their Commitment in a World of Change* (Regis College, Denver, 1969); A.A.

24. Ibid., p. 18.

25. *Guidelines for Jesuit Higher Education: The Consensus Statements, Recommendations, and Committee Report of the J.E.A. Denver Workshop on Jesuit Universities and Colleges: Their Commitment in a World of Change* (Regis College, Denver, August 6-14, 1969), pp. 1-3; A.A. A cautionary note is added to this Statement: "The term 'distinctive characteristics' is used to indicate traits that one finds or expects to find generally in Jesuit education. It does not mean that these characteristics are unique to Jesuit education or that they may not be found, separately or conjointly, in other types of education" (reference 1, p. 8).

26. Ibid., p. 3.

27. Ibid., pp. 4-7.

28. The search for the uniqueness of Jesuit education has always ended in frustration. The search for its distinctiveness has been more fruitful, even though it has led to a more sensitive understanding of the diversity of operations at individual campuses. It is interesting to note that in 1984 the Jesuit high schools began a search for the "distinctive characteristics of Jesuit education on a worldwide basis (see Vincent Duminuco, S.J., "JSEA: Document to Appear," *National Jesuit News*, January 1985, p. 5).

29. Minutes of the AJCU Board of Directors, October 8-9, 1971, Appendix II, p. 12; A.A.

30. Minutes of the AJCU Board of Directors, April 2, 1972, p. 1; A.A.

31. Minutes of the AJCU Board of Directors, November 10-11, 1972; A.A.

32. Minutes of the AJCU Board of Directors, January 13-14, 1973, pp. 2-6; A.A.

33. Ibid., pp. 5-6.

34. Michael J. Buckley, S.J., "Jesuit Catholic Higher Education: Introductory, Tentative Theses," a paper delivered at the November 4, 1982, AJCU Conference of Academic Administrators; A.A.

35. Ibid., p. 1.

36. Ibid., p. 3.

37. Ibid.

38. Ibid., p. 5.

39. Ibid., p. 6.

40. Fr. Buckley subsequently published his presentation in *Review for Religious* (May–June 1983), pp. 339–49.

41. David J. Hassell, S.J., *City of Wisdom* (Chicago: Loyola University Press, 1983).

42. John Paul II, Address to U.S. Catholic University and College Educators at the Catholic University of America, Washington, D.C., October 7, 1979.

43. Unpublished document in A.A.

44. Joseph A. Tetlow, S.J., *The Jesuit Mission in Higher Education: Perspectives and Contexts* (St. Louis: American Assistancy Seminar, 1984).

45. Merriman Cunninggim, "Categories of Church-Relatedness," in Robert Rue Parsonage, ed., *Church Related Higher Education* (Valley Forge, Pa.: Judson, 1978), p. 32.

46. Tetlow, *Jesuit Mission*, p. 52.

47. William J. Sullivan, "Jesuits in Higher Education: Yesterday, Today, and Tomorrow," address to the faculty of Fairfield University, September 26, 1980; A.A.

48. John W. Padberg, S.J., "How and Why the Jesuits Got Into Education," address given to a convocation of Loyola (New Orleans) faculty and professional staff on March 30, 1983; A.A.

49. James N. Loughran, S.J., speech to the faculty, September 19, 1984; A.A.

50. "Linking Religious Faith with the Learning Experience," *Boston College Bi-Weekly*, May 24, 1984, p. 8.

51. John Langan, S.J., "One and the Same: A Philosophical and Theological Meditation on the Catholic Identity of Catholic Institutions in a Pluralistic World," paper delivered on May 4, 1982, at the FADICA (Foundations and Donors Interested in Catholic Activities) Conference on the Catholic identity of Catholic institutions. A copy may be found at the Woodstock Theological Center of Georgetown University, Washington, D.C.

52. *Marquette University Annual Report*, 1982–83; A.A.

53. Richard P. McBrien, "The Case for Catholic Education," *Commonweal*, January 21, 1977, pp. 41–44.

54. David J. O'Brien, *The Jesuits and Catholic Higher Education* (St. Louis: American Assistancy Seminar, 1981).

55. Jeanne K. Neff, "Tradition and Quality: A Meditation," unpublished address at Wheeling College; A.A.

56. Quentin L. Quade, "Jesus Christ and the Complex Institution," pamphlet printed by Marquette University, June 1984; A. A.

57. J. Barry McGannon, S.J., *Source Book: Jesuit and Catholic Aspects of American Jesuit Colleges and Universities*, 2 vols. (St. Louis University, Office of University Relations, 1983); A. A.

58. "Institutional Goal Statements: An Anthology and Commentary," unpublished material prepared for the May 14, 1977, meeting of provincials' and presidents' committees to discuss Project One and its conclusions; 4 vols., May 10, 1977; A. A.

59. The 21 AJCU conferences involve over 600 religious and lay representatives of special functions (e.g., academic vice-presidents, alumni direc-

tors, business deans) at Jesuit colleges and universities. They usually meet formally once a year to discuss issues of general interest. One of their major obstacles is the inability to carry on a sustained exploration of an important issue.

60. A new tension in the discussion of religious identity is that between mission and community. Jesuit spirituality has always given primacy of place to mission, fitting community into mission, not vice versa. Some new approaches, giving primacy to community over mission, are developing among other religious orders, particularly of women religious. The eventual outcome is not clear at this writing.

61. Andre L. Delbecq, *Business Schools in Jesuit Education: Four Reflections* (Santa Clara: University of Santa Clara School of Business and Administration, 1980).

62. The AJCU Conference of Nursing Deans was formed in 1982. One of its first efforts was to try to define its mission in a Jesuit context.

63. FitzGerald, *Governance*, p. 207 (M. 2, above).

64. The restructuring movement seems to have passed its peak. Today 20 Jesuit colleges and universities are separately incorporated, all have lay persons as trustees (often a majority), and their charters have been updated, where necessary, to meet modern legal requirements under U.S. law.

65. William C. McInnes, S.J., "The Integration of Liberal and Professional Education," *Thought*, 57:225, June 1982, pp. 205–18.

66. John R. Crocker, S.J., *Resource Book for International Education: U.S. Jesuit Colleges and Universities* (Washington, D.C.: Association of Jesuit Colleges and Universities, 1981).

67. The 33rd General Congregation of the Society of Jesus, held in 1983, gives a ringing affirmation of the work of educators. The first application of the mission of Companions of Jesus sent into today's world is education. "Of great importance among the ministers of the Society are the educational and intellectual apostolates." Even more significant is the reason given: not because education is one of the traditional works of Jesuits but because *it is appropriate to our mission today*. "When carried out in the light of our mission today, their [i.e., Jesuits working in the schools] efforts contribute vitally to 'the total and integral liberation of the human person leading to participation in the life of God himself'" (Documents of the 33rd General Congregation of the Society of Jesus, the Institute of Jesuit Sources, 1984, p. 61).

Notes to Chapter 4

1. Edwin A. Abbott, *Flatland: A Romance of Many Dimensions* (New York: Barnes & Noble, 1963), p. 84.

2. Ibid., pp. 93–94.

3. Ibid., p. 98.

4. Ibid., p. 107.

5. Rudolph Arnheim, in *Toward a Psychology of Art* (Berkeley: University of California Press, 1972), p. 297.

6. Ibid., pp. 297–99.

7. Monika Hellwig, "Theology as a Fine Art," in *Interpreting Tradition:*

The Art of Theological Reflection, Jane Kopas, ed. (Chico: Scholars Press, 1983), pp. 3–12; here citing p. 6. Also, in an article entitled "Appreciative Awareness: The Feeling-Dimension in Religious Experience," J. J. Mueller, S.J., describes B. Meland's notion of "appreciative consciousness" as "a regulative principle in thought which as an orientation of the mind makes for a maximum degree of receptivity to the datum under consideration on the principle that what is given may be more than one thinks." It involves "receptiveness characterized by wonder." See *Theological Studies,* 45 (1984) 57ff., esp. pp. 62, 65–66.

8. Hellwig, "Theology," p. 8; see also Mueller, "Awareness," pp. 66–67 on "identification" characterized by empathy as the second step in development of the skill of "appreciative awareness."

9. Bernard Lonergan, *Method in Theology* (New York: Herder and Herder, 1970), p. 293. I have taken the liberty of adapting his material rather freely.

10. *Method,* p. 268.

11. Ibid., p. 331 with my parenthetical interventions added.

12. Ibid., p. 336.

13. Ibid., p. 353.

14. Roger Hazelton and Dorothy A. Austin, "Emerging Images in Teaching Religion and the Arts," in *Humanities, Religion, and the Arts Tomorrow,* Howard Hunter, ed. (New York: Holt, Rinehart, and Winston, 1972), pp. 201–16, here citing p. 215.

15. For further provocative discussion of these and related issues, see T. R. Martland, *Religion as Art* (Albany: State University of New York Press, 1981).

16. Taking a lead on points 1 and 2 from *Flatland,* where the Flatlander's bright hexagonal grandson discerned that the ability to square a number and *infer* a plane surface also implied the ability to cube a number and infer the inconceivable (volume) — for if a line moving parallel to itself yields a square, a square moving so must make "Something Else." See *Flatland,* pp. 69–70.

17. *Flatland,* p. 91.

Notes to Chapter 5

1. The problem I am referring to here has been discussed in recent years in terms of the question of the specificity or distinctiveness of Catholic/Christian ethics. A good collection of essays that touch on this area is *Readings in Moral Theology No. 2, The Distinctiveness of Christian Ethics,* C. E. Curran and R. A. McCormick, S.J., eds.

2. "With renewed emphasis since the 32nd General Congregation, Jesuits are to be identified as *agents of change,* through a corporate mission of the service of faith and the promotion of justice." This is in #20 of *The Jesuit Mission in Higher Education,* a letter from the American Jesuit Fathers Provincial to those working in higher education in the United States. The numbering system used here and in later citations is that devised by Joseph A. Tetlow, S.J., who includes the provincials' letter to their brother Jesuits as an Appendix in his *The Jesuits' Mission in Higher Education: Perspectives and*

Contexts, which appeared as vol. 15, no. 5, and vol. 16, no. 1, of *Studies in the Spirituality of Jesuits,* published by the American Assistancy Seminar on Jesuit Spirituality.

3. The bishops are careful to distinguish various levels of principles, those universally binding and those subject to different types of change and interpretation, throughout their 1983 pastoral letter, *The Challenge of Peace: God's Promise and Our Response.* Moreover, they recognize that the application of principles is always both necessary and complex.

4. This was the September 10, 1984, issue.

5. See, for example, comments reported on page 48 of the *Time* article just cited.

6. Pope Paul VI, for instance, distinguishes between secularism and secularization: "On the one hand one is forced to note in the very heart of this contemporary world the phenomenon which is becoming almost its most striking characteristic: secularism. We are not speaking of secularization, which is the effort, in itself just and legitimate and in no way incompatible with faith or religion, to discover in creation, in each thing or each happening in the universe, the laws which regulate them with a certain autonomy, but with the inner conviction that the Creator has placed these laws there. The last Council has in this sense affirmed the legitimate autonomy of culture and particularly of the sciences. Here we are thinking of a true secularism: a concept of the world according to which the latter is self-explanatory, without any need for recourse to God, who thus becomes superfluous and an encumbrance. This sort of secularism, in order to recognize the power of man, therefore ends up by doing without God and even by denying Him." This is found in #55 of *On Evangelization in the Modern World (Evangelii Nuntiandi),* an apostolic exhortation released on Dec. 8, 1975. The translation is that of the Daughters of St. Paul edition.

7. This has been a much discussed series of issues in recent years. Curran and McCormick have edited a volume of essays that highlight many of the central issues — *Readings in Moral Theology No. 1, Moral Norms and Catholic Tradition.*

8. The *sensus fidelium* is the theological rubric under which this type of question has traditionally been treated. An example of the church's caveat here comes in the discussion of masturbation in the *Declaration on Certain Questions Concerning Sexual Ethics (Persona Humana)* published by the Sacred Congregation for the Doctrine of the Faith on Dec. 29, 1975: "Sociological surveys are able to show the frequency of this disorder according to the places, populations, or circumstances studied. In this way facts are discovered, but facts do not constitute a criterion for judging the moral value of human acts." This statement occurs in #9 of the document, and the translation is that of the United States Catholic Conference edition of 1976.

9. *On Evangelization in the Modern World,* #19.

10. Ibid., #21.

11. In the Tetlow edition cited in footnote 2, this is found in #52.

12. Ibid., #39.

13. Ibid., #44–45.

14. John 14:6.

Notes to Chapter 7

1. Ignatius of Loyola, *The Constitutions of the Society of Jesus*, George E. Ganss, S.J., trans. (St. Louis: The Institutes of Jesuit Sources, 1970).
2. Walter M. Abbott, S.J., ed., "The Church Today," *Second Vatican Council* (New York: Guild Press, 1966), nos. 55–56.
3. Alvin Toffler, *Future Shock* (New York: Random House, 1970).
4. "Excellence in Higher Education," *The Chronicle of Higher Education*, October 24, 1984, pp. 35–49.
5. W. J. Bennett, "To Reclaim a Legacy," *The Chronicle of Higher Education*, November 28, 1984, pp. 16–21.
6. *U.S. News & World Report*, 96 (1983) 21–22.

Notes to Chapter 9

1. Faherty, William B., S.J., *Better the Dream — St. Louis: University and Community 1818–1968* (St. Louis University, 1968), p. 49.
2. FitzGerald, Paul A., S.J., *The Governance of Jesuit Colleges in the United States, 1920–1970* (University of Notre Dame Press, 1984), p. 46.
3. Brubacher, John S., and Rudy, Willis, *Higher Education in Transition: A History of American Colleges and Universities, 1636–1976* (New York: Harper & Row, 1958), p. 174. This book is recommended as an excellent source on this historical section; I have used it generously. I also gratefully acknowledge the assistance of Glenn R. Pellino of the University of Scranton.
4. *AJCU-JSEA 1984–85 Directory* (Washington: Association of Jesuit Colleges and Universities, 1985)´, p. 8.
5. Remarks delivered by Pope John Paul II on October 6, 1979, at the Catholic University of America, Washington, D.C.
6. *Documents of the 31st and 32nd General Congregations of the Society of Jesus* (St. Louis: The Institute of Jesuit Sources, 1977), p. 122.
7. Ibid., p. 424.
8. Pedro Arrupe, S.J., to the Society of Jesus, December 25, 1977, p. 4. (See also "The Jesuit Mission in Higher Education," a letter from the American Provincials, Easter 1978.)

Notes to Chapter 12

1. For more complete lists and treatments, see, e.g., George E. Ganss, S.J., *St. Ignatius' Idea of a Jesuit University*, 2nd ed. (Milwaukee, 1956), pp. 191–201; idem, *The Jesuit Educational Tradition and Saint Louis University* (St. Louis, 1969), pp. 17–24; St. Ignatius of Loyola, *The Constitutions of the Society of Jesus: Translated, with an Introduction and a Commentary, by G. E. Ganss, S.J.* (St. Louis, 1970), pp. 210–11.
2. *Constitutions of the Society of Jesus* [446].
3. Ibid. [460].
4. Ibid. [466].

5. See *Constitutions* [622e], and especially section 15 of Ignatius's letter of Dec. 1, 1551, to Araoz, cited in English in Ganss, *St. Ignatius' Idea*, pp. 28-29. This letter as a whole (pp. 25-29) is a remarkable synthesis showing Ignatius's educational vision, ideals or objectives, plans, hopes, and procedures as they were in his mind in 1551.

Notes to Chapter 13

1. Statistics in this section were revised in May 1988.
2. This meeting was held; a report of it can be obtained from the International Center of Jesuit Education, Casella Postale 6139, 00195 Rome, Italy.

Notes to Chapter 14

1. Herbert Marcuse, *Five Lectures* (Boston: Beacon, 1968), p. 105.
2. Abraham Maslow, *Toward a Psychology of Being*, 2nd ed. (New York: Insight Van Nostrand, 1968), p. 189.
3. William Shirer, *The Rise and Fall of the Third Reich* (New York: Simon and Schuster, 1960), p. 966. More recently, I have used direct quotations from persons I have interviewed who justify terrorism for the sake of defending family, homeland, or religion. Such persons have been from the left in Central America, from the IRA, from the right in South Africa, from the right in the USA, and from liberation movements in India and Africa.
4. In preparing the final draft of this essay, I am aware that there have been recent indictments of "relativism" and subjectivism in American life. Unfortunately, in most cases, the indictments have come from persons who remain remarkably uncritical of the ways that capitalism as well as Americanism have themselves served to "deconstruct" the inherent dignity of the human person. Be that as it may, among the many fine treatments of value relativism and the lost sense of personal dignity there is, from the sociological perspective, *Habits of the Heart* by Robert N. Bellah et al.; from the psychological perspective, *The Minimal Self* by Christopher Lasch; from an economic-cultural perspective, *Money and Class in America*, by Lewis Lapham; and from the philosophical perspective, *After Virtue*, by Alasdair MacIntyre (with an excellent series of responses and rejoinders in serious philosophical publications).

About the Authors

REV. LAWRENCE BIONDI, S.J., dean of the College of Arts and Sciences at Loyola University of Chicago, studied several languages including Italian, French, Russian, Polish, and Spanish, which led him to be the chairman of the Modern Languages Department from 1977 to 1980. Fr. Biondi received his Ph.D. from Georgetown in sociolinguistics in 1975. He has served on various committees encompassing administrative, academic, and student-related areas. He has been a consultant and editorial staff member of *Physicians Communications* and *Current Concepts in Patient Counseling*.

ROLANDO E. BONACHEA, Former dean of the College of Arts & Sciences at St. Louis University from 1980–85, and acting president at Duquesne University, Pittsburgh, he is currently president of Salem College, Salem, Massachusetts. He received his Ph.D. from Georgetown University in Latin American History in 1974. His professional field of concentration is Central America and the Caribbean. Dr. Bonachea is the co-editor of *Revolutionary Struggle, Collected Works of Fidel Castro 1947–1958* and *Cuba in Revolution*, among others. He is a past member of the St. Louis Archdiocese Commission on Human Rights. He is the recipient of the *Honoris Causa* appointment by Mexico's National Academy of International Law (1984).

REV. ROBERT A. BRUNGS, S.J., director of ITEST (Institute for Theological Encounter with Science and Technology) at St. Louis University, received his Ph.D. in physics from St. Louis University in 1962. Fr. Brungs is the author of *A Priestly People* and *Building a City: Christian Response and Responsibility*.

REV. GEORGE E. GANNS, S.J., director of the Institute of Jesuit Sources, St. Louis, received his Ph.D. in Greek, Latin, and philosophy in 1934.

REV. JOHN F. KAVANAUGH, S.J., associate professor of philosophy at Saint Louis University, has been a syndicated columnist in social commentary and has written and lectured in the areas of cultural ideology, consumerism, and social justice. His published books are *Human Realization*, a philosophy of the person, and *Following Christ in a Consumer Society*.

REV. WILLIAM C. MCINNES, S.J., president of the Association of Jesuit Colleges and Universities since 1977, was president of Fairfield University (1964–1972) and the University of San Francisco (1972–1977). He received a Ph.D. in business administration from New York University in 1954. He has served as trustee for several Jesuit universities, and has been a member of the board of directors of the Washington Center for Learning Alternatives, Better Business Bureau Foundation, InterFuture, and the Association of Catholic Colleges and Universities.

LAURENCE J. O'CONNELL, S.T.D., associate professor of theology at St. Louis University, has been director of the corporate ministry program in the Department of Theology at St. Louis University and chairman of the Department of Theology. He received a Ph.D. from the Catholic University of Louvain

189

(Belgium) in 1976. He has served in different capacities on the Commission on Human Rights, Board of Directors of the Association for Clinical Pastoral Education, and chairperson of the Mercy Hospitals Ethics Committee.

REV. JOHN W. O'MALLEY, S.J., professor of history at the Weston School of Theology since 1979, received his Ph.D. in history from Harvard University in 1966 and a Doctor of Letters (*honoris causa*) from Loyola University in 1982. He has been a Scholar in Residence at the American Academy in Rome and was awarded a research fellowship from the N.E.H. His principal publications include *Giles of Viterbo on Church and Reform: Praise and Blame in Renaissance Rome*, which received the Best Book Award on Italian Studies by the American Historical Association, and *Rome and the Renaissance*.

REV. J. A. PANUSKA, S.J., president of the University of Scranton since 1982, received his Ph.D. in biology from St. Louis University in 1958. He has taught at Emory University School of Medicine, Georgetown, Boston College, and Scranton. He has served on many and varied boards of directors and boards of trustees, is a member of professional associations, and is involved in scientific research on environmental physiology.

REV. JAMES R. POLLOCK, S.J., assistant professor at St. Louis University in the Department of Theological Studies, received his Ph.D. in philosophy from St. Louis University. Through the years, he has gained experience in counseling and spiritual direction and is a fluent speaker of six languages. He holds an S.T.D. from the Pontifical Gregorian University in Rome. He has been chairman of the board of advisers for *Theology Digest* and a pastoral consultant at St. Louis University Hospitals.

REV. G. JOHN RENARD, S.J., associate professor of theological studies at St. Louis University, received his Ph.D. in Islamic Studies from Harvard in 1978. He has been on the board of trustees for Cupples House and a member of many professional organizations such as the American-Oriental Society and the National Council of Churches Task Force on Christian-Muslim Relations.

CHARLES SCHROEDER, vice-president for student development at St. Louis University since 1981, received a Ph.D. in education from Oregon State University in 1972. He is a contributor and author of books and articles on student-related topics.

REV. JAMES SAUVÉ, S.J., secretary for education at the Curia, Rome, since 1978, received his Ph.D. in mathematics from Johns Hopkins University in 1965. Between 1968 and 1978 he held positions at Marquette University as director of campus ministry and assistant to the vice-president for student affairs.

REV. DONALD SUTTON, S.J., director of campus ministry at St. Louis University since 1983, received his Ph.D. from St. Louis University in psychology in 1974. He has conducted workshops and served as an organizational consultant to a number of groups, including the Stigmatine Fathers and the Sisters of St. Joseph. He has done book reviews for *Human Development*, a journal on religion and the social sciences, and has published in that journal.

REV. JOSEPH TETLOW, S.J., professor of history at Xavier Hall in Texas, studied theology at St. Louis University School of Divinity and received his Ph.D. on American Social-Intellectual History at Brown University. He has contributed to a number of magazines, such as *New Orleans Review* and *America* and is the author of "The Jesuits' Mission in Higher Education: Perspectives and Contexts."

Acknowledgments

This collection of essays had its origins in the Interdisciplinary Conference on *Jesuit Education: The Challenge of the 1980s and Beyond* held at St. Louis University in December 1984. Father John H. Gray, S.J., then Academic Vice President, encouraged me to explore the concept for the conference, and Father William V. Stauder, S.J., then Dean of the Graduate School, contributed many ideas to the interdisciplinary organization of the conference. Father Walter J. Ong, S.J., who always had the time to discuss topics for papers and concepts that should be addressed and who suggested and contacted many of the contributors, and to Father Anthony C. Daly, S.J., who assisted me in the actual editing of this volume and in taking care of multiple details, I am gratefully indebted.

Both before and after the 1984 conference, Father Daly and Father Thomas N. Lay, S.J., shared with me their boundless enthusiasm, support and encouragement as we worked toward the publication of these essays.

Miss Leslie Valentine, student assistant, along with my administrative assistant Suzie Pool, provided logistical support and personal touch in greeting the participants. Emma Easteppe gave invaluable assistance with the research involved in my own presentation. To all of them a grateful acknowledgement, for it is they who made our volume possible.

A special word of thanks to Father Paul C. Reinert, S.J., Father J. Barry McGannon, S.J., and Father George E. Ganss, S.J., for advice and encouragement in the early stages of planning, to Father Peter-Hans Kolvenbach, Superior General of the Society of Jesus, who encouraged our project, and to Father James W. Sauvé, S.J., whom Father Kolvenbach sent to the conference as his personal representative.

Finally, the conference was funded by an internal grant through a program supported by a grant from the Andrew W. Mellon Foundation. The help of the Foundation and of Saint Louis University itself is respectfully acknowledged. It was Saint Louis University which brought us together, and through its outstanding faculty in the College of Arts and Sciences provided me as Dean with an experience of personal and professional growth that I will never forget.

Rolando E. Bonachea